AROUND THE WORLD IN 72 DAYS

THE RACE BETWEEN PULITZER'S NELLIE BLY AND *COSMOPOLITAN'S* ELIZABETH BISLAND

By Jason Marks

D1293534

GEMITTARIUS PRESS

AROUND THE WORLD IN 72 DAYS:
THE RACE BETWEEN PULITZER'S NELLIE BLY
AND *COSMOPOLITAN'S* ELIZABETH BISLAND

Copyright © 1993 by Jason Marks

Printed in the United States of America

Published by Gemittarius Press, Post Office Box 20151, New York, N.Y. 10025-1511

Portions of Chapter 8 are from *Wandering Ghost* by Jonathan Cott, copyright © 1990 by Jonathan Cott. Reprinted by permission of Alfred A. Knopf, Inc.

Designed by Carson Ferri-Grant

Publisher's Cataloging in Publication
(Prepared by Quality Books Inc.)

Marks, Jason.
   Around the world in 72 days : the race between
Pulitzer's Nellie Bly and Cosmopolitan's Elizabeth
Bisland / Jason Marks.
      p. cm.
   Includes bibliographical references and index.
   Pre-assigned LCCN: 92-073586.
   ISBN 0-9633696-1-X (library binding)
   ISBN 0-9633696-2-8 (trade pbk.)
   ISBN 0-9633696-3-6 (trade text)
   1. Bly, Nellie, 1867-1922—Journeys. 2. Bisland,
Elizabeth, 1861-1929—Journeys. 3. Voyages around the
world. I. Title. II. Title: Around the world in seventy-
two days. III. Title: The race between Pulitzer's Nellie
Bly and Cosmopolitan's Elizabeth Bisland.

G440.B67136M37 1993   910.4'1
                                 QBI92-20201

 Produced at The Print Center., Inc., 225 Varick St., New York, NY 10014, a non-profit facility for literary and arts-related publications. (212) 206-8465

Printed on recycled paper

With deep gratitude to three other women in my life — my beloved wife Edith who encouraged me to take the trip, my secretarial assistant Grace Haislet who kept the manuscript shipshape, and my editor Doris Kuller who guided AROUND THE WORLD IN 72 DAYS: THE RACE BETWEEN PULITZER'S NELLIE BLY AND *COSMOPOLITAN'S* ELIZA-BETH BISLAND into sunlit harbor.

TABLE OF CONTENTS

There are two versions of how Elizabeth Cochrane adopted her famous pen name. The first gives Cochrane credit for quick thinking as she was persuading Madden (of the *Pittsburgh Dispatch*) to accept her piece on divorce: the editor wanted her to use a pen name; Erasmus Wilson, his assistant, was humming the popular Stephen Foster song "Nellie Bly," and Cochrane seized upon it. The second gives all the credit to Madden: he had made inquiries, learned of Cochrane's old family name, and decided it would be improper to link the family with commentary on divorce; this time an unidentified office boy was the whistler who gave Madden the idea. The choice proved to be symbolic: the girl in the song uses a broom to "sweep de kitchen clean"; Nellie Bly the reporter used her writing to clean up abuse and corruption.

Lea Ann Brown, Southern Illinois University
Dictionary of Literary Biography

AROUND THE WORLD IN 72 DAYS:
THE RACE BETWEEN PULITZER'S NELLIE BLY
AND *COSMOPOLITAN'S* ELIZABETH BISLAND

INTRODUCTION

Early in the 1950s I worked as a writer for a company that made flanges to seal tight the openings of steel drums. I was hired by the vice-president who asked me to publicize his activities as a businessman, artist, and psychic healer as well as to ghost a book that would go to the firm's clients or to thousands of manufacturers of metal barrels used to carry oil, syrups, and other liquids throughout the world. A romantic, impractical sort who had been trudging the streets of Manhattan with holes in the soles of his shoes, I was grateful for the job and determined to succeed at it. But how could I write a book that publicized the company? All I knew about the flange was that it surrounded the bunghole, and fitted the screwcap so snugly it made the barrel leakproof. I took my problem to a bright young executive in the company. He thought for a moment then asked, "Did you ever hear of Nellie Bly?"

Nellie Bly.....the name sounded vaguely familiar. She was famous for something or other. Hadn't they named a race horse after her?

"She was a newspaper reporter," my fellow employee said. "She went around the world in less than eighty days—a fantastic feat for her time."

All well and good. But what did Nellie Bly have to do with flanges?

"Her husband was one of the first manufacturers of metal barrels in America. Formerly, barrels were made of wood and they leaked a lot. She took over his business and turned it into a multi-million-dollar enterprise."

I did a little preliminary research and concluded, What a terrific idea! Loaded with romance! Filled with adventure! Nellie Bly was amazing! A daring and doubtless beautiful manufacturer of words, steel barrels, and legend! Wow! The book would be both entertaining and informative. I took the idea to the vice-president and was given the green light. The book about Nellie Bly described the history-making trip of a twenty-two year-old woman journalist who in 1889-1890 girdled the globe as a circulation-boosting stunt for Joseph Pulitzer's *New York World* and did it in seventy-two days, six hours, and eleven minutes, thus beating the record set by the fictional Phileas Fogg in Jules Verne's popular novel *Around the World in Eighty Days*. At the age of twenty-eight, Nellie married Robert L. Seaman, a wealthy Brooklyn manufacturer of metal barrels and more than forty years her senior. A footnote to the Nellie Bly story was the fact that another woman had gone around the world the same time Nellie did. Her name was Elizabeth Bisland, an associate editor for *Cosmopolitan* magazine. She too beat Fogg's record, but because she made the trip in seventy-six days she was consigned to oblivion.

Shortly before the book came out, *Life* magazine in New York condensed it into an article of about 5,000 words in length. With the innocence of the romantic, I presumed that if *Life* went to all that trouble, it would publish the condensation.

I was looking forward to a permanent job. The article never appeared in *Life*. So near, but so far—like Elizabeth Bisland. If only *Life* magazine had printed the article! If only Miss Bisland had not missed the steamship at Le Havre! Was luck self-perpetuating? Not long after my near-miss, I was let go by the company. Because, I wondered, I was now publicizing the firm's vice-president much more that the firm? Or because I wasn't aggressive and should have blown my own horn in the one office that counted—the main one down the hall? Had my inaction done me in, just as Elizabeth Bisland's had ruined her when she took at face value the erroneous report that the *S.S. Le Champagne* had sailed without her? I felt devastated, just as she must have felt devastated when she returned from her trip around the world to be met at the pier by "the glad faces of my friends." I went on to become a newspaper editor and reporter. I wrote novels and short stories and had some more near-misses. So near, but so far. "Hurrah for Nellie Bly!" the crowd cheered. "She's a winner!" Nellie Bly was Destiny's Darling, but did that take anything away from Elizabeth Bisland? After all, she too, had performed a remarkable feat, and but for a twist of fate—or was it fate?—it might have been she who was welcomed by throngs of roaring admirers and Nellie Bly who, as the heartbroken runner-up, was met by "the glad faces" of consoling friends.

In 1970, the humorist S.J. Perelman announced his intention to travel around the world using the same means of transportation that Phileas Fogg had employed. I wrote a story pegging Nellie Bly's trip to the news about Perelman and it was published in the *New York Times* travel section (January 24, 1971) under the headline, "S.J. Perelman, Meet Miss Nellie Bly." The sixty-six year-old Perelman planned to travel accompanied by his secretary on railroad, steamer, and elephant (a reliable one, for wet pachyderms were a major problem during the monsoon season). Young Nellie, unchaperoned, had ridden variously on train, ship, sampan, gharry, catamaran, burro, barouche and bullock cart, climaxing her effort to beat Fogg's record with a frantic dash across the American continent on several railways including the Atchinson, Topeka and Santa Fe.

I was grateful to Nellie Bly for helping me to break into *The Times*. Numerous other stories by me appeared in that newspaper's travel section over the next fourteen years but none gave me quite the same pleasure as the maiden one for which I did not need to travel. I had finally laid the ghost of Nellie Bly to rest, but not that of Elizabeth Bisland. Because I identified so strongly with her, she continued to haunt me. Who was she? Didn't she—every bit as much as Nellie—deserve the accolade? I started to research the life of Elizabeth Bisland. She was, I learned, the unsung heroine in the piece; she swallowed a bitter defeat and with no outward sign of resentment went back to the business of ordinary daily living. Miss Bisland was like those nominees at the Academy Awards ceremony, set smiles on their faces, hoping against hope to hear their name called.

As the winner—not them—raced forward to accept the Oscar, that set smile never left their faces. They wore the Bisland smile; they were, or so it appeared, game losers.

The more I learned about Elizabeth Bisland, the more she and Nellie Bly came to seem inseparable in their giddy quest for inconstant Fame. To my mind, you could not understand the importance of either woman without first understanding the importance of the other. And so, I began to write.....

AROUND THE WORLD IN SEVENTY-TWO DAYS:
THE RACE BETWEEN PULITZER'S NELLIE BLY
AND *COSMOPOLITAN'S* ELIZABETH BISLAND

CHAPTER ONE
WHAT THIS GIRL IS GOOD FOR

Folks in Cochran's Mills, Pa., including members of his own family, had nourished the impression that Michael Cochran was a man of means and wealth. Starting as a laborer, the enterprising Irishman had risen to become a mill owner, then a learned judge, and founded the town which took his name. So that following his demise, in 1880, those close to him were shocked to learn from his executors that his estate of $17,000 had melted away; Judge Cochran died broke.

Left with the upbringing of a daughter, Elizabeth, age thirteen, and her six older brothers, Mary Jane Cochran must have felt cruelly betrayed. But in those final decades of the Victorian era, the American husband reigned supreme in the home. It must be presumed that Judge Cochran had governed his family's finances as if by divine right, revealing little about their condition and allotting to his wife the role of homemaker. In any event, he was a good father. With laudable earnestness, he undertook the education of his daughter, introducing her to the realms of law, politics, and economics in his wondrous library and sending her off to a boarding school in Indiana where she spent a year before frail health forced her to return home. Young Elizabeth idolized her father; he sharpened her faculties, inculcated in her a love of learning. From her mother she learned how to be a lady, what to wear in society, and how to comport herself. But her father gave her an inquiring mind. At her tender age particularly, the loss of a father was a grievous blow.

What to do with her life? How to earn a living? Elizabeth Cochran's dilemma typified that confronting any young female groping to find her path in the male-dominated late nineteenth century. Her options were painfully limited. A respectable woman remained home until she married, and if she could not find a husband, she might train to become a teacher or nurse—provided she had the money. Otherwise, she was forced to live with relatives the rest of her days and accept the role of houseworker or nursemaid, without pay. Elizabeth persuaded her mother in the mid-1880s to move to Pittsburgh, a growing city with greater opportunities for employment. Already an impassioned feminist, she soon made her feelings known. The result was the following notice buried inside a local newspaper of November 22, 1885:

> Will the gentleman who wrote a letter to the *Pittsburgh Dispatch*, criticizing our editorial of Friday entitled "What Girls are Good for," please send his name and address to the editor? Mr. Madden wishes to discuss with the unknown contributor the possibility of his writing a feature article on the same subject for this paper.

The editorial had affirmed that Woman's place was in the home and had deplored the current trend of hiring women to work in shops and offices. As Elizabeth Cochran read the notice she trembled with excitement. For it was she who had written the letter, the gist of which was that girls had the same ability, talents, and intelligence as men but lacked the same opportunities. Without telling George A. Madden that the critic of his editorial was female, she wrote him requesting an appointment, signing the missive simply "E. Cochrane." (She retained thereafter the "e" added to her surname.) If she did not hear from him to the contrary, she wrote, she would be in his office next Wednesday afternoon at three o'clock. Madden did not reply.

Wednesday came. Madden was amazed to discover that the writer of that brilliant, scorching letter was not a man. No woman wrote that well, and the rough-and-tumble newsroom certainly was not the proper place for a lady! He stared in wonderment at the slip of a girl who was telling him she wanted a job with the *Dispatch*! How young she at first appeared, how meek and ingenuous! But her wide green eyes were searching, the jut of her jaw suggested determination, and her reddish-brown bangs hid a broad, thoughtful brow. Although she was small and slender, there was a presence about her that made her seem taller. Madden told her that she was too young and that he didn't hire women, but Elizabeth Cochrane was resolved to prevail against him. She and her mother, she said, were penniless, and the only way she knew to earn a living was to write. She knew also, she told him, that she had what it took to be a reporter: When her father, a lawyer, developed a case, he would send her out to interview families and neighbors and get information from them that might prove useful in the courtroom. Was not that, she asked, a form of reporting? With mesmerizing logic, her eyes flashing, she proceeded to convert the reluctant editor to her cause. Unlike the male hacks in his office, she had fresh pioneering ideas; they poured out of her as she paced restlessly before him. She wanted, she said, to go into the slums of Pittsburgh and expose the poverty and oppression there. It was not enough to describe an event;—a reporter must *participate*. Because she was one of them, she could readily identify with the poor. She would talk to the women who slaved in the shops, stay with families in the overcrowded tenements, explore the mills and factories where young children were required to work long hours, uncover the evil conditions in the poorhouses, hospitals, orphan asylums, prisons. As she spoke, Madden marveled at how sensitively her face reflected her feelings. She cared about the poor and the downtrodden with such an intensity that she *became* them, sharing their sorrows and aspirations, taking part on some deep emotional level in their daily lives. There was something of the actress about her, but her sincerity was not simulated. Madden was impressed; he hired her and let her pick her own topic for her first story. She wrote about divorce, arguing that spouses should have the right to dissolve a marriage that had become unendurable. Madden admired the style and cogency with which she handled this touchy subject. He bylined the article by Elizabeth Cochrane with the pen name he had assigned her, "Nellie Bly." She went on to champion the victims of callous industrial America. With an indignation that thrilled her readers, she wrote a series of articles deploring the filth and degradation that workers, mainly women, suffered in the factories of Pittsburgh. The circulation of the *Dispatch* soared, but Nellie Bly's "meddling" incurred the wrath of local civic leaders and factory owners, who pressured Madden into reassigning her to less explosive investigations. He had her cover the opera, concerts, recitals, lectures, the theatre. Nellie stewed at these restraints. When she demanded to be put on more consequential stories, he sent her out to interview the warden of Western Penitentiary, a modern facility for its time. Nellie talked not only to the warden but to the prisoners in their cells. Her story, which described in graphic detail the horrible conditions in other jails, infuriated city officials. Who did she think she was to judge their prison systems? How dare she soil the honor of womanhood and wander shamelessly, unchaperoned, through a prison filled with men? An editorial in a rival newspaper advised decent women everywhere to have nothing to do with the infamous Nellie Bly. Threatened with a loss of advertising, George A. Madden put her back on covering cultural events. While he raised her salary from five to fifteen dollars a week, a substantial wage for a young girl in the 1880s, Nellie was not mollified. She knew the time had come for her to venture into the wider world and find new challenges.

CHAPTER TWO

THE RACE AROUND THE WORLD BEGINS

When Nellie Bly got the idea, she thought, Wonderful! She rushed to tell Jules Chambers, her managing editor at Joseph Pulitzer's *New York World* and was informed that they had dreamed up the same idea a year ago with the intention of sending a man and then discarded it. Chambers, however, was supportive and took her to George W. Turner, the *World's* business manager. Turner, who nowadays might be labeled a sexist, opposed Nellie's notion on three counts: A woman traveling alone would need a protector; a woman would carry so much baggage she would lose precious time when required to make rapid changes; and Miss Bly spoke only English. No one but a man could pull it off.

Nellie Bly was not accustomed to taking "No" for an answer. At twenty-two she had already carved out a reputation for herself as an investigative reporter. She had exposed the plight of the poor and the oppressed in Mexico; feigning insanity, she had gotten herself committed to the notorious mental asylum on Blackwell's Island in New York City and uncovered the brutal treatment of the patients there. So she snapped at the business manager: "Very well! Start the man and I'll start the same day for some other newspaper and beat him!"

"I believe you would," said Turner, caught up like others before him in the intensity of those questioning green eyes. Before she left the *World* office, Nellie Bly convinced them that if anyone made the trip, it should be she. But it must have crossed her mind that the idea she thought was so fantastic had already been turned down twice by the *World*, once when they dreamed it up and once again when she did. How sold could they be on a notion that was second-day merchandise on the market shelf? She wanted to race around the world for her newspaper as a circulation-boosting stunt and beat the "record" set by fictional character Phileas Fogg in Jules Verne's *Around the World in Eighty Days*.

Almost a year later, Nellie Bly was summoned by Joseph

15

Pulitzer to meet with him on his yacht in New York Harbor away from the noise and commotion of the city. Already, at the age of forty-two, this man, remarkable for his energy, ambition, determination, and intellectual curiosity was a physical wreck. His eyesight, weak since childhood, was failing, and he suffered from what in those times doctors would have called a nervous breakdown but nowadays the symptoms of a burned-out case. Pulitzer had already lived several lifetimes. Born in Hungary, he received a good private-school education but at the age of seventeen ran away from home to join an army—any army. Rejected by the Austrian Army, French Foreign Legion, and British armed forces as physically unfit for military service, Pulitzer volunteered for the Union Army in the Civil War and was enlisted by a recruiting agent who shipped him to America. As an immigrant, he arrived in New York City virtually penniless and handicapped by language difficulties. Pulitzer served with the Lincoln cavalry regiment organized by Carl Schurz, with whom he would later become associated in the newspaper business. He suffered a series of painful, short-term job experiences, including one as a waiter in St. Louis but he persevered: Pulitzer learned English and became an American citizen, was hired in St. Louis as a reporter for Schurz's leading German-language daily, the *Westliche Post*, and at the age of twenty-two was elected as a Republican to the Missouri Legislature (he would later switch to the Democratic Party). Pulitzer became part-owner of the *Post*. In 1872, he sold his stock in that paper to Schurz. With money in his pocket now, he returned to Europe to tour the continent and visit his relatives in Hungary, married beautiful and accomplished Georgetown socialite Kate Davis, and satisfied the bar requirements to practice Law in the District of Columbia. Pulitzer campaigned for Samuel J. Tilden, the 1876 Democratic presidential candidate, and reported for the *New York Sun* on the work of the electoral commission which decided that disputed election in favor of Rutherford B. Hayes. Now equipped with an excellent command of English and a thorough knowledge of his adopted country, Pulitzer took bold action in the field of journalism. He bought two failed St. Louis newspapers and built them into the *Post-Dispatch*, a newspaper which thrived under his leadership, promoting itself as a champion of the people and crusader against abuses committed by the wealthy and powerful. In 1883, he sold that publication and bought from millionaire Jay Gould the ailing *New York World*, whose daily circulation had declined to about 11,000. For practical as well as philosophical reasons, Pulitzer wanted to appeal to the masses in New York City, for as he said "Circulation means advertising, and advertising means money, and money means independence." As a champion of the people, Pulitzer made the editorial page his pulpit for education and enlightenment, for fighting injustice and promoting social reforms. The result in the *World* was a rather odd mixture of idealism and stories on sex (within Victorian limits) and crime. Nellie Bly's sensational reports on life in a madhouse, poverty in Mexico, and the working conditions of shop girls in New York fitted perfectly into the Pulitzer formula. As a two-cent morning daily, the *World* undercut its competition, forcing the *Times, Herald,* and *Tribune* to reduce their price per copy. Like publisher William Randolph Hearst, who would come to New York in 1905 and become his arch-competitor in the battle for readers, Pulitzer raided the staffs of rival newspapers to obtain the finest journalists. At a time when the average salary of a reporter was $20—$25 per week, Pulitzer was paying some staff reporters as high as $50—$80 a week. During the 1880s, Pulitzer exposed political corruption including the award of a street-car franchise in New York and fought against such industrial giants as the New York Central, Standard Oil Company, and the Bell Telephone monopoly. He also campaigned in his newspaper to raise funds to complete the pedestal of Bartholdi's Statue of Liberty. By 1889, the *New York World* had around 340,000 readers and wanted more.

This was Joseph Pulitzer, at the age of forty-two, already a towering figure. Nellie Bly burned with excitement as she was rowed out for her audience with the man who had shown supreme confidence in her ability and hired her in the summer of 1887 to work for the *World*. She knew that the decision whether to send her around the world must come from the top. Why else would the great publisher want to see her? Despite his physical condition, Pulitzer's mind was as brilliant, penetrating, and imaginative as ever. He gave Nellie Bly the green light she had so anxiously waited for, painting with visionary clarity the opportunity now being presented her. He wanted her to go around the world and beat the incredible "record" set in the Verne novel. The *World*, he promised, would spare no expense to ensure that she won her race against time and Phileas Fogg. It would arrange her itinerary, cement her connections with trains and ships around the globe, gather information for her on the countries she was to visit, keep its readers fully apprised of her whereabouts and adventures, and prepare the network by which she could cable her stories daily to the *World* office in New York. A special courier service would conduct her reports and messages onto ships, and fleet pilot boats would get them off the ships; fast mail trains would carry them over land. The *World* would help Nellie with every means at its disposal on each step of her journey, and if she broke the record she would make history. Pulitzer added a note of mystery and menace to the Great Adventure: To maintain secrecy, Nellie would use a special code in her communications to the *World*, and she must—for now—keep everything he told her absolutely confidential, for if word leaked out, others would start to race her and would get there first. The *World* would get back to her, Pulitzer concluded, as soon as the details of her trip were worked out.

Nellie Bly was ecstatic. She was ready to start out *now* but she would have to wait. And the waiting was pure agony. What was holding up their completion of the details? What if the plans for her fell through? She poured her energies into an exposé of charlatans who claimed to teach scarfmaking and glovemaking to women in quest of a trade. Then one cold, rainy evening in November, 1889, Nellie was called in by editor Chambers and asked, "Can you start around the world day after tomorrow?"

Nellie's heart pounded. Her dream come true!

"I can start this minute," she said. The indomitable Nellie Bly had never doubted she would succeed when she set out to achieve something others believed was impossible. She thought now, If you want to do it you can do it. The question is, Do you want to do it? She wanted to do it.

Next morning, Nellie Bly went to fashionable Ghormley's. In exchange for a promise to plug their apparel in her stories, she was fitted in one day for a durable blue broadcloth dress and a checked camel's hair coat with jaunty visored cap that matched. Nellie purchased a steamship ticket to England solely, relying upon the *World*, with which she would be in continual contact while traveling, to keep her informed regarding whatever further was available in the way of ship and train connections and hotel accommodations. Perhaps to show the business manager he was wrong about women, Nellie packed her belongings into a single handbag, quipping that if one traveled simply for the sake of traveling and not for the purpose of impressing one's fellow travelers, the problem of baggage became a simple one. Nellie radiated optimism; she put her trust in the *World* to make everything come out all right. Pulitzer had laid down the grand design of her trip, and now his editors were arguing furiously over the details, cabling American consuls in Europe to be ready for her arrival, contacting railroad companies and steamship lines, cutting red tape and securing from Secretary of State James G. Blaine a temporary passport for Nellie, who had no passport. In a world in which America was not yet recognized for her industrial capacity and her image of herself as a mighty power had little psychological currency abroad, Nellie was also provided with some American gold and paper money to see if it would be honored in foreign lands, together with 200 pounds in good old solid, reliable English gold and Bank of England notes. Nellie brushed aside the suggestion that she carry a revolver, trusting to the chivalry of men in those times for a damsel in distress.

Nellie Bly had vowed to travel light, but true to her femininity she was unable to give up her jar of cold cream which was the bane of her existence whenever she tried to close her satchel. It seemed to her that the whole thing had happened like magic! A day-and-a-half ago she had been told to get ready to go around the world, and now she was going! But the last-minute rush of uncertainties was nerve-racking. For the past year Nellie had suffered daily from headaches which eminent physicians attributed to overwork and for which they recommended taking a vacation; nowadays they would prescribe aspirin. When she went to the *World* office to say goodbye, what she found exacerbated her anxieties. There was as yet no firm itinerary; some doubt was expressed as to whether the Brindisi mail train she expected to catch left

London every Friday night, or whether the week of her scheduled arrival in London was the one in which that same mail train connected with the ship for India or China. In a last-minute effort to patch together an itinerary, the *World* roughed out a schedule as best it could this side of the water. It called for Nellie Bly to arrive in London on November 21st, Paris on the 23rd, Brindisi the 25th, Suez the 27th, Ceylon on December 10th, Singapore December 18th, Christmas in Hong Kong, Yokohama on January 7th, San Francisco on January 22nd, and due back January 27th in the *New York World* office.

As Nellie Bly waved goodbye to her friends on the pier, she told herself what she had told them—that she was going on a much-needed vacation and the most enjoyable time of her life. She also told herself it was "only a matter of twenty-eight thousand miles, and seventy-five days and four hours" and she would be home again. But as the *Augusta Victoria* steamed down the sparkling bay, she brooded about the horrors she had been advised awaited her—the blazing heat, the biting cold, terrible storms, fevers, shipwrecks. She was, she knew, traveling the Atlantic at the worst time of year. She marveled at her boldness to go around the world when she was wholly unused to sea-voyages; still, there was no doubt in her mind as to the result of her quest. She saw the journey as a glorious adventure.

* * *

The 1880s marked the rise of monthly magazine journalism. A number of these ambitious new publications cut their prices from 35 cents to 15 cents in order to compete with the daily newspapers; *Cosmopolitan* was not among them. Founded in 1886 by writer and publisher Paul J. Schlicht, this handsome magazine retained its high yearly subscription price of four dollars. In accordance with its motto "The world is my country and all mankind my countrymen," *Cosmopolitan* featured articles on a wide range of subjects including how ancient people lived, climbing Mount Vesuvius, and the life of Mozart, as well as European travel sketches and African wild animal adventures. But the elitism of the magazine was not at all successful. After a financial struggle, Schlicht sold it to John Brisben Walker, who had a completely different idea of what a magazine should be. Whereas

Schlicht's approach had been too precious and had focused on a small audience, Walker's was geared to a more common denominator of readership as well as to what he called "dignified sensationalism." With these techniques, he was to build *Cosmopolitan* into one of America's leading illustrated periodicals (the noted novelist and critic William Dean Howells was for a time his co-editor) and, after seventeen years as its head, in 1905 he sold the magazine to William Randolph Hearst (it remains a Hearst publication to this day). Walker was a man of wide experience. Before taking over *Cosmopolitan* in 1888, he had been a cadet at West Point, a diplomat in China, an unsuccessful Republican candidate to the 43rd U.S. Congress, an alfalfa farmer in Colorado, and managing editor of the *Washington Chronicle*. (Walker would also go on to organize the Mobile Company of America, buy and rebuild a factory in Kingsland Point, Tarrytown, to manufacture Stanley Steamer automobiles, lecture at Catholic University in Washington, D.C., on: "The Church and Poverty," deliver an address at Cooper Union in New York City on whether Woodrow Wilson's administration stood for the people or for special interests, and during World War I become chairman of Friends of Peace and Justice, a national organization "working toward a higher justice for men and women.")

So that John Brisben Walker was a man to be reckoned with.

His challenge, in 1889, was: How to get *Cosmopolitan* out of the red ink and enable it to compete in the cutthroat world of journalism in New York? As its new owner and publisher, the shrewd and resourceful Walker announced that he was introducing "the newspaper ideas of timeliness and dignified sensationalism into periodical literature." It is hard to believe that in the tight little world of publishing he did not glean advance word of powerful Joseph Pulitzer's intent to send Nellie Bly around the globe to beat the record set by Jules Verne's fictional character Phileas Fogg. Walker must have seen a golden opportunity to outperform the daily newspapers at their own game. *Cosmopolitan*, as a periodical that came out once a month, simply was not geared to compete with publications that reached readers on a quotidian basis. But if it could somehow latch onto their formula for success—

Pulitzer's brainstorm ideally combined the journalistic elements Walker was pitching. It was dignified, it was sensational, and it was timely in the sense that Nellie Bly's trip was pegged to the American public's expanding curiosity about the world at large—its peoples, cultures, and modes of travel. But how to involve *Cosmopolitan*? Then Walker hit upon the idea: Why not send his *own* woman around the world to beat Nellie Bly? Such a race was bound to create tremendous excitement, and if his woman *won*, she would not only boost the circulation of *Cosmopolitan* she would put the magazine on the journalistic map with the heavyweights. And Walker's preliminary research gave him every reason to believe that his woman *could* beat Pulitzer's, for Miss Bly's promise to girdle the globe in seventy-five days erred on the side of caution; surely, what with today's efficiency of travel by train and ship, the journey could be accomplished in less time than that. He must, he thought, send a woman;—it wouldn't make sense to send a man! But which woman? Walker thought of Elizabeth Bisland. As associate editor on his staff, she had previous experience as a feature writer for the *Times-Democrat* in New Orleans and was a contributor of articles in *Cosmopolitan* and other magazines. When, on November 14, 1889, Walker read in the *New York World* the announcement that Nellie Bly was already setting sail for Europe, he plucked Miss Bisland out of the anonymity she cherished and, summoning her to his office, offered her the chance to become a star in the journalistic firmament. The war was on. Both publishers were more concerned about winning than about the reportage involved. Each vowed to spare no expense to guarantee that his representative emerged victorious. Elizabeth Bisland, a statuesque Southern belle who jealously guarded her privacy and her dignity, was appalled by her employer's request. She wondered what the warped male mind found funny or exhilarating in tearing a woman from her home and forcing her to get ready for a seventy-five day (or less) race around the world. She protested that (1) she did not want to go around the world, (2) she had no time to assemble a decent wardrobe, (3) she hated notoriety and seeing her name in headlines, and (4) she was expecting guests to tea tomorrow and did not want to disappoint them. One must assume Walker either offered Elizabeth Bisland a huge sum of money to undertake the assignment or he threatened to fire her if she turned it down. During the next few days, Walker and his business manager A.D. Wilson bent every effort to ensure that Miss Bisland would win the race against Nellie Bly. They secured travel arrangements whereby she would sail from San Francisco—it was her idea that she go from West to East—on November 21st, and reach Yokohama, Japan, on December 11th. They also cabled for a fast government boat to take her from Yokohama to Hong Kong in five days, at a cost to the magazine of $8,000 for this segment alone of her world tour. This tactic, it was planned, would gain time for her, as Nellie Bly would have to wait at Hong Kong four days for the regular boat. The rest of Elizabeth Bisland's journey would be comparatively simple: She would sail from Hong Kong on December 27th and arrive at Brindisi, Italy, where she would take the steamer for Marseilles, arriving on Sunday, January 21, 1890. If Miss Bisland arrived at Le Havre on time, she would sail for New York that same day. If she arrived a day late at Le Havre, she would sail on Monday, January 22nd, from Southampton, arriving in New York on January 29th.

Elizabeth Bisland packed her belongings into a good-sized steamer trunk, a large Gladstone bag, and a strap-shawl. She hoped to manage the trip on two cloth gowns, half a dozen light bodices, and an evening silk, and she took the precaution of carrying plenty of hairpins and pins (to keep the layers of clothing in her trunk separate and accessible).

The evening of the same day Nellie Bly sailed for Europe, Elizabeth Bisland set out in the opposite direction. She was seen off by her friends in New York and left on a train for Chicago. Her brain reeled;—it all happened so fast...the summons to Walker's office...the heated argument with him...the pressures of getting ready...the kisses and farewells and flurry of advice...the glare of the lights in the station...the coffin-like smell of the sleeping car. For her this was no adventure; this was a chore, and one that she accepted with extreme reluctance. She felt lonely, confused, depleted by the day's events. As the train pulled out with her on it, Elizabeth Bisland thought, What am I doing on this ridiculous wild-goose chase?

CHAPTER THREE

NELLIE BLY VISITS JULES VERNE

This was Nellie Bly's first sea voyage and she wondered if she would get seasick. When "the disease of the wave" did overcome her, one of the men, obviously an experienced marine traveler, sneered within earshot, "And she's going around the world!" Instead of taking offense, Nellie joined in the general laughter. She had a gift for not taking herself too seriously that helped smooth out the rough edges of travel; the need, however, to upchuck was no laughing matter. Thrice one evening, her mighty will power no match for Nature's onslaught, Nellie fled the Captain's table and thrice returned, to be greeted the third time by a burst of kindly bravos. Captain Albers told her that the only way to conquer seasickness was to force oneself to eat. Queasy Nellie put on a happy face; she couldn't wait for the dinner to be over, but when it was, she told them all how delicious the food had been! She went to bed and slept as if drugged, for almost twenty-four hours. Advised by the Captain that a big dinner would do her some good now, she ate heartily. The weather was bad and the sea rough, but Nellie felt fine now; she had vanquished seasickness.

Amiable and easy-going, Nellie Bly made friends easily, an asset to her as a journalist seeking information. Aboard the *Augusta Victoria*, she cultivated the acquaintance of an American girl traveling to Germany to visit her parents and brilliantly conversant with subjects ranging from fashion to literature and from politics to music. There was also a streak of mischievousness in Nellie; she amused herself by studying the peculiarities of her fellow passengers—the man who took his pulse after every meal, the woman who had not undressed since she left her home in New York because if the boat sank, she was "determined to go down dressed!"; the family whose little Skye terrier "Homie," much to their disgust, was confined to the care of the ship's butcher, and who, much to the concern of the passengers, was losing weight. How could a dog in the custody of a butcher grow thinner?

Nellie Bly's journey around the globe was, of course, bound to arouse patriotic sentiment. America in 1889 was still a young country—barely a century old and only twenty-four years past Lee's surrender at Appomattox. But it was already a nation bursting with social, economic, and industrial development. Under Benjamin Harrison, our 23rd President, six states—North Dakota, South Dakota, Montana, Washington, Idaho, and Wyoming—were admitted, bringing the total in the Union to forty-four. Rail and telegraph lines spanned the continent; mining production flourished; the number of wage-earners and manufacturing plants boomed. Funded by private and government sources, colleges and universities began to make an education available to masses of people. Now that the nation was settled from sea to shining sea, its banking and industrial leaders started to think of looking beyond U.S. shores for business opportunities. Nellie Bly inevitably became associated with this growth; she exemplified in the public mind the spirit of independence of the American Girl and the youthful get-up-and-go of the glorious land she represented in her travels abroad. She must have been more than mildly surprised to hear the seasoned travelers on the *Augusta Victoria* say that people in foreign countries didn't even know where America was! The ship's captain said many foreigners thought the United States was "one little island, with lots of houses on it." Once a letter from Germany delivered to him at his house near the wharf, in Hoboken, was addressed to "CAPTAIN ALBERS, FIRST HOUSE IN AMERICA." As Nellie Bly's trip progressed, she learned that the rest of the world regarded America as a backward nation! Britannia did, indeed, rule the waves, and the sun, indeed, never did set on the British Empire. When the passengers kidded Nellie about her trip around the world, she adopted a forced gaiety. She was in no position to put on the airs of a heroine.

The *Augusta Victoria* reached Southampton early in the morning of November 22nd, after a voyage of seven days and seventeen hours. As a woman traveling alone and unprotected, Nellie Bly defied the conventions of her day, and by doing so, she freed herself as journalist to explore new experiences. If, she observed, she had had a companion, she would have had less time to get to know her fellow passengers, from whom she now parted with keen regret. Nellie's status as a vulnerable female—which would later provoke male amorousness—currently invited a male protectiveness she was secretly pleased to receive. The handsome and genial Captain Albers had for many years commanded a ship in the East, and cautioned her regarding the care of her health. And now at the dismal hour of 2:30 in the morning, when the *World*'s London correspondent was supposed to meet her, one of her male acquaintances from the ship expressed concern about her safety and offered to conduct her to London if the correspondent did not appear. The *World*, however, did not let her down; when a young man overheard somebody identify her as the woman making the trip around the world, he asked Nellie her name then introduced himself as that newspaper's London correspondent. Nellie's male acquaintance from the ship drew the man aside and checked him out. He then informed Nellie, "He's all right. If he had not been so, I should have gone to London with you anyway. I can rest satisfied now for he will take care of you."

Nellie Bly went away, she would later recount in her book about her trip around the world, with a warm feeling in her heart for "that kindly man who would have sacrificed his own comfort to insure the safety of an unprotected girl." The observation was perhaps a trifle coy, for while Nellie, like any woman, enjoyed being protected by a chivalrous gentleman, she was to prove more than a match for males who made advances toward her either because they liked her or because they mistook her for a rich American heiress gallivanting around the globe and wanted to marry her (she put one persistent suitor off her trail by mislaying his peg leg!)

The *World*'s London correspondent informed Nellie that he had received a special letter from Mr. and Mrs. Jules Verne. They wanted her to come visit them at their home in Amiens. Nellie was thrilled. How could she possibly turn down an invitation from the internationally famous novelist whose fictional character she was trying to outdo? Was she willing to go without sleep—even rest—for two nights? No problem, Nellie said, provided that the unplanned trip did not make her miss any of her other connections. It all depended, she was informed, upon her getting a train out of here tonight. All the regular trains for London until morning had left, and unless they decided to run a special mail train for the delayed mails, she and the correspondent would have to stay here in Southampton all night and that would not give them time to see the Vernes.

They caught the fast mail train to London, arriving there in a ghostly fog. As her horse-and-carriage clattered toward the local office of the *World*, Nellie Bly caught fleeting glimpses of Westminster Abbey, the Houses of Parliament, and the river Thames. Her "bird's-eye view" of London troubled her. A great many foreigners, she reflected, had in the same rapid, superficial fashion, taken views of the United States and "afterwards gone and written books about America, Americans and Americanisms." As an investigative reporter trained to seek truth-in-depth, she began to sense the limitations that racing against time might impose upon her reportage. Joseph Pulitzer and his editors in New York were sticklers for accuracy, and accuracy required probing deep. But they appeared more concerned about her winning the race than with her writing honestly about her travels. Still, Nellie Bly must have remained committed to Pulitzer's credo; whatever the pressures upon her, she would strive as before to turn out stories that were truthful, clear, intelligent, terse without sacrificing depth, and sympathetic toward people.

At the London office, Nellie picked up the cabled instructions to her from the *World* in New York. The horse-and-carriage sped her and the correspondent through the empty streets to the American Legation where the Secretary provided her with a regular passport but not until after the time-honored male bantering. He asked her "the one question all women dread to answer." Twenty-two, she answered laughing, adding gaily that the discreet correspondent could "come out of his corner now." What was the color of her eyes? Green, she replied with feigned indifference. As if doubting her, the Secretary of the Legation leaned closer for a better look. The two men agreed that her eyes were green. How Nellie loved to flirt!

The horse-and-carriage whirled Nellie Bly and the correspondent to the office of the Peninsular and Oriental steamship company where she purchased tickets that would cover at least half of her trip around the world, or from Brindisi, Italy, to Hong Kong in British China. The train ride

27

to Dover was slow and uncomfortable, the crossing of the English Channel bitterly cold, and the railway compartment so cramped that four passengers competed for the one foot-warmer (the glare of the Frenchman seated across from Nellie made painfully clear to her that it was his toes she had tramped on).

All that was forgotten when she was met by the Vernes on the station platform in Amiens. Accompanied by Paris journalist R.H. Shepard, their translator, they welcomed her with a warmth and cordiality that made her feel like a cherished friend. Nellie was enchanted with them. The white-haired Mrs. Verne, her complexion flawless, eyes bewitchingly dark, lips a lovely red, spoke no English but her glowing hospitality made Nellie feel at home. Her celebrated husband, now sixty-one, his tousled hair and long beard snowy-white, his face florid and eyes a brilliant black, captivated the young woman from America with his energy, enthusiasm, love of life. Nellie was shocked to see him walk with a limp.

It should be noted at this point that Jules Verne's *Around the World in Eighty Days*, published in 1872, was still immensely popular seventeen years later when Nellie Bly set out to encircle the globe. Over that span of time, the novel had been re-issued in several editions, so that Nellie was pegging her trip not to some dated, moribund tome but to a daringly prophetic work of romance and adventure which continued to excite the public imagination throughout the world.

Nellie watched the bright flames in the Vernes' fireplace shed a comforting glow over the large living room—the soft velvet rug and the hangings and paintings, the borders of polished hardwood floor, the fine pieces of bronze statuary, the several tall silver candlesticks. A white Angora cat rubbed against Nellie's knee then crawled into her mistress's lap. Nellie's French was pretty much confined to the word "Oui." She broke the social ice by asking Verne—through Shepard— if he had ever been to America. Yes, he replied, but for a few days only, during which he saw Niagara Falls. The renowned author said he greatly appreciated the hundreds of letters he received yearly from Americans who had read his novels. He longed to return to America, he added, but his state of health prevented him from doing so. (Verne's limp was the result of a gunshot wound that had never healed and was inflicted on him in 1885 by his poor nephew in a fit of madness.)

When Nellie described her itinerary, Verne asked her why she wasn't going to Bombay the way his Phileas Fogg had done.

"Because I am more anxious to save time than a young widow," Nellie said, cleverly alluding to the Parsee beauty who was rescued by Phileas Fogg's devoted servant Passepartout from being cremated by suttee or sacrificed on her husband's burning funeral pyre.

"You may save a young widower before you return," Verne said with a smile.

Nellie Bly smiled back. She knew that such a thing was not likely to happen but enjoyed being told that she was desirable.

Verne showed Nellie his huge library and the spare, simple study where he had written the books that were to lay the foundation for modern science fiction and where he was now working on his seventy-fourth. He also showed her the large wall-map upon which he had traced in blue pencil the course Phileas Fogg was to take in *Around the World in Eighty Days*. Nellie knew that Verne was a learned and experienced geographer who before becoming semi-invalided had sailed throughout the world in his yacht to study first-hand the locales he wrote about in his novels. She dearly wished to hear him say that he believed she could beat Phileas Fogg.

For reasons of health, Verne did not smoke or touch alcohol anymore. But this was a special occasion. He and his wife toasted Nellie and the success of her trip with vintage Madeira. The clinking of their glasses did not bring Nellie the word she wanted to hear.

"If you do it in seventy-nine days," Verne said to her in French, "I shall applaud with both hands." Nellie knew what he meant: He doubted that she would do it in seventy-five days, as she had promised—she was traveling during the Winter on a trip that was wholly north of the Equator. As a compliment to her and her courage, Verne spoke, haltingly, to her in English: "Good luck, Nellie Bly." She knew what he meant by that, too: she would need luck. Nellie Bly luck. Lots of it.

With Gallic courtesy, Mrs. Verne kissed her gently and affectionately on either cheek. Playful Nellie stifled an impulse to kiss Mrs. Verne on those sweet red lips—and show her how it was done in America.

The Vernes waved farewell to Nellie Bly from the front gate of their courtyard. As they faded from sight, time returned to obsess her. Time. Time. Pitiless and unforgiving. The Vernes had urged the driver to convey Nellie at top speed, but the carriage now rolled so quietly that she wondered if her visit to their home would jeopardize the success of her tour. She urged the driver on: Don't spare the horses, *Monsieur!* Faster! Faster! FASTER! They arrived in the station none too soon. The train to Calais was pulling in! She must get to Calais in time to catch the fast mail train to Brindisi! She could feel Father Time and Phileas Fogg breathing down her neck. She had no idea another woman was racing against her.

CHAPTER FOUR

ELIZABETH BISLAND CROSSES AMERICA

Roses.

A big bunch of pink roses.

They were a going-away gift from her friends who saw her off in New York.

How charmingly the pink complemented her traveling ensemble!

Elizabeth Bisland tried to fight off the depression by clinging to the image of the pink roses. Beauty would be her savior. She plucked a bloom from the bouquet and pressed it to her nostrils. No use. That funereal odor of the sleeping car overwhelmed the faint fragrance of the rose. She had always looked for beauty—as a means by which to transcend the disagreeable experiences of daily life. One sees this revealed in her account of her trip around the world particularly when she is feeling upset, angry, and fatigued.

Miss Bisland tried to sleep as the train roared through the dead of the American night. She fell into a worrisome daze of lucubration. What, she wondered, was she doing on this flight into nowhere? Twenty-five thousand miles to travel on this absurd junket! Just because Pulitzer's woman had promised to do it in seventy-five days and Walker thought *his* woman could do it in less! What idiocy. Ripped from her hearth and home to chase around the world after that publicity-hound! Nellie Bly thrilled to the prospect of racing around the earth; the very idea filled her rival with revulsion. From almost everything that can be learned about their lives, the two young women were a study in dramatic contrasts.

Hungry and unhappy, Miss Bisland arrived in Chicago only to find that the person who was supposed to meet her in the vast, gloomy, nearly empty railroad station was not there. Had *Cosmopolitan* made a mistake? She wandered around the station looking like an orphan in a storm. A friendly conductor took her under his wing and showed her where to switch to the train for Council Bluffs, Iowa. Like Nellie Bly, she enjoyed being protected by men. The conduc-

31

tor bade her a commiserating adieu. She sat down on a high stool at a restaurant counter. Skimpy meals are normally expected when one is on the move at odd hours, but Miss Bisland's of ham and tea left her cross and angry. She was furious at how events beyond her control had conspired to cast her in this preposterous role of a fame-seeker and a reluctant globetrotter. It was not her style to grovel for by-lines;—leave that to the headline-hunters!

Elizabeth Bisland boarded the train for Council Bluffs. Despite her anxiety about her earth-encircling journey and its purposes, she slept well and awoke at daybreak feeling she had recovered her sanity. She raised the curtain to her train window and was greeted by a sight that filled her with transcendental ecstasy. Sunrise! It was as if God in issuing his daily fiat of "Let there be light" was showing her a new Jerusalem! As far as the eye could see, the fields and uplands covered with hoar-frost glistened with silver and pearl. In a hymn to the dawn of day, Miss Bisland wrote in her journal:

> As the light grew, nacreous tints of milky blue and rose flushed the argent pallor of the land, and when the yellow disk rolled up over the horizon's edge, I travelled for some brief space in a world of intolerable splendor, where innumerable billions of frost crystals flashed back to the sun the reflection of his shining face. Even the engine-driver was moved, I fancy, by this marvelous morning vision, for though we were far from any stopping-place, there suddenly thrilled through the silence a long, keen, triumphant blast, and we trailed as we flew floating golden plumes of steam....

The exuberance of her observations here and elsewhere throughout her account of her travels suggests why John Brisben Walker chose to send Elizabeth Bisland racing around the globe. Miss Bisland was an aesthete, a devotee of beauty. (She was to take delight in painting lavish word-pictures of landscapes and the art and architecture of Japan; the sight of England's shores made her rhapsodize with quotes of Shakespeare's ringing patriotic verse.) If the purpose of travel writing is to make the reader want to "go there," Elizabeth Bisland was one of America's first great travel writers. Her prose, like her personality, was suffused with glamor, mystery, and romance. Nellie Bly, on the other hand, was a prob-

32

ing, aggressive hard-news reporter whose job was to dig up the plain—often unpleasant—facts about a person or a place and whose stories, therefore, were not likely to satisfy one's need to "get away from it all." As a prodigal romantic, Miss Bisland probably, like her readers in an already highly-industrialized society, yearned for more from life than it could give. As the train sped toward Council Bluffs, seated across the aisle from her was an amorous middle-aged couple whom she put down as "peculiarly un-interesting fellow-travelers." Herself twenty-eight, she regarded them as "ancient little lovers who numbered some hundred or more years between them." Now that their children were grown, they were on their way to sunny California to spend their second honeymoon, but their "quaint, antiquated billing and cooing" indicated to the alluring Southern belle that in addition to there being snow on their roof, there was no fire in the furnace.

That night, in Council Bluffs, thanks to *Cosmopolitan's* instigations, Elizabeth Bisland was able to catch a new fast transcontinental mail train instead of the regular train. The mail train, an experiment, was on a test run. The railroad stood to cinch a $750,000 contract with the U.S. Government if it demonstrated that it could get the mail there on time despite some of the most inhospitable territory known to man. The pace was tremendous from the start; the train began to climb the Great Divide or the great ridge of the Rocky Mountains which separates westward-flowing streams from eastward-flowing ones. Trees and shrubs became rare; vast stretches of plain and upland meadow were devoid of human habitation except for an occasional silent, lonely cabin. The terrain became so dreary and so desolate that it put Miss Bisland in mind of "the cursed site of some prehistoric Sodom, sown with salt." She added:

> The air shone with a luminous clearness undreamable in coast countries, and at night the stars were huge and fierce; not the soft-gleaming palpitant planets of tropic nights, but keen and scintillant as swords....There was something hideous and brutal in the doom laid upon this unhappy territory, as of a Prometheus chained on the mountain-tops, its blood dried to dust in its veins, and lifting a scarred face of gray despair to the rainless sky.

Elizabeth Bisland's fondness for romanticism and for making classical references was rooted in her youth when she learned to read French in an attempt to master the four volumes of philosopher Jean Jacques Rousseau's *Confessions.* Her luxuriant scholarliness was in marked contrast to Nellie Bly's matter-of-fact, down-to-earth reporting. The landscape now gave way to the Bad Lands of South Dakota—so-called because Indians and trappers found their arid wastes with their 500-feet-deep gullies difficult to cross. Here again, with the coming of daylight, Miss Bisland filled with elation at the heavens:

> The moon wan with the dawn, hung directly in the zenith, and on the eastern rim of the ghostly plain, under the quivering jewel of the morning star, burned the first vague flush of day. Slowly a dusky amethyst radiance filled the sapphire bowl of the sky, quenching the stars one by one as it rose, and when the sun showed over the world's edge the cup was brimmed, and the pale moon shone faintly in its depths, like the drowned pearl of the Egyptian queen. There was no eye but mine to see, yet in the midst of unpeopled desolation the majestic skies were fulfilled with the same slow pomp and splendor as if all the worshippers of the Sun knelt in awed wonder to see the Bridegroom come forth of his chamber.

More than seldom, the gorgeousness of Elizabeth Bisland's writing revealed more about her than she realized. Her taste for luxury showed itself in her likening the colors of Nature to those of precious gems. The morning star was a jewel, the dawn amethystine, the sky sapphire, and the moon a pearl. Also apparent was her delight in taking Nature personally. Thus the sun became a Bridegroom (God or Christ) emerging from his bedchamber. Miss Bisland's rapture with the cosmos was ultimately to be tested in the extreme, when the elements of wind and wave and storm would attack her with a violence that must have made her wonder if some form of Divine retribution was being visited upon her for having regarded the race around the world as a joke.

The mail train rocketed through the Bad Lands at a nerve-shattering pace, yet when it was five hours away from

Ogden, Utah, it was two hours and a half behind schedule. The $750,000 contract now hung in the balance and would be either won or lost by morning. A locomotive engineer with a reputation for derring-do was telegraphed to meet them at the next stop. The charismatic Elizabeth Bisland warmed instantly to the colorful Mr. Foley. He was "a gentleman of Irish extraction who labored under an entire absence of physical timidity, and who remarked with jovial determination, as he climbed into the cab, that he would get us to Ogden—or hell, on time." Foley pulled out the throttle and the train plunged ahead at 65 miles per hour, a speed not uncommon for American trains in those days, but this route lay through horrifyingly mountainous terrain. The officers of the train became alarmed and ordered Foley to reduce speed. That worthy consulted his watch then proceeded to ignore their warning. With what Miss Bisland described as a "cheerful indifference," he corkscrewed the train through gorges and canyons in a nightmarish five-hour ride. The betting stood ten-to-one among the passengers they would get to Hades. Throughout the hideous night of rocking cars and roaring engine and flying landscape and backward-reeling telegraph poles, they clung to their sleeping berths and many of them got wretchedly sick. Miss Bisland seemed above all this; from the rear car, she saw that the tracks were "two lines of fire in the night." She came back inside and watched a train official playing cards:

> One man rolled in an anguish of terror on the floor; and the General Manager, engaged in a late game of whist, regarded the sufferer with sympathetic interest as he took the odd trick with the thirteenth trump, remarked that it was such episodes as this in American life that made us a nation of youthful graybeards.

The tone of the writing was humorous and mildly mocking in the face of potential disaster. Despite her aversion to John Brisben Walker's challenge, Elizabeth Bisland accepted it courageously, as her response to the calamities that befell her in the climactic stage of her trip around the world was to demonstrate. What stuck in her mind on the highballing train was that the General Manager took the odd trick with the thirteenth trump. What also stuck in her mind was that after getting them to Ogden on time, the hearty Irish engineer disappeared forever behind the swinging doors of a saloon in quest of an "antidote," for as he put it, these night rides were prone to give a man a cold. Just as Miss Bisland admired the swagger and aplomb of Foley, there was an elegant dash and élan about her.

The altitude rose to 8,000 feet; the air grew dry; jack rabbits and coyotes were visible, and now and then an arrangement of teepees. Indians crowded about the train at every stop. Nellie Bly might have envied the resonance of the following reportage:

> Those of the female sex who were blessed with offspring permitted us to view the living contents of the corded parcels they carried on their backs in exchange for small current coin. The papoose, I discovered, is the original Baby Bunting. He slumbers with stoical composure in a nest of rabbit skins—presumably those for which "papa went a-hunting"—that line a portable wooden cradle into which he is strapped, and from which, I am told, he rarely emerges during infancy. The girls and boys from six to sixteen I found very pretty, with smooth red skins, glittering teeth and eyes, and black Vandyked locks. Those whom years had overtaken were indescribably wrinkled and parched. Old squaws squatted in the dust huddled in blankets, and were as impassive as ancient worm-eaten idols. A coin dropped into their hands brought a mumble and a glance from their rusted eyes; but indifference did not wound them, neither did the fast train or any of its passengers excite their curiosity—the vagaries of the white man were so numerous that nervous prostration would be a sure consequence of any attempt to interest themselves in his doings, and peace and composure lay only in entirely ignoring him.

As the train hurtled westward, Elizabeth Bisland's senses reveled in the countryside. The delicately perfumed dry air gave way to trees and flowers, grassy hills and watery marshes. Then Sacramento appeared briefly and "the first outer edges of that yellow wave from China which has broken upon the Pacific coasts." There was a strong resentment in

America toward the Oriental influx. In the 1850s and 1860s, Chinese coolies were in such demand as cheap labor that railroad builder Leland Stanford and other industrialists imported whole shiploads of them. By 1880, they numbered over one hundred thousand. With the completion of the transcontinental railways, white immigrant laborers came to California in increasing numbers and found themselves competing for jobs with a people whose standard of living enabled them to toil for incredibly low wages. So that Elizabeth Bisland was not alone in her foreboding regarding the Chinese newcomers; she reflected a widespread sentiment.

Miss Bisland arrived in San Francisco on November 19th. Thanks to Mr. Foley, she reached the Golden Gate a whole day ahead of her schedule. She had crossed the continent in four days and twenty hours. (Nowadays, the same trip would take an Amtrak train two days, twenty-two hours, and fifty-three minutes—or 18:53 hours from New York to Chicago and fifty-two hours from Chicago to San Francisco.) *Cosmopolitan*, Miss Bisland soon discovered, had left nothing to chance. Her arrival did not go unnoticed; she was, in fact, met by a crowd of prying reporters who bombarded her with questions about her trip around the world. For a woman who wanted to stay out of the limelight, this was a trying experience. She was invited out to luncheon by the editors of the *San Francisco Examiner*, owned and published by William Randolph Hearst who would, as previously noted, one day buy *Cosmopolitan* magazine from John Brisben Walker. Again more questions. The men from the *Examiner*, however, treated her the way she was accustomed to being treated—with courtly courtesy. She needed that, for she felt exhausted by the wild journey across the continent. Thus when she learned that *Cosmopolitan*'s efforts to get her ship for Japan to leave earlier than scheduled had failed, she did not grieve. She would lose two days in her race against the Bly woman, but she would lose them in delightful San Francisco!

Miss Bisland rode a cable car, saw Nob Hill where the bonanza kings had their palatial residences, and watched the barking sea lions frolic on the Seal Rocks.

The ship was a madhouse of people running back and forth, luggage thumping down the companion-way. Raked by the eyes of the sensation-hunters, Elizabeth Bisland felt inconsolably alone. And then something happened that made her day:

At the moment when the gong had warned all visitors ashore there was handed up to me from the wharf a great nosegay of white chrysanthemums and roses, to which was attached a card inscribed "J. M. Prather," and bearing "good wishes" and "New Orleans" pencilled in the corner. A hat was lifted from a handsome gray head, and two kind dark Southern eyes gave me a smile of such friendliness and good-will that it warmed my heart like a greeting from my own people. This unknown gentleman taking the trouble to bid me a silent, fragrant farewell seems to me the most delicate and charming impulse of that much-misinterpreted and scoffed-at Southern chivalry, and should he ever see this I wish him to know how pleasant and lasting was the perfume of his flowers and kindly thought.

CHAPTER FIVE

"WELCOME TO SUNNY ITALY"

From Calais, Nellie Bly mailed her account of the Verne interview to New York and cabled: "To all my kind friends in America, good-by for the present. It took sharp work to catch the Brindisi mail train, but I got it."

Back in the States, the drumbeat of publicity commenced. The *World* brayed that the whole civilized world was watching Nellie Bly and that she should be known instead as "Nellie Fly." Out-of-town newspapers picked up on the story. It had all the makings: Charming young woman traveling the world alone and unprotected...pioneering the independence of her sex...and trying to achieve the impossible. The British press declared that no mere female could beat the remarkable Phileas Fogg (an Englishman, whose trip began and ended in the Reform Club in London). Out-of-town U.S. papers as far apart as the *Auburn* (Maine) *Gazette* and publications in Pennsylvania, Nellie's home state, acclaimed her quest. As might be expected, Joseph Pulitzer's competitors in New York gave Nellie Bly and her trip little or no ink. *The New York Times*, for example, mentioned her by name only once, and that in a January 30, 1890 account of Elizabeth Bisland's arrival back in New York. Otherwise, *The Times* made a curiously oblique reference to her in a December 22, 1889 story about an English journalist who visited Jules Verne in Amiens and was told by the author's wife that he was a teetotaler. Whereupon Verne playfully reminded her that just the other day he drank to the health of "that little lady and wished her *bon voyage*.....And if she does have success, and does come home triumphant, I shall not be disinclined to take another glass of your Madeira, and to toast her across the sea. How, *Monsieur*, is that for a confirmed 'temperance man'?" Even more indirect and roundabout was an item in the *New York Evening Sun* of December 3, 1889, about a man named Folsom who—in an effort to validate Jules Verne's time-estimate—mailed himself a letter that went around the world in eighty-four days. In 1881, he publicly challenged in print anyone to "do it better if you can." So many people tried to do it that the postal service became overburdened with this unique kind of mail. On January 27th, in 1885, a young man named William L. Richards who was with Standard Oil in New York City joined the Folsom craze. He mailed a letter to himself care of R.G. Tilford with Walsh, Hall and Company in Yokohama. At the same time, he mailed a second letter to Mr. Tilford asking him to cross out the "Yokohama" address, mark the envelope "Not here," and forward it care of R.G. Tilford, 44 Broadway, New York City. The first letter was mailed to catch the Liverpool steamer, and the second to go via San Francisco. The second letter reached San Francisco on February 3rd, Yokohama on the 27th, and New York on April 23rd, having encircled the globe in eighty-four days. The first letter was sent without any word of explanation to anyone along the way. It reached London on February 7th and left on the 9th, arrived in Yokohama on the 16th and left on the 17th, and returned to New York May 12th, having been gone one-hundred and four days.

The vagaries of these letters are, to say the least, puzzling. If the success of the first letter was contingent upon Mr. Tilford's acting on the advice contained in the second, why would Richards dispatch them round the world in opposite directions? In any event, the story in the *Sun* continued:

> Since then, transportation lines have changed and improved their schedule, and last June, Mr. Richards determined to try again. He consulted Billings Guide and saw that a regular service around the world was in operation that consumed exactly seventy-three days to travel. Accordingly, he mailed a letter in London June 20th, and Yokohama July 31st, one day ahead of time. It left on August 2nd by regular mail boat and was delivered in New York on August 24th—seventy-three days after its departure. It had taken its chances with all kinds of storms and other things that delay travel, and by regular scheduled conveyances had made its long journey on time and without any fuss, except a deal of pounding by various postmasters in various countries.

The Tilford connection in Yokohama had again, it would appear, played a key role in this intricate game of postmarks.

So must have a global mail service by land and sea that was by now so fixed and well-established that a letter so meagerly supported by forwarding names and addresses could go around the world in quicker time than Joseph Pulitzer's Nellie Bly had promised! The route that Richards' letter took corresponded roughly to the one Nellie was now taking. The implication in arch-rival publisher Charles A. Dana's sprightly *Sun* was clear: If a letter could do it in record time, why send a woman?

No fuss in print, certainly, was made about Nellie Bly by *Cosmopolitan*. Never once did it mention her by name or even allude to her—at any time during the trip. Never once did Elizabeth Bisland indicate in print that she knew Nellie Bly existed—although she must have thought about her more than seldom. And the only public acknowledgement that Nellie would make of Miss Bisland's existence on the planet was a brief reference to her as "the other woman"—after she had been out of New York thirty-nine days and was informed by a travel agent in Hong Kong that "another woman" was racing against her. Why plug the competition? That would have defeated the purpose of the war between the publishers.

Nellie Bly's fan mail mounted while she was away. Readers of the *World* hungered for information about where she was and what was happening to her, where she was going to next and how well she was faring in her effort to beat the "record" set by the fabled Phileas Fogg. When Nellie had nothing to report, her editors would titillate readers with stories about the hazards she might run into, including fogs, siroccos, and the dreaded monsoon. They ballyhooed such tidbits as "Some of the Queer Things Nellie Bly Will See on Her Trip to Japan." They ran a contest in which the *World* promised a free trip to Europe to the person who guessed most closely how long her trip would take. Songs and verses were written about her, and one enterprising businessman manufactured and sold a "Nellie Bly wrapper" or ladies' negligee. The *World* ran a Nellie Bly game in which the reader used markers to indicate her progress and took chances on the precise minute she would reach her next destination. Heavy bets were made in gambling parlors on whether Nellie would beat the record and on the exact time she would arrive home. Inquiring minds wanted to know: Was Nellie Bly really a woman? What did she look like? Was she hitched? People wanted not only to adopt her, befriend her, honor her, advise her, warn her, and reprimand her;—they wanted to marry her! The circulation of the *World* thrived on this carefully orchestrated hoopla. An entire nation and much of the "civilized" world fevered for news of Nellie Bly.

The object of all this attention took the train to Calais where, at 1:30 in the morning, she caught the express train to Brindisi. Built to accommodate the mails to India and not passengers, it had but one passenger coach, a Pullman Palace sleeping car for twenty-two persons. One of those twenty-two passengers was by rule a guard. Today, with the return of sleeping-car thievery in Europe, travelers by rail would welcome such strict adherence to security. As the train sped forward, Nellie Bly found herself confronted with a challenge that often faces journalists—when the news is slow, how to make something out of apparent nothing. The next morning, she struck up an acquaintance with a rosy-cheeked, golden-haired English girl traveling with her father who suffered from a hacking cough. Nellie learned that just before their departure from England, the daughter put in her father's luggage a large prayer book, a gift from a clergyman who sought to comfort the ailing man in his suffering. Her father now thanked her for her thoughtfulness but asked her to return the prayer book with his compliments; he was chagrined at having deprived the good cleric of it for so long. Clasping to her breast her own out-sized missal, the daughter upbraided her father; she would not, she told him, return the sacred gift from a member of the Church. Jokingly, her father told her that *her* prayer book wasted valuable packing space and that a smaller, less pretentious one would have done just as good service. Nellie Bly observed:

> I was actually startled by the hard, determined light on her face. In everything else she was the sweetest, most gentle girl I ever met, but her religion was of the hard, uncompromising kind that condemns everything, forgives nothing, and swears the heathen is forever damned because he was not born to know the religion of her belief. She spent all the afternoon trying to implant the seeds of her faith in my mind, and I listened thinking from her words that if she was not the original

Catherine Elsmere, she at least could not be more like that interesting character.

Unlike those of her journalistic rival, Nellie Bly's allusions pertained to recent news events. Catherine Elsmere was a character in popular novelist Mrs. Humphry Ward's highly controversial *Robert Elsmere*, published in 1888. In the novel, when her husband, a young Anglican clergyman, left the church to perform social work among the people, Catherine continued to love him but was unable to share his changing belief that the function of religion lay outside the church and was to serve those in need.

The monotony of travel by mail train taxed not only Nellie Bly's ingenuity as a reporter but her patience as a passenger. The train windows looked as if they had never been washed; France was, for the most part, a dirt-smeared blur. The visibility was no better in "sunny Italy," which was hidden in a dense fog. It was so cold that night that shivering Nellie had to pile all her clothes on top of the single blanket that was provided for her sleeping berth. Next morning, the heavy gray fog obliterated everything more than three feet away. Nellie, fretful, checked her wrist watch. Ten a.m. How was it possible for the world to be virtually invisible at ten in the morning? She sought out the guard and demanded an explanation. This was, he told her, a most extraordinary thing;— he had never seen such a fog before. Nellie must certainly have wondered if the fog would make her late for the connection at Brindisi. The train was supposed to arrive there at 10:14 that evening, or in plenty of time for her to catch the steamship for Port Said at 2 a.m. the following morning. Nellie tried to calm her nerves by counting the days she had been away from New York and subtracting them from the number she had promised to do the trip in. It was November 24th, and she had been out of New York ten days. That left her sixty-five days. From Hoboken to Southampton to London was 3,041 miles and from London to Brindisi would be 1,450 miles. Four thousand, four-hundred, ninety-one— how many more to go? According to the *World*'s researches, she had at least another seventeen thousand miles to cover— not as the crow or gull flew but as the trains rode and the ships sailed. By that reckoning, she would have to do 26.15 miles per day or a little more than a mile per hour. Could she go at a mile per hour without let-up for sixty-five days! No, No, it was the trains and ships that would do the racing! Oh, this was maddening! In a frenzy of weary restlessness, Nellie Bly replaced counting the days with mulling whether the ubiquitous navy-blue uniforms of American railroad conductors and porters should be done away with and the neat brown uniforms with gold braid on cuff and collar of their Italian counterparts be introduced in the States. Anxiety gave way to ennuie. Nellie amused herself by noticing the difference between the whistles on Italian train engines and those at home. In Italy, they were plaintive and soprano; in America, deafening, an ear-tormenting bass. It also intrigued her that French and Italian trains were started by a blast on a tin horn that sounded much like the horns she had heard enthusiastic stumpers use at night in American presidential election campaigns.

The fog lifted briefly to reveal a beautiful beach and a smooth bay dotted with brightly colored, sun-kissed sails that looked to her like "mammoth butterflies, dipping, dipping about in search of honey!" How incisively that image captured what she was experiencing! On the other side of the train, white buildings were perched on the perpendicular side of a high, rugged mountain. Although the road winding upward on the mountain was walled on the ocean side, she would not, Nellie thought, care to travel up it. Her readers, seeing things through her discerning eye, must have felt the same tremor of anticipation.

At the next station, the passengers got out to have their dinners in an Italian restaurant. Here again, Nellie Bly showed her acute understanding of people, lending to an ordinary incident a warmth, humanity, and richness. When a little girl with enchanting dark eyes ran forward to greet her, Nellie drew forth a large copper coin to press into her outstretched hand (the bigger the coin in Italy, the less, generally, its value). The child's father was proprietor of the restaurant. A small man with delicately refined face, a diamond sparkling on his white shirt front, he chided the tot and she drew back. Nellie knew that he had told his daughter not to accept anything from her; she could have boxed the man's ears for his impudence! The guard from the train explained, "You have insulted him." As if Nellie didn't know that! "The

Italians are the poorest and proudest people on earth. They hate the English."

"I am an American," Nellie retorted.

The waiter, who spoke English, came forward and offered to intercede. Nellie was determined that the child should yet take the coin, but how to heal the hurt feelings of her father?

"What a beautiful restaurant!" she cried. She went on to lavish praise not only on the quality of the food in Italian eating places but on that lovely baby whose exquisitely beautiful eyes looked exactly like her father's—or at least he must, judging from the similarity of their eyes, be her father—although he looked so young! The waiter smiled and bowed and translated, as Nellie knew he would. She described the restaurateur's reaction as follows:

> Then the little man's pride melted away, and a smile replaced the frown on his face. He spoke to the baby who came up and shook hands with me. I gave her the coin and our peace was sealed. Then the little father brought forth a bottle of wine, and with the most cordial smiles and friendliest words begged me to accept it. I did not intend to be out-done, so I told the waiter that I must take some wine with me. I insisted on paying for it, and with low bows and sweet smiles we took leave of one another, and I rushed after the guard to the train, boarding it just as the horn blew for it to continue on its way.

A little flattery went a long way in Italy! And there as everywhere else, the road to a father's heart lay through his love for his daughter.

The train arrived in Brindisi after one o'clock in the morning—two hours late. There were two boats in the harbor—the one that was to sail for Alexandria, and the *Victoria*, the ship Nellie Bly was to take for Port Said and the Suez Canal. As she climbed the gangplank, she began to experience an ailment even worse than seasickness: namely, Anglophobia. She had heard about the snootiness of the English, and her anxieties were confirmed the moment she stepped aboard ship. She hardly expected at that hour of the morning the trial that was to confront her. The deck was crowded with men waiting up to see the new passengers. They must have felt ill-paid for their loss of sleep, Nellie thought, for besides the men who came on board, there were "only the two large English women and my own plain, uninteresting self." As the two English women were "among their own people," Nellie waited for them to take the lead. They, however, were more helpless than she. Under the scrutiny of those male eyes, the three new female arrivals waited for someone to come forward and assist them. So much for Nellie's assurances to her editors in New York that if a woman traveling around the world was ever in distress she would always find a man to protect her. Was this, she asked, the usual manner of receiving passengers on English boats? The males were polite enough; it was strange, very strange, they told her, that a steward did not come to their assistance. Finally, one of the men who stood about dared to speak without having first been introduced to the females. He gave her directions to the purser's office. Accompanied by the train guard, she went there with her letter of introduction from officials of the Peninsular and Oriental Steamship Line requesting that the commanders and pursers of all P. and O. boats on which she traveled give her all the care and attention it was in their power to bestow. The purser of the Victoria received Nellie Bly with infuriating indifference. She described his behavior as follows:

After leisurely reading the letter, the purser very carelessly turned around and told me the number of my cabin. I asked for a steward to show me the way, but he replied that there didn't seem to be any about, that the cabin was on the port side, and with this meagre information, he impolitely turned his back and busied himself with some papers on the desk before him.

The cabin, Nellie was dismayed to find, was already occupied. Two disheveled women stuck their heads out from the lower berths and exclaimed in annoyance, "Oh!" Nellie echoed with an "Oh!" of her own, but in a tone that was caustic rather than supercilious. She returned to the purser and informed him that she would neither sleep in an upper berth nor occupy a cabin with two other women. The glacial purser re-read her letter of introduction from the P. and O. as if to determine how much weight he should attach to it. Then he summoned a steward who escorted her to another cabin. The single occupant, a pretty girl, greeted her with a friendly smile. As Nellie was fond of saying, when she set her mind to something she usually got what she wanted.

CHAPTER SIX

BOWING DOWN TO FUJI

Elizabeth Bisland watched the green hills of America sink out of sight in the level sunshine. Night came on, the wind turned cold; Chinese passengers flung paper prayers overboard to ensure a safe voyage. In steerage, the "four hundred pigtails" kept up a shrill, cheerful chatter; most of them were going home to settle down upon money made from the "foreign devils." Like many of her countrymen, Miss Bisland felt threatened by the "yellow tidal wave" of immigrants to America and their unwillingness to assimilate. In Chinatown in San Francisco, she had noticed that they held to their own national dress, manners, and food, and in their tiny shops sold wares which "no American seeks." And now, from high on the hurricane deck of the steamship, she sniffed again "the Chinese smell"—that effluvium compounded of the pungent fumes of opium and the smoke of incense sticks. The *Oceanic* was "wonderfully clean from stem to stern," but no amount of scouring, she knew, would rid the vessel of that sickening, all-permeating odor; all China reeked of those "strange, stifling fumes." The French novelist Pierre Loti, she noted, wrote that the smell could be detected while a ship was still miles off the China coast. What Elizabeth Bisland, the avid Anglophile, did not mention was that Indian opium was introduced into China toward the end of the 18th century by the British, who hoped to obtain in exchange more of the silk, porcelain, and tea for which their home markets clamored. In the Opium War (1839—1842), China fought the British in a futile attempt to stop the import of opium.

Which is more tedious—prolonged confinement on a train with dirt-smeared windows, or being cooped up seemingly without end on a ship at sea? Elizabeth Bisland soon found herself reduced to playing games with her agitated brain. For the next four days, a storm confined her to her cabin where she watched the "foaming flood of emerald" of the Pacific roar past her porthole, "making a dull green twilight within." All she saw was this and the slats of the upper berth.

48

There were six slats, of that she was certain, for she had already counted them several thousand times:

It was the only mental process of which I was capable during the long nights while I lay and listened to the loud combat of the thundering squadrons outside, whose white plumes flashed into sight again with the first gray gleam of day the battle still raging. Every plank in the ship creaked and groaned and shrieked without once pausing to take breath, and I regarded with contemptuous indifference the frantic tobogganing of all my most treasured possessions all over the stateroom. What were the fleeting things of this world to one to whose unexampled sufferings death must soon put a period? It was comforting to think that one's last will and testament was made, but hateful the contemplation of burial at sea. It was such an unnecessarily tragical end to this ridiculous wild goose chase.

Her terrible predicament rekindled her anger at her employers. She had not asked to be jerked away from home and friends to become entombed half way across the world in a ship battered by wind and storm and ocean and any moment about to sink to the bottom! Trapped in her heaving cabin, Elizabeth Bisland raged not at the elements but at the farcical misadventure upon which she had been dispatched and which now threatened to take her life. Still, she maintained her presence of mind amid the chaos; she had a job to do. Whatever her feelings about the assignment, she prided herself on her professionalism. She must have been paid handsomely to perform an undertaking that was fraught with hardship and peril and that, initially, she had declined to accept. On the fifth day out from San Francisco, the "boiling pot of the sea" subsided. She began to take beef tea; her will to live revived. Other passengers straggled back on deck, looking pale and wan. A week passed before the whole ship's company was able to assemble at table.

Elizabeth Bisland depended upon the officers and crews of the *Oceanic* to get her—come Hell or High Water—to Hong Kong in time to catch the special mail ship for Ceylon and thus save her a delay of ten days. They were a cosmopolitan (no pun intended) mix: Norwegians, Russians, English,

French, Japanese, Americans, Germans, and Hungarians. Miss Bisland was delighted to find that the chief engineer was a Manxman, or a native of the Isle of Man (a dependency of the English Crown in the Irish Sea and rich in folklore and legend). The passengers, comprising Americans and English, included "a full cargo of missionaries—fifteen in all—mostly young women, and on this occasion, all Presbyterians." It was a time when missionaries were busy propagating the Christian faith in China and Japan and they used the steamships of the Occidental and Oriental Line regularly to travel back and forth. A note of incredulity regarding Religion with a capital "R" crept into Miss Bisland's description of the "cargo" of missionaries:

> Among them is a young doctor who has just taken her degree, and is going to the East to save both souls and bodies. She wears "reform" clothes, and has a strong, well-cut face, from which the heavy hair is brushed smoothly back. She regards the ten years' exile into which she is entering as merely the apprenticeship of her professional career, and is likely to consider the physical welfare of her patients of more importance than the acceptance of her creed.

Much like the fictional Robert Elsmere to whom Nellie Bly had alluded, the young doctor put her faith in good works rather than in spirituality. She was "the plain, wholesome product of Northwestern life and a Northwestern female college—speaking the speech of that region with a broad and burring 'r'." And since her job was to treat diseases of the body, not to save souls, the physician's future, Miss Bisland allowed, was likely to be a "simple and pleasant one."

Not so with another young missionary, who suffered from "an undue spirituality of nature." At war with the "enchanting dimples in her fresh young cheeks" was the "maiden severity of her eyes." It saddened Elizabeth Bisland to think what the girl of twenty was giving up by condemning herself to "a decade of lonely exile in a remote Japanese town." Miss Bisland reported:

> She is not indifferent to a young girl's natural joys, though she mentions them loftily as things in the remote past appealing to her now forever put away. It would be

pretty and amusing, as a young girl's *exalté* fancies are sometimes, were the sacrifice of her best years to indifferent heathen not so real and melancholy to think on. One is tempted to pray that some Cymon may come to rescue this Christian Iphigenia from her squalid little Oriental altar before the knife of distaste and ennui shall have murdered her youth and charm.

The young girl's particular mission struck the hedonistic Elizabeth Bisland as the height of folly. To relinquish all the joys and pleasures of life when she so clearly deserved them! And for what? A fanciful delusion! She should be rescued from that fantasy!

As the *Oceanic* steamed toward Japan, the "emerald" of the ocean gave way to a "burning azure" and Miss Bisland's prose to a luscious outpour:

Sapphire would be pale and cold beside this sea—palpitating with wave shadows deep as violet, yet not purple, and with no touch of any color to mar its perfect hue. It flames with unspeakable, many-faceted splendor, under a sky that is wan by contrast with its profundity of tint, and the very foam that curls away from our wake is blue as the blue shadows in snow. The cutter-like prow of our ship flings up two delicate plumes of pearl, and the sunlight shining through these has wrought upon the blue floor beneath us a rainbow arch that encircles our onward path, moves with our moving, and shimmers upon the waving flood as the iris shimmers upon a peacock's breast.

The ship plowed forward at the rate of 350 miles per day. Elizabeth Bisland filled with a kind of despair at getting up each morning to see the same sea, the same horizons, the same "sword-winged" birds that had followed them from San Francisco. The voyage through these blue solitudes was a lonely one. Like Nellie Bly on the Atlantic, Miss Bisland reached out and socialized with the passengers in her own little floating world on the Pacific. She reported that they swapped life-histories, took photographs of each other, exchanged warm professions of friendship and advice about the future. They played draughts and quoits and cards, and got together in corners to "criticize the missionaries" and were criticized by them. It is interesting to note that seventeen years later, in 1906, in her autobiographical *The Secret Life: Being the Book of a Heretic*, an accumulation of philosophical observations, Miss Bisland would write:

> The very name of Saint is a stench in my heretical nostrils. I never knew or read of one who was not a vain egoist, with all the cruelty, obstinacy, and selfishness of the egoist. Read the Lives of the Saints. Not one of those absurd chronicles but is a repulsive tale of an insane vanity trampling on the rights and feelings of others to achieve notoriety.

A free-thinker for her time, Elizabeth Bisland dismissed the saints out of hand as vain, warped, and self-serving. She compared St. Theresa (1515—1582), for example, to playwright Henrik Ibsen's Hedda Gabler who was destructive to herself and others. Yet St. Theresa was one of the most remarkable women of her time. Giving up her life with a noble, well-to-do family, she entered the Carmelite order and traveled tirelessly throughout Spain to found houses and convents for members of that faith and free them from the unreformed clergy. Her extraordinary energy, good humor, intelligence, and spiritual power helped spread the movement beyond Spain and across Christendom. Her written works, which were models of beauty, richness, and eloquent simplicity became celebrated as literary masterpieces and were the founts of modern mysticism. Why, instead of presenting rounded portraits of the saints, in their strengths as well as their weaknesses, did Miss Bisland excoriate them? Her romanticism did not extend to a belief in life after death or in miracles on earth.

Nellie Bly was straightforward; with Nellie, what you saw was what you got. Whereas Elizabeth Bisland was a person of riveting complexity. She fancied herself a model of dignified and genteel Southern womanhood yet she discreetly hankered after half-naked coolies and crewmen. She started out detesting the race around the world yet ended up wanting to win it in the worst way. And while, as a product of her culture, she condescended toward classes of people not of her skin color, she cared about individuals *within* those classes. Many of the four hundred yellow people in steerage were going home with their earnings. Many others were merchants with a merchant's pass which would enable them to return to America once their business across the ocean was finished. Among the Chinese going home to stay was a "Forty-niner," an old gentleman with an iron-gray pigtail:

He came to California during the gold fever, and was now going home to die in China, having thriftily calculated that it costs less to cross the waters alive than it does in a coffin. He was rich in those early days, but, as he explains in fluent and profane American, fan-tan, poker, euchre, and horse races have reduced his store to an immodest competence. However, as he nears the Chinese shore he feels he can afford to wear a magnificent and lurid pair of brocaded trousers, of the sort popular in China when he left, and still—after forty years —of the very latest fashion.

With similar compassion, Miss Bisland described the plight of another, much younger, Chinese headed home to die:

Down in these Chinese quarters, placed where he can catch the best of the healing salt breezes, is a young fellow of six-and-twenty, who lies motionless all day, with crossed hands and half-closed eyes. These hands and the sunken face are the color of old wax, as impassive as if indeed they were cut from such substance. It is common among the immigrants to America to fall sick with a consumption and to struggle back in this way to die at home. He seems afraid to breathe or move, lest he should waste the failing oil or snuff out the dying flame ere he reaches his yearned-for home—the Flowery Kingdom—the Celestial Empire!

When the *Oceanic* reached Japan, all the missionaries landed. They were, Elizabeth Bisland reported in a mildly satiric tone, "full of happiness at arriving at the scene of their labors to save immortal souls." For herself, her divinity was not the Christian deity but Nature. When she saw Fujiyama soaring into the blue, she grew ecstatic. Fuji, the highest mountain on the islands. Yama, the general term for all mountains, "Fuji" meaning "Mother of Fire." Miss Bisland gazed at the sacred, snow-capped volcanic peak which had inspired Japanese poets and painters throughout the centuries. She reported:

For more than two hundred years the Mother of Fire has been clad in snows and has made no sign. Traces of terrible ancient rages lie along her ravaged sides; but her passions are stilled, peace and purity crown her; and he who hath seen Fujiyama's fair head lifted out of the blue sea and flushed with the dream of the coming day layeth his hand upon his mouth and is silent, but the memory of it passeth not away while he lives.

On the morning of December 8th, Elizabeth Bisland was twenty-four days out of New York. As the gray clouds about the base of Fuji resolved themselves into the green hills of Japan, she underwent a kind of religious conversion. She bowed her head in awe at "the real East, not east of any-where, but the East...the birthplace of Man, and of his Religions...of Poetry and Porcelains, of Tradition, and of Architecture." She was, she felt, in the portal of "the Great Temple of the World." She fell upon her knees actually in wonderment at the "mysterious age and vastness" of Nippon...Fan-land...a fairyland Eden...the Country of Chrysanthemums.

This was Elizabeth Bisland's paean to paganism. She was no missionary, but she had found her spiritual home.

CHAPTER SEVEN

THE BOAT! THE BOAT! I'LL MISS THE BOAT!

Nellie Bly asked the purser of the *Victoria* if she had time to go ashore and send a cable.

"If you hurry," he replied.

The train guard took her along several dark streets to a building where he spoke to the cable operator in Italian. But hearing Nellie speak in English, the operator replied in the same language. Nellie told him she wanted to send a cable to New York. She was astonished to hear him ask her where New York was. At first she thought he was spoofing, then she realized he spoke out of ignorance. Captain Albers and his passengers were right! America was in the middle of nowhere as far as people in foreign countries were concerned! Didn't the man know that New York was becoming a center of Finance? Hadn't the word yet gotten to him that New York was attracting people from his very own Italy in quest of greater freedom of opportunity? How was it possible that a cable operator in Brindisi, a focal point for travel from America and western Europe to India and the Orient, had not heard visitors allude to the wonders of New York City? Didn't he know that New York was fast becoming America's Number-One metropolis? Didn't he know that New York was now a magnet for Americans fleeing the drudgery of the farms or pushed off them by mechanization? Didn't he also know that New York was now a mecca for young, ambitious dreamers eager to carve out their careers and enjoy the diversions that only a great city could afford? Had no one ever enlightened him to the fact that already during the 1880s upwards of five million immigrants had entered the United States and that nearly all of them settled in the cities, New York chiefly among them? Nellie Bly would have apprised him that private homes could not keep pace with the growth of population in New York and that town houses were becoming too expensive—even a modest one rented for $1,800 a year, and servants needed to maintain such an establishment demanded salaries as high as $15 or $20 a month.

She would have acquainted him with Rutherford Stuyvesant who introduced a new, more compact and economical structure—the apartment house. Located on East 18th Street and patterned after Parisian buildings, it featured six-room-and-a bath units that rented for $1,000 to $1,500 a year. More elaborate apartment houses were later erected, she would have added, including the nine-story Dakota on Central Park at West 72nd Street, which boasted fifteen-foot ceilings, mahogany paneling, marble floors, and nine rising-and-falling hydraulic elevators that made tenants complain of "elevator sickness." The Dakota was so-named because its builders joked it was so far north of the center of the metropolis that it might as well have been in Indian territory. Nellie would have explained that New Yorkers regarded "civilization" as lying farther South—on 14th Street, for example, which was a shopper's paradise. She would have cited the visiting English lady who remarked:

> It is a perfect bazaar. Not only is there a brilliant display in the windows of everything from Paris-imported bonnets to pink-satin boots, but the sidewalk is fringed with open-air stalls, heaped high with pretty things, many of them absurdly cheap.

The Italian cable operator's not knowing where New York was may have reflected more than native lack of awareness; it may have mirrored a feeling of superiority among Europeans. After all, Paris was the center of art and fashion, Rome of sculpture and classical architecture, and legend attributed the founding of Brindisi to Diomedes, the companion of Ulysses. New York was a babe in swaddling clothes culturally. But just as she loved America, Nellie Bly loved the city that had opened the doors of opportunity for her. If she hadn't had a more immediately pressing matter of communication on her mind, she probably would have informed the cable operator that while New York had no Louvre and no Michelangelo or da Vinci, it was progressing in ways that Rome and Paris had not begun to dream of. New York had skyscrapers that soared up to twenty stories high, with elevators running up and down inside. New York had John Augustus Roebling's 1,600-foot Brooklyn Bridge, the first suspension span to be supported by steel cable. New York had elevated trains and something new called the trolley which ran electrically on tracks and bid fair to replace the horsecar. New York had Central Park, created by landscape architect Frederick Law Olmsted whose Greensward plan transformed eight-hundred acres of rocky wilderness in the middle of Manhattan into a playground for the people, with carriage roads, bridle paths, a zoo, a lake for boating and skating, and afternoon concerts that attracted audiences of forty-thousand. True, the streets of New York were not paved with gold; the immigrants—the Irish, Germans, Italians, Rumanians, Hungarians, Slovaks, Greeks, Poles, Turks, and Jews from Russia—were crammed into a squalid, noisy, over-crowded two-square-mile area known as the Lower East Side, in grim tenements right next door to factories belching smoke and soot. Typhoid and cholera raged through the slums; gangs roamed the streets; the people's clothes and the East River itself stank from the pollution. That, Nellie Bly knew from her experience as a reporter, was the negative side of the New York story. But these were hard-working people who believed in America! Despite the hardship, disease, and deprivation, they worked as peddlers, toiled in sweatshops, entered the expanding needle trades. They were determined to become American citizens, succeed at their business or profession, educate their children. These were the people whom Nellie Bly and Joseph Pulitzer were trying to help through their stories and editorials.

All that Nellie might have told the cable operator who didn't know where New York was—but the important thing of the moment was that she cable her editors. She watched him hunt through a lot of books to ascertain, he said, by which line he could send the message and how much it would cost. Nellie was so amused by the situation that she forgot all about the departure of her ship until she had completed her mission to the cable office and stepped outside.

The loud, warning blast of a whistle brought Time crashing in on her consciousness. Nellie and the train guard exchanged looks of alarm. Her boat! Her boat was gone—and with it her few belongings!

"Can you run?" the guard asked in a husky voice.

Nellie said she could. He grasped her hand tightly and rushed her through the dark streets. Her heart beat like a drum. She could see the headlines back in New York, *NELLIE*

BLY IS A LOSER! They raced like maniacs through the streets past astonished watchmen and early-morning pedestrians. A sudden bend brought the harbor into view. They ran down to the wharf. Nellie, breathless, saw that the boat for Alexandria had gone and that hers, the *Victoria*—was still there!

Close calls and delays were her pitfalls, and this was a very close call.

•

CHAPTER EIGHT

ELIZABETH BISLAND'S LOVESICK ADMIRER

While Elizabeth Bisland was falling in love with Japan, Lafcadio Hearn was wasting away for her back in New York.

Miss Bisland's association with the bohemian journalist and inveterate traveler began in the early 1880s when they worked together on the *New Orleans Times-Democrat*. The diminutive (five-foot-three), half-blind Hearn (he had lost his left eye in a childhood accident) became fascinated with Japan and with Miss Bisland as well. He was captivated by the beauty and intelligence of the seventeen-year-old girl who had already established herself as a poet and a writer of short newspaper features and would soon become a fixture among the New Orleans glitterati. He nursed her devotedly through a bout of yellow fever in her room in the quaint little hotel but after she recovered he resumed his exquisite shyness toward her. His feelings about her turned ambivalent. Asked to describe her, he told an acquaintance:

> Tall, fair-skinned, large black eyes, and dark hair. Some call her beautiful, others, pretty; I don't think her either one or the other; but she is decidedly attractive physically and intellectually. Otherwise she is selfish, unfeeling, hard, cunning, vindictive; a woman that will make inferno in any husband's life, unless he have a character of tremendous force.

The love-goddess of Hearn's fantasies regarded him as a witty, delightful, marvelously sensitive companion. But she was ambitious; when the opportunity presented itself, she went on to New York to work as an editor for *Cosmopolitan* magazine. When Hearn called upon her in the Big Town, he found her to have "expanded mentally and physically into one of the most superb women you could wish to converse with.... It now seems to me as I had only seen the *chrysalis* before; this is the silkmoth!" Miss Bisland held forth in her salon above a candy shop on Fourth Avenue, her rich and handsome suitors vying with one another for her attentions.

She was an altogether formidable woman. Hearn observed:

> She is a witch—turning heads everywhere, but some
> of her admirers are afraid of her. One told me he felt as if
> he were playing with a beautiful dangerous leopard,
> which he loved for not biting him. As for me, she is like
> hasheesh. I can't remember anything she says or any-
> thing I myself say after leaving the house; my head is all
> in a whirl, and I walk against people in the street, and
> get run over, and lose my way—my sense of orientation
> being grievously disturbed. But I am not in love at all—
> no such foolishness as that; I am only experiencing the
> sensation produced upon—alas!—*hundreds* of finer men
> than I.

Hearn's infatuation with Japan was somewhat less dramatic. It began when he visited the impressive Japanese
exhibits of bronzes, porcelains, silks, and ink-brush painting
at the New Orleans Exhibition of 1885. Like other members
of the American public, Hearn was intrigued by this mysterious, exotic land which Commodore Matthew Perry in 1854
had officially opened up to Western trade and diplomatic
relations and which had been isolated from the West for more
than two centuries. He once told Elizabeth Bisland he felt
frustrated at being "unable to find the Orient at home." He
started mulling a visit to Japan. Ironically enough, Miss
Bisland, who wanted to stay at home, got to the Orient before
he did. But he must have shared with her his fascination for
Japan so that she went there with rising expectations for an
Elysian experience. Not long after she left New York to race
Nellie Bly around the world, Hearn was overcome by an
access of jealousy for her:

> Did you often wish to stop somewhere, and feel
> hearts beating about you, and see the faces of gods and
> dancing girls? Or were you pelted like the Lady of the
> *Aroostook* by officers and crews—and British dignitaries
> eager to win one Circe-smile—and superb Indian
> colonels of princely houses returning home—that you
> had no chance to regret anything? I have been so afraid
> of never seeing you again, that I have been hating splen-
> did imaginary foreigners in dreams—which would have
> been wickedly selfish if I had been awake.

Poor Lafcadio!

But if he could not have the love-goddess of his dreams, he could have his Orient! Late in 1889, he sent Harper & Brothers a proposal for his next travel book: He would live among the common people in Japan and write about their daily lives. (Hearn would subsequently go to Japan, marry a lady of high Samurai rank there, become a professor of English literature at the Imperial University of Tokyo, and write books and shorter pieces about the country and its people, with Miss Bisland editing his letters and writing a biography of him.) Still, Hearn was an astute observer; he would not let his adoration of his "Lady of the Myriad Souls" cloud his discernment. He had, after all, nursed her through a life-threatening illness when her emotional defenses were down and she relied upon him. He knew from their past relationship the essence of her—the good in her that she seemed to have concealed, at least temporarily, under all that dazzle she put on, all that smart repartee. She had changed, all right, since she left New Orleans; she seemed to have acquired a superficial personality that covered up the Elizabeth Bisland he once knew. He left a letter with her doorman to be given her upon return from her trip around the world:

> What I want to say is, that after looking at your portrait, I must tell you how sweet and infinitely good you can be, and how much I like you, and how I like you— or at least some of those many who are one in you. I might say love you—as we love those who are dead (the dead who still shape lives); —but which, or how many, of you I cannot say. One looks at me from your picture; but I have seen others, equally pleasing and less mysterious. Not when you were in evening dress, because you were then too beautiful, and what is thus beautiful is not that which is most charming in you. It only dazzles one, and constrains. I like you best in the simple dark dress, when I can forget everything except all the souls of you.

Hearn further anguished:

> It seems to me that all those mysterious lives within you—all the Me 's that were—keep asking the Me that is, for something that is always refused;—that you keep saying to them: "But you are dead and cannot see—you

61

can only feel—and I will not open to you, because the world is all changed. You would not know it, and you would be angry with me were I to grant your wish. Go to your places and sleep and leave me in peace with myself." But they continue to wake up betimes, and quiver into momentary visibility to make you divine in spite of yourself—and as suddenly flit away again. I wish one I saw that night when we were looking at...what was it? Really, I can't remember what it was; the smile that effaced the memory of it—just as a sun-ray blots the image from a dry-plate suddenly exposed. There was such a child-beauty in that smile...Will you ever be *like that always* for any one being?

For all his wisdom, Lafcadio Hearn kept chasing the shimmering phantasm that tortured him. After he had married plain, conventional, non-English-speaking Setsu Koizumi, in January 1891, he made an oblique, bitter reference to Elizabeth Bisland:

How diamond-hard the character of the American woman under the idolatry of which she is subject. In the eternal order of things, which is the highest being, the childish, confiding, sweet Japanese girl—or the superb, calculating, penetrating Circe of our more artificial society, with her enormous power for evil, and her limited power for good?

He had given up hoping to resurrect the Child of Innocence he had nursed back to health in that quaint little hotel in New Orleans and with whom he had developed a passionate intimacy. Whether they ever had sexual intercourse is not known, but the openness with which he shared with her his fantasies about her (however veiled they were by Victorian euphemism) suggests they were very close. Clearly, his emotions toward her were mixed; he regarded their relationship as symbiotic. She was good for him, yet she was bad for him. In any event, he was hopelessly and helplessly enchanted by her. In 1903, after a silence of almost eight years, Lafcadio Hearn renewed his correspondence with Elizabeth Bisland, informing her from Japan that he often dreamed of seeing her again. He longed, he wrote her in America, to meet her "even for a moment, and to hear you speak (in some one of the Myriad Voices), would be such a memory for me. And you would let me 'walk about gently, touching things'?" The side of Hearn that viewed Miss Bisland negatively felt threatened by this august female who combined sexiness with intellect and with a drive for power and position. With docile Setsu, at least, he felt secure. It must have seemed to him quite consistent with Elizabeth Bisland's personality as he understood it that his *inamorata* in the States would choose (twelve years earlier) as her husband someone who was both successful and socially acceptable—Charles W. Wetmore, a prominent New York corporation attorney and financier. Lafcadio Hearn was destined never again to meet his demon-angel—except in his fantasies. He had prepared a series of lectures on Japan for delivery at Cornell University, Ithaca, NY, in 1904. That same year, however, he died before he could return to the United States. He was fifty-four years old.

Upon Hearn's death, Elizabeth Bisland published the first biography of him, remembering him with warmth and devotion. She described him as a "fantastically witty companion" and a man of "astounding sensitiveness"—shy, composed, modest and deferential, a brilliant talker but an attentive listener, and caressing, affectionate, and confiding with "those whom he loved and trusted." His voice was musical and very soft, and there was "an almost feminine grace and lightness in his step and movements." Nothing escaped his observation—no object or tint, not the slightest nuance or change in tone or facial expression. Miss Bisland wrote of his affliction:

> The enormous work which he demanded of his vision had enlarged beyond its natural size the eye upon which he depended for sight, but originally, before the accident—whose disfiguring effect he magnified and was exaggeratedly sensitive about—his eyes must have been handsome, for they were large, of a dark liquid brown, and heavily lashed. In conversation he frequently, almost instinctively, placed his hand over the injured eye to conceal it from his companion.

They must have been very close for her to be able to write about him with such honesty and depth of understanding.

* * *

When Elizabeth Bisland first saw Japan she was overcome with admiration. But while she loved the beauty of the country, she idealized its inhabitants. She saw the Japanese themselves not as a shrewd, upwardly-striving people with problems and practical concerns but as little children—sweet, innocent, imaginative, charming, doll-like, elfin, eternally smiling:

> I am refreshed and cheered to find that the writer of each book fails, as signally as I shall fail to convey, any idea of the fairy charms of the Land of Chrysanthemums...Shall one then paint a dragonfly with a whitewash brush? Nevertheless, I gather from these books much confirmatory of my own swiftly gathered impression. The very faults of the Japanese are such as are misdemeanors in adults but quite forgivable in children. They are hopelessly immodest, with the unconscious shamelessness of babies, and they fib imaginatively with an infant's inability to discern the relative value of truth and falsehood. They are brave with the headlong courage of the child who is ignorant of the meaning of danger, and in matters of honor they have youth's reckless passionate exaltation. They are unfailingly sweet-tempered and courteous. Their artistic consciousness ascends into the realm of morality. They are frugal and temperate; they detest all ugliness, dirt, and squalor; they are unique; they are delightful—they are Japanese!

For a "swiftly gathered impression," this was pretty strong stuff! Enchanted by Nippon, Miss Bisland moved about as if in "a joyous dream." She had come ashore at Yokohama in a sampan piloted by an "elfin" ferryman and been welcomed with friendly smiles by "more medieval folk in blue" who chartered jinrickshas. She rode in one down the handsome waterfront Bund and visited the business section and the street markets heaped high with fresh fruits, vegetables, and enticing sweetmeats. There was an air of friendliness everywhere in this land of "fairy children." She beguiled the reader:

> Tonsured doll-babies in flowered gowns, such as one buys at home in the Oriental shops, are walking about here alive, and flying queer-shaped kites, with a sort of calm unconscious elfishness befitting dwellers in fairy-

land. Two little Japanese ladies with pink cheeks, and black hair clasped with jade pins, toddle by on wooden pattens that clack pleasantly on the pavement. Their kimonos are of gay crepe, and their sashes tied behind like bright-tinted wings. Every one—even the funny little gendarme who stands outside of his sentry-box like a toy soldier—gives us back smile for smile.

If Lafcadio Hearn had not found his Orient in America, Elizabeth Bisland had found hers in Japan. She attached herself to "an agreeable group of Americans" and attended the theatre where they were entertained by artful acrobats and by actors in a play in which one of the leading actors was:

> ...the great shogun himself, stern of mien and with fierce, orgulous brows; a very impressive figure. He is the embodiment of the sterner side of the Japanese character—the aristocrat spirit that kept alive a haughty feudalism long after Europe had forgotten it; the haughty pride and courage that bid a gentleman expiate his offences only by his own hand; the spirit that has allowed no conqueror to set foot on Japanese soil, and still makes these people the bravest and freest race in Asia.

Miss Bisland, like the great shogun, was an elitist. The coolies who transported her around town by magical moonlight in jinrickshas reminded her of "sandalled steeds"'; on the fashionable shopping street of Schichiu, everything looked "ridiculously tiny by day, and deliciously absurd. One has a feeling that this is all a game that one is playing to amuse the children." The train that took her to Tokyo was "a funny train, as absurdly toy-like and doll-housey as is everything else in this country." Her appreciation of the finer things of life almost caused her—and others—to miss that train. She and her friend Madge were so charmed by the fabrics in the silk-shops of Yokohama that they kept other Americans waiting for them in the railroad depot and were upbraided for their inconsiderateness. Elizabeth Bisland stayed in Tokyo at the residence of the American minister. An astonishing profusion of flowery plants bloomed in every corner of the mansion. For Miss Bisland, Japan was the paradise she had dreamed existed:

It is revealed to those who live long enough and who go up and down the earth, and to and fro upon the face of it, that man has never conceived an ideal that is not somewhere a reality. There are women living as beautiful as any of the marble Venuses; there are even men as pure and high-minded as Galahad; there are Edens in existence—perchance, somewhere, there is something nearly resembling Paradise—and certainly the enchanting fairy dreams of our childhood, ravished from us by the cruel misrepresentation of our elders, have an actual existence, yet more fantastic and delicious than our baby minds could ever have imagined, in these islands lying hard by the coast of China. Let no one scoffingly set this down as a figure of speech. All who have ever set foot on these shores bear the same testimony to the elfin witchery of Nippon—the land of the rising sun.

It was brilliant of her to suggest that nothing was impossible if the imagination was open. This was Elizabeth Bisland at her most profound.

Japan was a land where she took her tiffin in a "little lattice glove-box of a teahouse" and drank delicious tea from tiny cups without handles, dined on rice and crisp, freshly broiled eels with polished black chopsticks; a land where she watched the pretty lanterns swinging and the yellow moon turn the bay to wrinkled gold; a land where the "frolicsome, chattering crowd" clacked about in wooden sandals or slid soundlessly past in Chinese cork soles, where the houses were delicate little "match-box" structures with paper window-sashes, where the little oranges in bamboo nets were set about in their green leaves, and where a "nipping and eager" air (she could not resist quoting Shakespeare) blew among the rose trees.

In Tokyo, Elizabeth Bisland jinricksha'd past the Mikado's palaces to the famous temples at Shiba. She visited the tomb of Ieymitsu, the ruler who "consolidated the feudal system" and during whose reign chivalry flourished, the Japanese were "respected at home and abroad," and Japanese art "blossomed into its supreme, consummate power." She failed to tell the whole story or to point out that under the Tokugawa shogunate which lasted from 1603 to 1867, farmers were heavily taxed to pay for their feudal lords' taste for grandeur and for ostentatious tombs to commemorate them. Elizabeth Bisland perceived Ieymitsu as follows:

> Laying down a life of power, he yearned for an immortality of beauty—to be magnificent and impressive even in death; and choosing his spot, he spent millions in glorifying his resting place. He had a nice taste in tombs, had this splendid old Japanese.

The beauty of the setting Ieymitsu had selected and the opulence of the tomb he had ordered built for himself moved Miss Bisland to indulge in one of her most glowing bursts of scene-painting:

> The hill is clothed in pines, through which the light winds go softly sighing. The westerling sun shines slantingly along the green arcades and makes golden shadows across the path we have come. The mild-moving air has stolen red blossoms from the glossy-leaved camellia-trees and shred them upon the hoary gray lanterns and mossy stairs...Never monarch slept among sweeter verdure, space, and calm...The tomb has, as have all these shrines and temples, walls of a deep rich red, whose clear color three centuries have not dimmed...Above is a broad frieze of gorgeous carving— dragons, birds, lotus, and chrysanthemums tangled in fantastic intricacies, and all lacquered and gilded with such honest pains that Time's teeth cannot gnaw through the color or his breath tarnish the gold. Above the frieze leans the green and gray tiled roof, with its fretted ridges and airy, upturned gables, of a fine lightness and unmatched grace of outline...The interior is octagon-sided and mosaic-paved, and up from the center where the great shogun lies, curls the cup of a giant lotus, whose calyx is the jewelled shrine, springing to the roof which rests on a ring of polished columns, and each of these in turn on a base of lotus leaves. Everywhere, from pavement, shrine, and wall, shines the shogun's golden crest of three lotus leaves meeting at the stems...Space does not avail to tell of the splendor of this tomb...the plating of gold and silver bronze; the myriad-tinted lacquers, hard and polished as gems; the untarnished gilding, the inlaying of precious stones,

and, most wonderful of all, the grace and gorgeousness of the myriad delicate fantasies wrought out by art to soothe the king's last sleep.

The magnificence of what she had just witnessed drove Elizabeth Bisland to exclaim to the shaven-headed priest who had shown her the royal grounds and edifices, "*Et ego in Arcadia*—I too have been in fairyland!" The lay brother may, or may not, have known that Arcadia was, according to the Roman poet Vergil, a district of the Peloponnesus which was the home of simplicity and happiness. There was certainly nothing simple about Ieymitsu's tomb! In any event, Miss Bisland reported that the priest had "warned" her about the extraordinary loveliness of the place. What, possibly, could rival this experience which she would treasure remembering the rest of her life? She felt moved to observe, "...and having seen it (Ieymitsu's tomb), I am fain to declare that I forgive fate in advance for any future trick, because of this one day of unmarred delight."

Time drove Miss Bisland, just as it did Nellie Bly. She raced across Tokyo in her ricksha to the great park of Uyeno, to see the sun go down behind Fujiyama. She looked out across the city's "vast hive with its million or more folk whose myriad lights begin to twinkle in the violet dusk." Miss Bisland could not know that Lafcadio Hearn would shortly come to Japan and take up Japanese ways, nor could she know that six years from now, in 1895, he would describe the Tokyo she presently gazed at as "the most horrible place in Japan—a den of dirty shoes, absurd fashions, wickedly expensive living—airs—vanities—gossip." The new Tokyo was not for him. Elizabeth Bisland worshipped a moment before a gigantic, calm-lidded stone Buddha set on a little hill, amid a thicket of roses. That sort of experience—the old Japan and its mysticism and folklore—was what Hearn's sensibilities would attune to in the twelve books about his adopted home he was to publish during his lifetime.

Back on the train, Elizabeth Bisland watched through her window the broad, yellow moon shining on the ever-present Fujiyama. She returned to Yokohama where she bade regretful farewells to "the charming Americans" and caught the steamship *Oceanic* for Hong Kong. It was vital that she get to Hong Kong in time to connect with the special mail ship for

Ceylon and thus save herself a delay of ten days. The *Oceanic* left Yokohama on December 10th; Miss Bisland had been out of New York twenty-six days. She spent much of the voyage in her cabin devouring books on Japan from the ship's library. She read into the interpretations by the various authors that they corroborated her "swiftly gathered impressions" regarding Japan and the Japanese people. Part of her willingly admitted that the thirty-six hours she had spent in Nippon was scarcely enough time to know Nippon, but another part of her—her Romanticism—trusted implicitly in the power of her intuitions.

CHAPTER NINE

NELLIE BLY ON THE SUEZ CANAL

Nellie Bly's life aboard the English steamship *Victoria* bound for Suez was a series of disagreeable experiences, but she took them in stride. Her first morning at sea, she awoke to find herself standing upright beside her berth. She was drenched. The sounds of vigorous scrubbing on the deck above told her what had happened; she had gone to sleep with the porthole open, and inasmuch as her berth was just beneath it, she had received the full force of the scrub-water as it came pouring over the sides. No sooner had she managed to close her heavy window on the Mediterranean and go back to sleep when she heard a voice call, "Miss, will you have your tea now?"

A steward stood at the door awaiting her reply. Nellie refused the tea, as did the English girl on the other side of the cabin. Managing to answer the girl's bright smile with a very tired one of her own, she was off to sleep again.

"Miss, will you have your bath now?"

It was a stewardess in a white cap. She was bending over Nellie, who felt tempted to retort she had already had her bath, or shower—in scrub-water. Instead, she mumbled, "In a few minutes," and was asleep again.

"Well, you are a lazy girl," the voice reprimanded her. "You'll miss your bath and breakfast if you don't get up the instant!"

Nellie had always liked to sleep late. She wondered if she was back in school being punished by the teacher for not paying attention. But she held her temper and replied stiffly, "I generally get up when I feel so inclined." Again, Nellie nodded off.

The interruption next time was the same steward, telling her that the ship was inspected every day and that her cabin must be made up for the captain, who would be here presently.

Nellie had no choice but to get up. She went into the bathroom and found she was unable to turn on the water; the faucet-mechanism was unfamiliar to her. When she asked another steward where the stewardess was, he replied to her amazement, "The stewardess is taking a rest and cannot be disturbed."

It is hard to imagine Elizabeth Bisland would have been treated uncivilly by the personnel aboard the *S.S. VIctoria*. Her grand manner would have intimidated them, and since she was accustomed to insisting upon respect for her dignity, they probably would have accorded her the utmost courtesy. Nellie Bly, for her part, took none of the folderol personally. She went up on deck and admired the velvety-blue of the sea, enjoyed the balmy air which was "soft as a rose leaf, and just as sweet, air such as one dreams about and but seldom finds; standing there alone among strange people on strange waters, I thought how sweet life is!" There was a touch of the poet about her despite her down-to-earth nature. Nellie was not alone for long, for just as was true while she crossed the Atlantic, she was now quick to socialize with her fellow passengers. Her English cabin-companion introduced her to friends, and an Englishman who was in the Civil Service in Calcutta and had been in India for the past twenty years took a special interest in her. The trip from Calais on the India mail express was an old story to him; he had noticed her on the train and, learning that she was traveling alone, he devoted most of his time to looking out for her comfort and pleasure. It cannot be emphasized too strongly how courageous Nellie Bly and Elizabeth Bisland were just from a social standpoint. In the year 1889, a woman traveling alone would be regarded as an oddity, and for a woman to travel *around the world alone* would be unthinkable! There were times during their respective journeys when the strains of social pressure seemed as punishing as any monsoon to Nellie Bly and Miss Bisland. The bugle blew for tiffin, the Indian word for luncheon aboard ships traveling in Eastern seas. The English Civil Servant invited Nellie to go with him to tiffin, and since she had gone without breakfast, she was anxious to eat, whatever the slights she had already endured aboard ship. It was becoming evident to her that not all the English were prigs. As an experienced journalist, she smelled out easy generalities and scrupulously avoided committing them. Soon again, her powers of objectivity were to be tested.

There were over three hundred passengers on the *Victoria*, and the dining room, she observed, was never meant to accommodate a ship carrying more than seventy-five first-class passengers. Instead of showing Nellie and her English gentleman to a table, the headwaiter suggested politely, "Sit anywhere." So they sat down at the nearest table, and were soon joined by four women of ages "ranging from twenty-four to thirty-five" who snorted indignantly at their presence. Nellie Bly reported:

> They were followed by a short, fat woman with a sweeping walk and air of satisfied assurance, who eyed us in a supercilious way and then turned to the others with an air of injured dignity that was intensely amusing. They were followed by two men and as there were only places for seven at the table the elderly man went out. Two of the girls sat on a lounge at the end of the table, which made room for the young man. Then we were made to suffer. All kinds of rude remarks were made about us. "They did hate people coming to their table;" "Too bad papa was robbed of his place;" "Shame people had to be crowded from their own table," and similar pleasant speeches were hurled at us. The young woman who sat at my left was not content to confine her rudeness to her tongue, but repeatedly reached across my plate, brushing my food with her sleeves without one word of apology. I confess I never had a more disagreeable meal.

Yet despite the obvious harassment, Nellie Bly again showed that distinctive capacity of hers for perceiving all sides of a story:

> I thought at first that this rudeness was due to my being an American and that they had taken this means of showing their hatred for all Americans. Still, I could not understand why they should subject an Englishman to the same treatment unless it was because he was with me. After-experiences showed me that my first conclusion was wrong: that I was not insulted because I was an American, but because the people were simply ill-bred. When dinner came we found that we were debarred from the dining room. Passengers who got on

Nellie Bly with checked camel's-hair coat, visored cap, and single handbag, traveled light. *(The Bettman Archive)*

Elizabeth Bisland, the statuesque beauty who prized her dignity as a Southern gentlewoman, regarded the trip as a "ridiculous wild-goose chase." *(Lafcadio Hearn Collection, Howard-Tilton Memorial Library, Tulane University, New Orleans, LA)*

Joseph Pulitzer: His proven formula for success was a curious mixture of moral crusading and sensationalism. *(Brown Brothers)* Painting by John Singer Sargent.

John Brisben Walker wanted to put *Cosmopolitan* on the map with the journalistic heavyweights. *(Brown Brothers)*

Jules Verne: "If you do it in seventy-nine days I shall applaud with both hands." *(The Bettman Archive)*

Lafcadio Hearn in Japanese attire. *(The Bettman Archive)*

The *Oceanic*, the first steamer of the White Star Line between Liverpool and New York. *(The Bettman Archive)*

Nellie Bly, triumphant, waved to the cheering crowds. *(The Bettman Archive)*

Around the world in seventy-two days and six hours—reception of Nellie Bly at Jersey City on the completion of her journey—from sketches by C. Bunnell. *(The Bettman Archive)*

Front page of the *New York World*, January 26, 1890—Nellie Bly victorious. *(The Bettman Archive)*

Nellie Bly in a pensive mood. *(Brown Brothers)*

Elizabeth Bisland enjoying Nature. *(Brown Brothers)*

They raced against Jules Verne's legendary fictional creation.
(*Brown Brothers*)

At the age of 22, she became an international celebrity. *(The Bettman Archive)*

Cover of *The Nellie Bly Book: Around the World in 72 Days* (*Pictorial Weeklies*, 1890).

Elizabeth Bisland

Frontispiece of Elizabeth Bisland's *In Seven Stages: A Flying Trip Around the World* (*Harper & Brothers*, 1891).

at London were given the preference, and as there were not accommodations for all, the passengers who boarded the ship at Brindisi had to wait for second dinner.

Dinner is a major event in one's life aboard an ocean liner, and Nellie Bly soon discovered that hers aboard the *Victoria* was no better than the service. Since she was among that group of wretches who had gotten on ship at Brindisi, she had to wait until 9 p.m. for her repast. It comprised cold soup, left-overs of fish, beef, and fowl from the first dinner, and cold coffee. A cry of objection went up from the late-dinner passengers, who wanted to get up a protest to serve on the captain. Nellie Bly, siding with the conservatives, refused to join with the would-be complainants. Again, that shrewdly balanced judgment of hers—particularly remarkable for a person in her early twenties—enabled her not only to report the event but to penetrate to the more significant layers of truth beneath the event. Making further inquiries, she learned that two women with whom she had traveled on the express-mail train to Brindisi had been treated even worse than she aboard ship. She ascertained further still that places were reserved only at dinner on the *Victoria* and that at breakfast and tiffin it was first-come, first-served. Acting on this information, Nellie and the two women went to early tiffin the following day and were informed by a young man who sat at the head of an otherwise empty table, "You can't sit there. I've reserved those places for some of my friends." They went to another table and after sitting down, were requested by late-comers to get up and give the places to them. The one woman cried bitterly, telling Nellie, "I am a grandmother, and this is the sixth trip I have made to Australia, and I was never treated so insultingly in my life." Thus once again, as Nellie Bly made clear to her readers back in New York, the rudeness aboard the *Victoria* could not be attributed simply to the ship's personnel or to English class-consciousness; rather, it was a manifestation of human nature at its pettiest. People were like that, and Nellie Bly, with her microscopic eye for the follies and foibles of mankind, reported their behavior with telling accuracy. Still, she must have felt somewhat disappointed that thus far her trip around the world had challenged little more than her ability to make something out of apparently trivial incidents. Reduced to working with the material that her journey threw at her, she must have yearned for the days of not long ago when she uncovered the oppression toward women who toiled for slave-wages in the sweatshops of New York, exposed the brutal treatment of mental patients in the asylum on Blackwell's Island, and trapped the notorious Ed Phelps, the lobby king of Albany, into accepting a bribe to kill a legislative bill that would eliminate the sale of quack remedies in the state. Those were important stories. Writing about loutishness at tiffin was scarcely likely to prove of earth-shaking consequence.

Boorishness toward the passengers on the *Victoria* was one thing; a calculated neglect of their needs was quite another. When a woman who looked as if she was dying of consumption needed help to get to the deck with her rugs, Nellie Bly asked a stewardess to assist her. The ship's employee replied that she would not help anyone until they came and requested her to do so. When the *charge d'affaires* to China and Siam for the Spanish government walked up to the Captain of the ship and said he wished, as a matter of diplomatic protocol, to pay him his respects, the commander glared at him and said, "What of it?"

Finally, even Nellie's vaunted broadmindedness cracked under the strain. In a scathing outburst, she editorialized back to her readers in New York:

> Travelers who care to be treated with courtesy, and furnished with palatable food, will never by any chance travel on the *Victoria*. It is all rule and no practice on that ship. The impudence and rudeness of the servants in America is a standing joke, but if the servants on the *Victoria* are a sample of English servants, I am thankful to keep those we have, such as they are.

Notwithstanding the annoyances on the voyage to Port Said, Nellie Bly continued to keep herself open to people. The passengers on the *Victoria* ranged from "some of the most refined and lovely" to "some of the most ill-bred and uncouth." Most of the women with whom she socialized wanted to know all about American women and envied Nellie for her spirit of independence and her happy nature. During the daytime on the Mediterranean, the men played crickets and quoits; at night, the passengers held songfests, and a little girl with a pale, slender face sang "Who'll Buy My Silver Earrings?" so sweetly that Nellie knew "If she had tried to sell any, we should all have bought." What Nellie liked to do most of all was sit in a dark corner of the deck and listen to the tomtom beat and weird musical chanting of the lascars (East Indian sailors) below, that always accompanied their evening meal. By day they were a "grim, surly lot," climbing about the ship "like a pack of monkeys" and chanting, as all sailors did when hoisting sail. Occasionally, there was dancing on deck, Nellie Bly reported, to the "worst music it has ever been my misfortune to hear." She sympathized with the members of the band, which had been newly hired:

> The members of the band also washed the dishes, and though I could not blame the passengers who always disappeared at the appearance of the musicians (?) still I felt sorry for them; it was both ridiculous and pathetic that they be required to cultivate two such inharmonious arts! One of the officers told me that the band they had before were compelled to scrub the decks, and their hands became so rough from the work that it was impossible for them longer to fill the role of musicians, so they were discharged and the new band were turned into dish-washers instead of deck-scrubbers.

Not that the entertainment aboard ocean liners has developed that rapidly since Nellie Bly's day. Until the 1950s, passengers still entertained each other (an exception being games such as bingo, supervised by pursers or other ship's officers). After World War II, entertainment departments such as the Cunard Line's started presenting amateur performers, then expanded to featuring professional bands ranging from Harry James and his orchestra to shipboard musical aggregations. Nowadays, passengers are treated to lavish stage productions with computerized light and sound and boasting big-name stars the likes of Tony Bennett and Connie Francis from Las Vegas or Broadway shows. Unionization has helped performing artists to secure decent pay and working conditions aboard ships. Nowadays, that violinist in the ship's orchestra may well have studied music at Juilliard or be on a busman's holiday from the Philharmonic. No more scrubbing decks or washing dishes to earn one's musical keep on an ocean liner!

How little the name NELLIE BLY meant to most people outside America during her race around the world was vividly illustrated by two incidents on the *Victoria*: The first involved some cabled messages, and the second, Nellie's reputation among the passengers. When she boarded the ship at Brindisi the purser gave her some cables that had been sent to her care of the *Victoria*. After she had been out at sea several days, a young woman came to her with an unsealed cable and asked if she was Nellie Bly. Nellie said she was;—whereupon the woman said that the purser had given the cable to some of the passengers, as he did not know who Nellie Bly was, and that it had traveled among them for two days. Talk about a short memory! The same churlish purser who had so ill-manneredly welcomed her aboard proceeded to forget who Nellie Bly was with shocking alacrity.

Even more suggestive of her anonymity overseas, Nellie had not been on the *Victoria* many days before one of the passengers told her it was rumored on board that she was an eccentric American heiress traveling alone with a toothbrush and a bankbook. Nellie was quick to surmise that much of the attention she was receiving from males on the ship owed to this story about her that reputed she was wealthy. One fellow told her that she was the kind of girl he liked and that since he was the second son and his brother would get both the money and the title, his sole ambition was to find a wife who would settle one thousand pounds a year on him. Another chap informed her that he had been traveling ever since he was nine years old and that his despair at ever finding a woman who could travel without innumerable trunks and bundles had quenched his desire to love and marry. He must, apparently, have been drawn to her not only by the rumor that she was filthy rich but by the fact that she came on board ship with one little traveling bag. Nellie noticed that he was exquisitely dressed and that he changed his apparel at least three times a day. When she asked him how many trunks he carried with him, he replied, amazingly, "Nineteen." "I no longer wondered," Nellie mocked to her readers, "at his fears of getting a wife who could not travel without trunks."

The *Victoria* anchored off Port Said at the mouth of the Suez

Canal at 5:30 p.m. on November 27th. She had been out of New York thirteen days. While the ship was being coaled, the passengers looked forward to going ashore for a few hours and seeing some new faces. They came armed with sticks and parasols to beat off the beggars. A fleet of small boats piloted by half-clad Arabs descended upon them. Greedy for a few pence, the boatmen fought savagely among themselves for customers, yanking each other into the water and clinging to the rope ladder that had lowered from the ship. When they refused to let go, Nellie Bly reported, the Captain had to order the sailors to beat them off with long poles before the passengers could venture forth. Nellie tempered justice with mercy in her description of the scene:

> This dreadful exhibition made me feel that probably there was some justification in arming one's self with a club. Our party were about the first to go down the ladder to the boats. It had been our desire to go ashore together, but when we stepped into the first boat some were caught by rival boatmen and literally dragged across to other boats. Then men in the party used their sticks quite vigorously, all to no avail, and although I thought the conduct of the Arabs justified this harsh course of treatment, still I felt sorry to see it administered so freely and lavishly to those black, half-clad wretches and marvelled at their stubborn persistence even while cringing under the blows.

In "quaint and sleepy" Port Said, Nellie Bly and the other passengers, yelling and bouncing in the saddle, rode burros through the streets. They bet recklessly on the wheel in the local gambling house and laughed to see the man rake in their English gold. Her purse lighter now, Nellie resisted buying the tempting low-priced lace and the Egyptian curios in the shops; like everybody else, she purchased a sunhat, and a pugaree to wind about it, as was customary in the East. On her stroll through the town, Nellie Bly the reporter, as was her wont, scrupulously avoided over-simplification. She noted that whereas the tenants in the houses were clearly poor, the carved-wood fronts of their abodes "would have been worth a fortune in America." She recognized, too, with remarkable clarity and swiftness, the complexities involving the mendicants in the streets:

> We saw a great number of beggars who, true to their trade, whined forth, with outstretched hands, their plaintive appeals, but they were not so obtrusive or bothersome that they necessitated our giving them the cane instead of alms. The majority of the beggars presented such repulsive forms of misery that in place of appealing to my sympathetic nature, as is generally the case, they had a hardening effect on me. They seemed to thrust their deformities in our faces in order to compel us to give money to buy their absence from our sight.

Thus while Nellie Bly as journalist was a champion of the poor and the oppressed, she was no "bleeding-heart liberal" by our definition. Poverty, to her mind, was not necessarily ennobling, and the beggars were using her the way they used all the tourists who passed through Port Said. She saw through their peculiar form of blackmail, by which they let her know she need only give them *baksheesh* to make them stop shoving their crooked bones and toothless maws in her face.

That same evening, Nellie Bly and the other passengers returned to the *Victoria*. The next morning, she awoke earlier than usual and rushed up on deck to see the famous Suez Canal. The *Victoria* was passing through what looked like a mammoth ditch, enclosed on either side by high sand banks. The ship seemed to be scarcely moving, which made Nellie Bly doubly aware of the oppressive heat. She was informed that according to law, vessels must not travel the canal at a speed exceeding five knots an hour, because a rapid passage would cause a current strong enough to erode the sand banks. To help the passengers tolerate the swelter and the tedious hours on the canal, one of them, Nellie reported, described its history:

> It was begun in 1859 and took ten years to build. The work is estimated to have cost 18,250,000 pounds sterling, although the poor blacks were employed to do the labor commanded at the lowest possible wages. It is claimed that the lives of one-hundred thousand laborers were sacrificed in the building of this canal, which is only one-hundred English miles, eighty-eight geograph-

ical miles in length. When first completed the width of the canal was three-hundred and twenty-five feet, but the constant washing in of the banks had reduced it to one-hundred and ninety-five feet. The bottom is said to be seventy-two feet wide and the depth is but twenty-six feet. The trip through the canal can be made in from twenty to twenty-four hours.

It is interesting to note that by the late 20th century, the transit time through the Suez Canal had been reduced to fourteen hours, and that in 1870, the canal's first year of operation, there were fewer than two transits per day—whereas nearly one-hundred years later, the average number of ships passing through had grown to fifty-six per day. It is also interesting to note that although the Suez Canal was built by the French and financed by them (Great Britain did not become the major shareholder until six years after the canal was completed), Nellie Bly's source for information about the canal put the estimated cost of construction in English pounds sterling, not in French francs (Hail Britannia! Britannia rules the waves!). But perhaps most interesting of all was Nellie's journalistic approach to the Suez Canal as compared with Elizabeth Bisland's to the tomb of Ieymitsu in Tokyo. Nellie was careful to point out the dark side that so often attended the construction of man's great wonders;—all those people who died building the Suez Canal! Miss Bisland let her awe at the splendor of the shogun's final resting place blind her to mentioning the possibility that it had been erected at a cost in human lives and suffering.

That night, the *Victoria* dropped anchor in the Bay of Suez. Some jugglers came aboard. Among them was a black man who wore a sash, turban, and baggy breechclout in the lining of which he carried two lizards and one small rabbit. He was, Nellie Bly reported, very anxious to show the passengers his tricks and get money from them, but he refused to do anything with the lizards and the rabbit until he had performed his trick with a handkerchief and some bangles. He selected Nellie from among the crowd to hold the handkerchief, which he had first shaken as if to show them that it contained nothing. He must have singled her out because he felt he could count on her to be not only a good actress but an ally. Nellie reported:

He then showed us a small brass bangle, and pretended to put the bangle in the handkerchief; he then placed the handkerchief in my hand telling me to hold it tightly. I did so, feeling the presence of the bangle very plainly. He blew on it and jerking the handkerchief loose from my grasp, shook it. Much to the amazement of the crowd the bangle was gone.

The trick, however, was on the black juggler! While he was performing, some of the passengers had stolen his rabbit and one of his lizards crawled off somewhere. At last, one young man produced the rabbit from his pocket and returned it to the juggler, much to the poor fellow's relief. The migratory lizard was nowhere to be found; as it was time for the ship to sail, the juggler was forced to return to his boat. Nellie Bly observed:

> After he had gone, several people came to me to know if I had any idea how the trick with the handkerchief had been done. I explained to them that it was an old and very uninteresting trick; that the man had one bangle sewn in the handkerchief, and the other bangle, which he showed to the people, he slipped quietly out of sight. Of course, the one who held the handkerchief held the bangle, but when the juggler would jerk the handkerchief from the hand, and shake it, in full view of his audience, the bangle being sewn to the hand-kerchief, would naturally not fall to the floor, and as he carefully kept the side to which the bangle was attached turned towards himself, he successfully duped his audience into thinking, that by his magic, he had made the bangle disappear. One of the men who listened to this explanation became very indignant, and wanted to know if I knew positively how this trick had been done, and why I had not exposed the man. I merely explained that I wanted to see the juggler get his money, much to the disgust of the Englishman.

The air was suffocating as the *Victoria* sailed down the Red Sea. The passengers tried to forget the heat by entertaining each other. Their blackened faces streaked with perspiration, a number of the young men put on a minstrel show. Those passengers who could sing at the songfests sang, and those who realized they had no voice kept quiet. Otherwise, people lounged about on deck in easy chairs. A few of the women appeared at dinner in dresses with long trains—much to the amusement of those passengers who felt that full dress was out of place on a steamship. Nellie Bly simply changed from her heavy-waist dress to her silk bodice and felt "cool and comfortable and lazily happy." Men normally, she observed, felt freer than women did to enjoy themselves under such straitened circumstances. The men aboard the *Victoria* played cricket and quoits, gambled for high stakes in the smoking-room, and rendezvoused in dark corners of the deck with females who were congenial. The weather was so hot that the men spent their nights on deck instead of in their cabins. Nellie as feminist in the Man's World of 1889 reported:

> It is usually customary for the women to sleep on deck, one side of which, at such times, is reserved exclusively for them. During this trip none of the women had the courage to set the example, so the men had the decks to themselves. Sleeping down below was all the more reason why women arising early would go on decks before the sun began to boil in search of a refreshing spot where they could get a breath of cool air. At this hour the men were usually to be seen promenading about in their pajamas, but I heard no objections raised until much to the dismay of the women the Captain announced that the decks belonged to the men until after eight o'clock in the morning, and that the women were expected to remain below until after that hour.

Because of the intense heat, the passengers had been warned by the ship's officers not to go ashore at Aden. The women, their timidity unabated, stayed on board to bargain with the peddlers who came to the ship to sell ostrich feathers and feather boas. Not all the women, that is. Nellie Bly and a few of the more-reckless passengers decided to brave the torridness and went ashore to see what the port city at the southern entrance to the Red Sea had to offer. The release from the inhibitory atmosphere of the *Victoria* seemed to freshen Nellie' reportorial instincts. The inhabitants of Aden, she noted, brushed and polished their teeth to a dazzling whiteness with "tree branches of a soft, fibrous wood which they cut into pieces three and four inches in length"; the small man whose boat brought her ashore had legs so thin that they reminded her of "smoked herrings, they were so black, flat and dried-looking," the fashion-conscious males bleached their hair yellow by coating it with lime which remained on for several days exposed to the hot sun and the water, and the bright yellow against the black skin made Nellie think of the craze to bleach one's hair that had burst upon America some years ago and since become "an old and tiresome sight." The black natives of the English seaport were bejeweled from head to toe and wore little else, inasmuch as "in a place as hot as Aden, jewelry must be as much as anyone would care to wear." Whereas, interestingly enough, Elizabeth Bisland seemed obsessed with the men she saw during her trip around the world, Nellie Bly felt drawn to the way the women presented themselves to attract the male:

> To me the sight of these perfect, bronze-like women, with a graceful drapery of thin silk wound about the waist, falling to the knees, and a corner taken up the back and brought across the bust, was most bewitching. On their bare, perfectly modeled arms were heavy bracelets, around the wrist and muscle, most times joined by chains. Bracelets were also worn about the ankles, and their fingers and toes were laden with rings. Sometimes large rings were suspended from the nose, and the ears were almost always outlined with hoop rings, that reached from the inmost edge of the lobe to the top of the ear joining the head. So closely were these rings placed that, at a distance, the ear had the appearance of being rimmed with gold. A more pleasing style of nose ornament was a large gold ornament set in the nostril and fastened there as screw rings fasten in the ear.

Nellie's need, however, for the whole truth required her to cite as well the grotesqueness—to her western eye—of their appearance:

> Still, if that nose ornamentation was more pleasing than the other, the ear adornment that accompanied it was disgusting. The lobe of the ear was split from the ear, and pulled down to such length that it usually

rested on the shoulder. The enormous loop of flesh was partially filled with large knobs.

Despite their fondness for jewelry and for adorning their bodies with it, the tribespeople of Aden, Nellie Bly observed, were poor and their shops dirty and uninviting. Nevertheless, the town itself was of great strategic importance to the British Empire; dominated by a steep mountain with an English fort on top, it was regarded as the strongest gateway to India. As Nellie and her fellow passengers rode back to the pier in their hired carriage, little naked children ran after them for miles, "touching their foreheads humbly and asking for money. They all knew enough English to be able to ask us for money."

The passengers boated back out to the *Victoria* where they looked downward from the deck. In the water to one side of the ship, a number of men and youngsters called "the Somali boys" were giving an exhibition of diving and swimming. Nellie Bly, whose speciality as a stunt reporter had required that she be a good actress (she had feigned insanity so convincingly on Blackwell's Island that she fooled even the doctors!) knew a good performance when she saw one. The Somali boys were putting on a show for the tourists. Nellie reported:

They would actually sit in the water looking like bronze statues, as the sun rested on their wet, black skins. They sat in a row, and turning their faces up towards the deck, would yell methodically, one after the other, down the entire line: "Oh! Yo! Ho!" It sounded very like a chorus of bull-frogs and was very amusing. After finishing this strange music they would give us a duet, half crying persuasively, in a sing-song style: "Have a dive! Have a dive! Have a dive!" The other half, meanwhile, would put their hands before their widely opened mouths, yelling through their rapidly moving fingers with such energy that we gladly threw over silver to see them dive and stop the din.

But like all exciting entertainers, the Somali boys had much more than charm going for them. Beneath the glitter was a disciplined talent; just as she was to become bewitched by the geisha dancers in Japan, Nellie Bly was enthralled with the divers in the Bay of Aden:

> The moment the silver flashed over the water all the bronze figures would disappear like flying fish, and looking down we would see a few ripples on the surface of the water—nothing more. After a time that seemed dangerously long to us, they would bob up through the water again. We would see them coming before they finally appeared on the surface, and one among the number would have the silver between his teeth, which would be most liberally displayed in a broad smile of satisfaction. Some divers were children not more than eight years old, and they ranged from that to up to any age. Many of them had their hair bleached. As they were completely naked, excepting a small cloth twisted about their loins, they found it necessary to make a purse out of their cheeks, which they did with as much ease as a cow stows away grass to chew at her leisure.

Nellie Bly's acute powers of observation enabled her to penetrate the fog of mystification that surrounded the divers. Why were they impervious to attack in these shark-infested waters? She observed:

> No animal, waterborn and bred, could frisk more gracefully in the water than do these Somali boys. They swim about, using the legs alone, or the arms alone, on their backs, or sides, and in most cases, with their faces under water. They never get out of the way of a boat. They merely sink and come up in the same spot when the boat passes. The Bay at Aden is filled with sharks, but they never touch these black men, so they tell me, and the safety with which they spend their lives in the water proves the truth of the assertion. They claim that a shark will not attack a black man, and after I had caught the odor of the grease with which they anoint their bodies, I did not blame the shark.

The black divers may have liked to think that the color of their skin magically protected them from the sharks. Nellie Bly may well have been the first white traveler through Aden who refused to "buy" the local folklore. The divers were human beings to her, not tourist attractions. It was the smell of the grease that repelled the sharks, not the divers' pigmentation or their glandular secretions.

After their seven-hour stay in Aden, Nellie Bly and the intrepid companions who had gone ashore with her now boated back to the *Victoria*. From the deck of the moving ship, she watched the divers swim after them a long ways out from the land. One of them, a little boy, came aboard to be with Nellie and the other passengers. Shortly he took his departure from them, she reported, with a splendid salute:

> ...and when he left us he merely took a plunge from the upper deck into the sea and went happily back towards Aden, on his side, waving a farewell to us with his free hand.

The *Victoria* sailed for Colombo on the Island of Ceylon. It was December 2nd and Nellie Bly had been out of New York eighteen days. One day ahead of schedule, she remained blissfully unaware that another woman was racing against her.

CHAPTER TEN

THE PLEASURES OF HONG KONG

Elizabeth Bisland caught one more glimpse of Fujiyama, then Japan sank out of sight. As the *Oceanic* steamed toward Hong Kong, Miss Bisland's thoughts turned to that far-famed port. Hong Kong! The name clangored in her consciousness like "two slow loud notes of some great brazen-lunged bell." Hong—Kong!

The first day out from Yokohama, tragedy struck. The young Chinese fellow who had lain motionless and sick with consumption died. He had struggled hard to "keep the flame burning," Miss Bisland reported, and now that flame had flickered out. A canvas was hung across the screen, and she watched the comings and goings of the doctor. The young man's death inspired in her a flight of poetic fancy:

> They will carry him back to his country, though he will not be glad or aware. But the sea knows she is being defrauded of her rights, and wakes and rages. She comes in the nights and beats thunderously with her great fists upon our doors. She leaps to look over our bulwarks for her hidden victim; she roars with wrath and will not be appeased. For two days we steam in the face of the northwest gale she has raised, and for three, the ship plunges like a spurred horse.

Elizabeth Bisland put herself at war with the storm, which raged for five days and which forced her to "go leaping and plunging about the ship," unable to keep her seat or to prevent her soup and entrees from spilling. It was then she had "retired to bed" and, wedging herself in tight with pillows, read the books about Japan from the ship's library.

At 2 p.m. on Sunday, December 15th, the *Oceanic* dropped anchor in the harbor of Hong Kong amid a host of ships from all nations. Elizabeth Bisland was now thirty-one days out of New York and twenty-three days out of San Francisco. She must by now have become profoundly impressed by her boss John Brisben Walker's powers of persuasion and manipulation. She knew that he had tried unsuccessfully to bribe Cunard White Star steamship line officials in San Francisco to permit the *Oceanic* to leave two days ahead of the scheduled time of departure. But she also knew that the same officials felt compelled to make it up to him and instructed Captain Kempson to make all due haste for Miss Bisland's sake and thus help her gain an edge in her race against Nellie Bly. The result was that the ship took sixteen days to cross the Pacific to Japan and five days to steam to Hong Kong from Yokohama—one of the fastest voyages known for that time of year, when the winds were unfavorable or coming from the East.

Cosmopolitan's plan, Miss Bisland reported, was for her to stay with personal friends in Hong Kong so that she might "see something of domestic life in the East." She was taken ashore in their private launch and carried through the waterfront business quarter in a silver-trimmed chair of bamboo borne by four Chinamen dressed in her friends' livery. The residential section was "cool and shadowy" with tall bamboo trees, gigantic ferns, and the "prodigious shiny leaves of tropical lilies." There were flowers everywhere—in the courtyards, at both ends of every flight of stairs, and on balcony railings. Miss Bisland personified the flowers:

> Every nook and corner that will hold a jar is filled with bloom, and the rarest orchids are strewn carelessly about, industriously producing flowers, in a delicious provincial ignorance of their own value and of what they might exact in the way of expensive attention.

The people of Hong Kong elicited a mixed response in Elizabeth Bisland. Her descriptions of them were eminently journalistic—clear, vivid, and evocative—yet expressed a tendency to regard beauty as skin-deep. She reported:

> We meet the most astonishing variety of the human race. All sorts and conditions of Chinamen—elegant dandies in exquisitely pale-tinted brocades; grave merchants and compradors, richly but soberly clad; neat amahs with the tiny, deformed Chinese feet, sitting at the street corners, taking in sewing by the day; street sellers of tea, shrimp, fruit, sweetmeats, and rice; women working side by side with the men, mending the

streets...horrible old women, weazened and wrinkled beyond all imagining, all the femininity shrivelled out of them, their only head-covering a bit of black cloth across their seamed and humble foreheads, and the last pathetic spark of the female instinct for adornment displaying itself in the big jade and silver rings in their ears.

That these "horrible old women" might have earned their wrinkles by mending the streets side by side with the men did not strike Miss Bisland. Her class-consciousness surfaced as she surveyed the polyglot mix in this strange locale:

From windows shaded by light bamboo blinds look out coarse olive faces—heavy and dull of eye, repulsively sensual. These are Portuguese descendants of the hardy sailors who explored and ruled these seas before the English supplanted them. They have bred in with the natives everywhere and have grown an indolent mongrel race...Plump and prosperous-looking gentlemen go by in European dress and with tight-fitting purple satin coal-hods on their heads. Their complexions are dark and their features—dug out of a mat of astonishingly thick beards—are aggravatedly Hebraic in their cast. They are Parsees, and look uncommonly like the lost tribes—exhibiting also, I am told, the same eminent abilities in business probably possessed by those much-sought-for Hebrew truants.

Elizabeth Bisland's feeling of exclusivity toward people of ethnic origin and skin color different from her own coalesced with a passion for them if they were attractive males. This intriguing mixture of provocation and prohibition may well have been what that frustrated suitor in New York was describing when he confided to Lafcadio Hearn that he felt as if he were "playing with a beautiful dangerous leopard" which he loved for not biting him. In any event, the next target of her gaze in the streets of Hong Kong was a Sikh policeman:

At the corner stands a haughty jewel-eyed prince of immense stature—straight and lithe as a palm—in whose high-featured bronze countenance are unfathomable potentialities of pride and passion....He wears a soldier's dress and sword, and a huge scarlet turban of the most intricate convolutions. I cry out with astonishment at the sight of this superb creature. "Is it an emperor?" I demand, in breathless admiration. "An emperor! Poof! It's only a Sikh policeman. There are hundreds about the place as splendid as he." When the Arabs who had seen Europeans only in trousers fled before the magnificent onslaught of the kilted Highlanders at Tel-el-Kebir, they exclaimed in amazement: "If these are the Scotch women, what must the men be!" So, though a bit dashed, I say to myself, "If these are the Sikh policemen, who must their princes be?", and secretly resolve to go some day and discover.

In Elizabeth Bisland's rich and vivid fancy, if she was going to conduct a clandestine tryst it would be with a potentate, not with a policeman. Miss Bisland knew by what chain of circumstances Sikhs from India had come to the streets of Hong Kong. And now, surveying this splendid "creature" she reported:

It gives me my first real impression of the power of England, who tames these mountain lions and sets them to do her police duty. It would seem incredible that this rosy commonplace Tommy Atkins who comes swaggering down the street in his scarlet coat can be the weapon that tamed the fine creature in the turban....What is it makes this cheerfully vulgar Anglo-Saxon the lord of the Hindoo? Physically, he is not the Sikh's superior, and in profound and passionate sentiment, if one may judge by the countenance, the Hindoo is infinitely above the Briton. Nor is the latter greater in courage or dignity, for these Indians made a noble resistance to English encroachment, and after submission were enrolled in the army of the conquerors as their bravest and most loyal troops....What is the secret?...Is it more beef and mutton perhaps—or more of submission to orders and powers of self-discipline?

Miss Bisland's speculations about the British Tommie were interrupted by her sight of one of Queen Victoria's best and bravest warriors striding toward her:

Here comes one of the conquerors of India, a kilted Highlander, swinging down the road in his plaid petticoats, with six inches of bare stalwart pink legs showing, and a fine hearty self-confidence in his utter disbelief in the power of anything human to conquer him.

Elizabeth Bisland's Scottish blood tingled at the sight of those six inches of rosy male thigh peeping above the Scottish knee.

* * *

The friends' house where Elizabeth Bisland stayed in Hong Kong afforded her all the comforts a Southern gentlewoman could have required. From the rear veranda, she enjoyed a wide view of the precipitous, verdure-filled city ringed with tawny hills that sloped down to the flashing harbor bay. In the mansion itself, she admired the lofty hall filled with potted plants and massive furniture of Indian ebony, the great drawing room fifty feet long and eighteen feet high with its rich European fittings and Eastern bric-a-brac. She noted with particular interest the photographs scattered about of members of the Hohenzollern dynasty, the ruling house of Imperial Germany since 1871, for her friends were German. She pleasured in her bedchamber, "another huge shadowy place," which had a dressing room and bath "as large as the ordinary drawing room at home" and which was furnished with "old mahogany and silver fittings brought from Germany two generations ago." Its airy unencumbered spaces, she reported, "remind me of the fine old bedchambers in the plantation houses at home in the South." When she was a child she lived in Mount Repose (built prior to 1824 on the estate founded by her great-grandfather John Bisland, one of the earliest cotton planters), the large, dignified family mansion in the Pine Ridge neighborhood north of Natchez.

Although to the manor born, Elizabeth Bisland felt solicitude for the masses of the destitute on the streets of Hong Kong:

There is a general public amiability—without the gay and gracious vivacity of Japan—in all save the lowest class of laborers. These toiled terribly and incessantly for infinitesimal sums, and by the most minute economies manage to exist—to continue these labors and privations. They are old in youth, parched, callous, and dully indifferent. Incapable of further disappointment, they exist with the stolid patience of those who expect only stones and serpents, having abandoned all hopes of bread and fish.

This same woman would later in life found in Washington, D.C. an evening clinic to provide health services for the working girl who could afford only moderate charges. At twenty-eight, however, Miss Bisland's true emotional allegiance lay not with the downtrodden laborers of Hong Kong but with the wealthy and powerful whose decisions made the city prosper. Accordingly, she proceeded to catalogue the financial assets of the town: The shops, hotels, clubs, and handsome counting-houses...the "massive and imposing" banks and public buildings...the warehouse and the huge dry docks and shipyards on land reclaimed from the harbor basin...the enormous export trade in cotton, tea, silk, spices, and rice...the development of manufacturing industries...the international flavor of Hong Kong, whose government business was conducted by the English, Germans, Parsees, and Chinese...and the port-city's strategic importance, which was so great that four or five warships were always in its harbor or cruising in the neighborhood and that two full regiments were kept in the garrison. At the time of Miss Bisland's visit, one of those regiments was of her favorite Highlanders:

> They are being put through a rapid and vigorous drill one morning when we pass the parade ground, and the pipes are shrilly skirling—music to stir the heart in which runs the smallest drop of Scottish blood. Not even the Sikh policemen stand first in my affections at this moment, as, to that wild keen sound, the solid ranks of brawny red-haired Caledonians trot by, with their petticoats fluttering about their bare knees and their bayonets set in a glittering hedge....Oh, braw sight!...Oh, bonny lads!...Scotland forever!

The climate in Hong Kong was delightful at this time of year, and Elizabeth Bisland's friends were "loath that I should lose a single pleasure." They visited the Botanical Gardens which inspired in her another of her lavish verbal paintings of scene:

We pass under the tremulous, lacy shadows of ferns twenty feet high, through trellises weighted with ponderous vines that blow a myriad perfumed purple trumpets up to the golden noon, and emerge upon banks of crimson and orange flowers. The flaxen-haired muslin-clad English children play here, cared for by prim trousered Chinese amahs; and we meet pretty blue-eyed German ladies in their chairs taking this road home.

As members of the Nordic race, the English and the Germans not only shared the House of Hanover which had already given four Georges to England as kings, they also enjoyed in common blond hair and blue eyes! Contrast those descriptions by Miss Bisland with those by her of the coarse, lazy, leaden-eyed "mongrel" Portuguese and the dark, hirsute Parsees who looked "aggravatedly Hebraic." Her Anglophilia and her insularity were inextricably intertwined.

Elizabeth Bisland's friends took her by tram to the top of Victoria Peak which dominated Hong Kong. They gazed down at the harbor whose beauty was rivaled only in Rio de Janeiro and Sydney, then descended in chairs past the "white palace-like bungalows with smooth-shaven tennis courts where ruddy-cheeked, spare-loined young Englishmen toss the ball to fair-haired light-footed English girls." They wound downward in a smooth, easy motion to "the regular *pad, pad, pad, pad* of the bearers' feet." The sun set, gilding the heights; below in the harbor, the lights of the town, the ships, and the flitting sampans sparkled through the evening "like multitudinous fireflies." As they passed, magically, it seemed, from the light into the heavy gloom of a grove of trees, the woman who hated making this "ridiculous" race around the world, felt pangs of homesickness:

> A great pure calm reigns here where we sink into this cool flood of darkness;...half-naked figures go by noiselessly on unshod feet....I know all this; I remember it well....Somewhere—once—I passed through just such shadowy ways in the warm nights. This silent peace of darkness after long hours of burning light is quite familiar to me. I try to recall where it was—but it was a long, long time ago and I have forgotten the name of the place and the people who lived there....I only remember that I

used to pass under the great trees...that some wonderful secret delight waited for me beyond them. Alas! That was very long ago; tonight only an excellent dinner attends my coming.

Home was not New York; home was Elizabeth Bisland's childhood on the plantation, and the grove of trees may well have put her in mind of that stand of gnarled live oaks festooned with Spanish moss that faced the big white house on the rise.

Miss Bisland dined royally in Hong Kong, in the palatial townhouse of a "handsome dark gentleman" reputed to have made a huge fortune financing the reclamation and development of the waterfront on Kowloon Peninsula opposite Hong Kong. She likened her host to Kubla Khan and his abode to Khan's stately pleasure dome in Xanadu, in the poem by Samuel Taylor Coleridge. The sumptuous banquet featured many courses and costly wines and was served by "a phalanx of tall Celestials in rustling blue gowns." The nabob's national identity was diversified. "For convenience and brevity," Miss Bisland reported, "he gave it out that he was a British subject, resident in China, born in India, and with a certain mixture of Greek and American blood in his veins." If one's pedigree was important to her, so was his degree of financial stability. Before they banqueted in his pleasure dome, the businessman took Elizabeth Bisland and her friends on a tour of the Kowloon waterfront:

It had been his fancy to come to Hong Kong twenty years before, neglecting to bring with him any drafts on his treasury, and in the interim he had collected something like a million pounds it was said. It was he who had made the long waterfront at Kowloon, rescuing it from the sea, and had covered it with great godowns filled with merchandise of the East, and it was he who was proposing the same feat on the opposite side of the harbor. He had interested himself more or less in the banks, the shipyards and manufactures of various sorts....

Miss Bisland's admiration of wealth and power commingled with her resplendent style of writing to glamorize Hong Kong. She captured brilliantly the scenic color—the sights and sounds and smells of the town: The steep narrow streets...the odor of opium and dried ducks and fish hanging exposed for sale in the sun...the hiss of "many strange repulsive" meals cooked in the braziers...the richly gilded fretwork of the shops...the houses lime-washed with tints like those found on Chinese porcelains...the long perpendicular signs lettered with large black characters. She caught the place, and the bustling commotion of the place:

> ...streets that climb laboriously up and down stairs, and so narrow that there is hardly room for our chairs to pass through the multitudes who swarm there. Sixteen hundred residents to the acre they average in this part of the town, buzzing and humming like the unreckonable myriads insects breed from the fecund slime of a marsh.

It was December 18th and Elizabeth Bisland's three-day stay in Hong Kong would soon become a memory. Time. Time. Time was inexorable and beauty fleeting; she felt the old pressures return. *Cosmopolitan* was pulling the strings back in New York, and Miss Bisland was the reluctant puppet. The plan had been for her to sail from Hong Kong on the North German Lloyd ship *Preussen*, but there was a Peninsular and Oriental steamer that sailed three days earlier. Advised to take that ship as far as Ceylon by O. and O. Steamship Line agent Mr. Harmon, Miss Bisland acquiesced. She was a prisoner of the race against Time and Nellie Bly. She found herself on the deck of the *Thames*, "surrounded by the charming friends and acquaintances of this Hong Kong episode, who have come to give me a final proof of their goodness, and wish me speed on my journey." She waved goodbye to her friends and the beautiful city with keen regret. The ship was as polyglot as the land she had just left; it swarmed with "queer people" including lascar sailors "clad in close trousers and tunic of blue cotton check and red turbans" and Parsees in their "purple coal hods" who had come aboard to "bid farewell to a parting friend." Among the passengers was a Highlander going home. His comrades had brought their bagpipes to give him a last tune. "Grief and Scotch whiskey," Elizabeth Bisland reported, "move them finally to 'play a spring and dance it round,' in spite of the heat, which brings the sweat pouring down their faces." Proud that she was descended from the Britons, she watched the Union Jack, the national flag of the United Kingdom, flying bravely above the ship as it steamed toward Singapore.

CHAPTER ELEVEN

HOORAY FOR THE RED, WHITE, AND BLUE?

The Union Jack flew as well above the *Victoria* as it sailed toward Ceylon, but Nellie Bly did not gaze at it with feelings of exultation. The young women aboard ship asked her if she would like to participate in some *tableaux vivants* one evening in which they wished to portray the different countries. They invited her to represent America but she refused. Then they asked her what the American flag looked like! They wanted to fabricate one and to drape it around the young woman who was to represent America. To hear that people didn't know what the Stars and Stripes looked like came as a shock to Nellie, but she graciously allowed to her readers that the young women put on some "really very fine" living tableaux. Despite their ignorance about her country's flag and despite the miserable service aboard the *Victoria*, Nellie Bly expressed high regard for the English. With characteristic even-handedness, she reported:

> The loyalty of the English to their Queen on all occasions, and at all times, had won my admiration. Though born and bred a staunch American, with a belief that a man is what he makes of himself, not what he was born, still I could not help admiring the undying respect the English have for their royal family. During the lantern slide exhibition, the Queen's picture was thrown on the white sheet, and it evoked warmer applause than anything else that evening. We never had an evening's amusement that did not end by everybody rising to their feet and singing "God Save the Queen." I could not help but think how devoted that woman, for she is only a woman after all, should be to the interests of such faithful subjects.

Nellie Bly spoke not a word in behalf of her own country during the outpourings of allegiance to their sovereign Queen by her subjects aboard the *Victoria*. The steadfastness of their homage shamed Nellie into telling herself that there was little good she could say about her own leaders in the United States. "There I was," she reported, "a free-born American girl, the native of the grandest country on earth, forced to be silent because I could not in honesty speak proudly of the rulers of my land, unless I went back to those two kings of manhood, George Washington and Abraham Lincoln." The presidents most familiar to Nellie at the age of twenty-two were Grover Cleveland and Benjamin Harrison. In her up-close view of his first administration, Cleveland was ineffective because of his abrasiveness and bull-headed refusal to compromise. (Based on his two terms of 1884—1888 and 1892—1896, history would ultimately evaluate him as a man of great integrity who fought valiantly against government job-patronage, pension give-aways for Civil War veterans, protective tariffs and "cheap" silver money.) In the election of 1888—probably the most corrupt campaign in American history—Cleveland ran for re-election and was defeated by Harrison, an Indiana lawyer and U.S. Senator who had served as a Union officer in the Civil War but was mostly famous for being the grandson of the ninth U.S. President, William Henry Harrison (elected 1840), celebrated for his victory over the Indians at Tippecanoe, Indiana, in the War of 1812. The 23rd President of the United States had been in office only nine months when Nellie Bly set out on her race around the world. Harrison, a man who shrank from leadership, stayed above the fray in the campaign of '88, letting his supporters do the in-fighting. Nellie Bly knew that among his wealthy and powerful financial backers was John Wanamaker, the "Merchant Prince" of Philadelphia, who swelled the candidate's campaign coffers, raising, it was said, at least one-hundred thousand dollars in ten minutes, one million dollars in all, and had another two million dollars in reserve. "We raised the money so quickly the Democrats never knew anything about it," Wanamaker said. Even despite her short acquaintance with Harrison's abilities, Nellie Bly suspected that there was fraudulence connected with the election. She knew what the insiders knew—that although Harrison had lost to Cleveland in the popular vote, his henchmen won the Electoral College war for him by buying votes in Indiana and making a deal with Tammany Hall in New York that swung those two states into the Republican column. Benjamin Harrison, Nellie Bly saw, was either a political naif or corrupt:—the men who picked him to run for the presidency did so because they knew they could manage him. After the election, he proclaimed, "Providence has given us victory" —a statement which led Republican National Committee Chairman Matt Quay to observe that "Providence hadn't a damn thing to do with it." The hard reality set in for Harrison when he assumed office and discovered that the party managers had usurped all his power. "I could not," he was to say later, confirming Nellie Bly's suspicions about him, "name my own Cabinet. They sold out every place to pay the election expenses." President Harrison named the "Merchant Prince" his Postmaster General (Wanamaker dropped thirty-thousand Democrats from the payroll during his first year).

No wonder while the English passengers on the *Victoria* idolatrously sang "God Save the Queen," Nellie Bly felt tongue-tied—unable to praise America's recent Chief Executives. She was very patriotic toward her country, but she couldn't brag about its leaders. She was so patriotic she would have felt disloyal to explain to the English that it was her job as a reporter to dig up the disagreeable truths and that she took a jaundiced view of America's public servants because she knew where the skeletons were hidden—not only in the national but in the state and local closets. She was so patriotic she would have felt disloyal to tell them how she had trapped "the Fox," Ed Phelps, the corrupt lobbyist, by masquerading as the wife of a patent medicine manufacturer and persuading the "lobby king" to accept a bribe of two-thousand dollars to kill a legislative bill that would eliminate the sale of quack remedies in New York State. She was so patriotic she would have felt disloyal to mention the notorious Boss Tweed—Tammany Hall leader William Marcy Tweed (1823—1878), who with his "Tweed ring" cronies swindled New York City out of sums estimated at between thirty million and two-hundred million dollars. She was so patriotic she would have felt disloyal to tell them about Tammany tool Hugh J. Grant who became Mayor of New York in 1889 and, in deference to the public outcry, reopened the clip joints, brothels, disreputable dance halls, and other dives. She was so patriotic she would have felt disloyal to tell them about a New York City where politicians, police, and the underworld were in league to bilk the public and where, but for the press, the grievous social and economic problems would have gone unspotlighted. She could not speak without holding back about Joseph Pulitzer's *New York World* and its campaign against crowded factory conditions, brutalizing sweatshops, teeming deathtrap tenements, violence toward immigrants, and a tax system that lined the pockets of the rich and oppressed the poor. How could she boast about the *World*'s crusades when the conditions themselves existed?

CHAPTER TWELVE

MISS BISLAND CONFRONTS THE RODENT

Elizabeth Bisland gloried in life aboard the *Thames*. More like a fine yacht than a steamship, it was spacious and commodious, affording the traveler all the comforts of home away from home. Here and there hung canary cages "thrilling with songs"; narcissus bulbs in bowls blossomed with white flowers and jars full of palms and ferns were everywhere. Miss Bisland was assigned a large, pleasant stateroom on the water-side, with a view that left her "on intimate terms with the milky, jade-tinted sea." Worn out from the hectic round of pleasures in Hong Kong, she drifted into a balming slumber:

Beneath this window is a broad divan, and here, laved in tepid sea winds and soothed by rippling whispers against the ship's side, I sleep—the languorous, voluptuous sleep of the tropics...sink softly into that dim warm flood where one lies drenched, submerged in unconsciousness; a flood that ebbs slowly, slowly—bearing with it all fatigue and satiety—and leaves me on the shores of life again in a pale lilac dusk glimmering with great stars....

She awoke feeling rested and revitalized:

Yea, verily, life is good in this magnificent equatorial world! Again I am a great sponge, absorbing beauty and delight with every pore. Every day brings new marvels and new joys. I go to bed exhaustedly happy and wake up expectantly smiling. Everything pleases, everything amuses me; most of all perhaps the strong British atmosphere in which one finds one's self on board a P. and O. steamer.

There was only one other woman on the passenger list, and her affinity, too, for the British heritage was strong. She was "a charming little old lady from Boston," Elizabeth Bisland reported, "who after two years of travel in the East had suffered no diminution of her respect for the Common and Phillips Brooks." The Common was, of course, the Boston Common, a tract of public land purchased by the town in 1634 when it was loyal to the British Crown. (Brooks, now fifty-three, an American Episcopal clergyman, was famous for his stirring sermons in Trinity Church in Boston and for having written the Christmas hymn "O Little Town of Bethlehem.") At this point Miss Bisland once again evinced her lustiness: While she perceived the pronounced masculine flavor of the British atmosphere aboard the *Thames* to be a "limitation," she reacted to its bodily manifestation with hearty approval:

> The men, from captain to cook, are fine creatures. Their physical vigor is superb—such muscles! such clear ruddy skins, white teeth, and turquoise eyes. They are flat-backed and lean-loined; they carry their huge shoulders with a lordly swagger; they possess a divine faith in themselves and in England....

She went on to rhapsodize about the "astonishing collection of accents" among the males—passengers as well as officers and crew—with a bow to the diversity-within-unity of Her Majesty's subjects:

> No one of them speak alike; the burly bearded giant three places off from me at table speaks with a broad Scotch drawl; the handsome, natty little fourth officer with the black eyes and shy red face who sits opposite, in white duck from head to heel, has a bit of a Yorkshire burr on the tip of his tongue; the Ceylon tea-planter talks like a New Yorker, and there are fully a dozen variations more between his accent and that of the tall young blond, whose fashionable Eton and Oxford inflections leave one speechless with awe and admiration of their magnificent eccentricities.

Miss Bisland's veneration of things British extended to a rave review of the daily cuisine. This was her introduction to the food "upon which the folk of English novels are fed." The menu of well-prepared dishes on the *Thames* offered an international range of choices, but Elizabeth Bisland's Anglophilia imparted to the British cooking a special piquancy and zest:

I learn to know and appreciate the Bath bun and the Scotch scone. I make the greatly-to-be-prized acquaintance of the English meat pie, including Mr. Weller's favorite "weale and 'ammer," and I recognize touching manifestations of British loyalty to the sweets christened impartially with appellations of royalty—Victoria jelly-roll, Alexandra wafers, and Beatrice tarts. Waterloo pudding is one of our favorite desserts, and other British triumphs and glories adorn the bill of fare from time to time.

Samuel Weller, the center of comic interest in Charles Dickens' novel *The Pickwick Papers*, cleaned and polished gentlemen's boots and ladies' shoes at the White Hart Inn, and later was servant to Mr. Pickwick, to whom he became devotedly attached. Alexandra was a granddaughter of Queen Victoria. (She would marry Russian emperor Nicholas II and fall under the influence of the debauched "holy man" Rasputin after she took over the throne from her hemophiliac husband.) The Bath bun and Scotch scone are still popular in Britain, and so are meat pies of steak-and-kidney, chicken, veal-and-ham (Sam Weller's "weale and 'ammer"), rabbit and game, but the featured dessert nowadays is more likely to be bread-and-butter pudding or a trifle. Rarely is it named after royalty.

It was Sunday morning—and the day before Christmas—on the steamship *Thames* plowing southward on the South China Sea. Elizabeth Bisland attended a religious service which she found "fatiguing," then watched the officers and crew natty in their dress-uniforms undergo a ceremonial inspection under the critical eye of their commander. After that, she and the other passengers retreated to refresh themselves with cooling drinks. She was feeling prankish:

> As the little fawn-eyed punkah-wallah (to put it in American, the boy who pulls the hanging fan over the table) passes me, I snatch off his turban and find his round brown head shaved as smooth as my palm, except for the one lock over the brow by which Mahomet is to catch him up to heaven. He finds this liberty only an amusing condescension on my part, and smiles indulgently and shyly, following me about

always afterwards with little mute services and attentions—so sweet-natured are these Eastern folk.

This act of impudence could scarcely have gratified the Muslim punkah-wallah. But probably, he had long since learned that the best way to the heart and pocket of a rich tourist from Britain or America was to play the servile role of the charming mascot. But then the angelic side of Miss Bisland took over. As the *Thames* steamed toward the equator, she thrilled to a beauty so transcendental that it must have made her forget all about the war for circulation between John Brisben Walker and Joseph Pulitzer and about her race against "Time" and Nellie Bly:

> We sail through the blue days on an even keel. The sea does not even breathe; but it quivers in the terrible splendors of the noon with undreamable peacock radiances....The sky arches in a dome of intolerable vastness, filled with a blinding light. Hardly can its glories be borne, even in the shadow of the wide awning where one lies half the day in Indian lounging chairs, warmed to the very heart and soaked through with color and light....There are no pageants or sunsets. The burning ball, undimmed by any cloud, falls swiftly and is quenched in the ocean, and after an instant of crepuscular violet the prodigious tide of light vanishes abruptly, like some vast conflagration blown out suddenly, and as suddenly succeeded by "The night of ebony blackness, / Laced with lustres of starry clusters."

Her powers of description now reached a dazzling zenith:

> Then the constellations hang in the awful vaults of darkness like enormous gleaming lamps trembling in suspension. And from the swart deep beneath whirl up myriads of great ghostly jewels, glittering with unearthly fires and trailing a broad waving path of spectral silver along the black water in our wake.

On the morning of December 23rd, the passengers sighted Singapore, which was only seventy miles from the "centre of heat." ("Centre" was the chiefly British spelling of the word.) The voyage from Hong Kong through the South China Sea had taken five days; Elizabeth Bisland was now thirty-nine days out of New York.

The waters of the harbor in Singapore, Miss Bisland reported, were "curiously banded in broad lines of brilliant violet, green, and blue, each quite distinct and with no fusions of color." Fed by centuries of incessant heat and moisture, the tremendous rampage of tropical vegetation in the surrounding hills seemed to threaten burying "the City of Lions." Miss Bisland responded to Singapore much as she did to Hong Kong; she was impressed by the power, wealth, and prestige of the town, cataloguing its financial assets and proudly explaining its strategic importance to the British Empire. In the 12th century Singapore was the capital of the Malayan empire, but in 1824 the British purchased it from a Malayan sultan. It then was "scarcely more than a heap of ruins," but that didn't faze the indomitable Britons:

> Only those who travel to these Eastern ports can have any adequate conception of the ability which has directed English conquest in the Orient. When they bullied the Malayan sultan into selling Singapore, they were apparently acquiring a ruinous and unimportant territory. Today this port is the entreport of Asian commerce, a coaling station for vessels of all countries, a deep, safe harbor for England's own ships and men-of-war, and a point from which she can command both seas. The inhabitants of her Straits Settlements number considerably more than half a million, and the exports and imports are each in value something like ten million pounds yearly. The United States alone buys there, every twelve months, goods worth more than $4,000,000.

Elizabeth Bisland went ashore at Singapore accompanied by the lady from Boston, the Ceylon tea-planter whose twenty years' residence in the tropics had made him used to the heat, and a "tall blond" fellow whose "rosy skin" beaded with drops of sweat despite the fact that he was attired in "snowy silk and linen...and a Terrai hat with a floating scarf." The last-named was "grandson of one of the world-famous conquerors of the East." Immediately she was confronted with a mode of transportation that was new to her—the gharry, a "queer little square" carriage for hire that was "made for the most part of Venetian blinds" and drawn by "a disconsolate pony the size of a sheep." The encounter troubled her; in another of those evidences of caring that belied her egocentricity, she reported:

> Conveyance in the East is a constant source of unhappiness to me. I was deprecatory with the jinricksha men in Japan, I humbled myself before the chairbearers of Hong Kong, and now I go and make an elaborate apology to this wretched little beast before I can reconcile it to my conscience to climb into the gharry, or let him drag me about at a gallop.

As the gharry bore her into town, Elizabeth Bisland delighted in the riot of color: The deep red of the earth and the bright green of the trees...the burning blue of the sky and the rainbow radiance of the sea...the blinding white, azure, green, red, and yellow of the houses with their heavy squares of lime-washed brick. The interiors were "gloomily cool" but more than enough of the "huge fierce glare of day" entered through the open door.

Miss Bisland's little pony passed swiftly through the business part of Singapore. When he reached the broad red water-road where the houses faced the sea, the voluptuary side of her took over:

> One is suddenly aware that the sensory nerves awake in this heat to marvellous acuteness. The eye seems to expand its iris to great size and be capable of receiving undreamed potentialities of luminosity and hue. The skin grows exquisitely sensitive to the slightest touch— the faintest movement of the air. Numberless fine undercurrents of sound reach the ear, and the sense of smell is so strong that the perfumes of fruit and flowers at a great distance are penetrating as if held in the hand. One smells everything: delicious hot scents of vegetation...the steaming of the earth...and the faint acrid odors of the many sweating bodies of workers in the sun....

The water-road teemed with a cosmopolitan mix of folk: Hindu fruit vendors, English officials, Chinese and Malay merchants, and the "lower class of people." Elizabeth Bisland's response to the environment switched from the sensuous to the sensual; her desirous eye seized upon the male expanses of bare flesh:

Nearly all foot-passengers are half or three-quarters naked. It is an open-air museum of superb bronzes who, when they condescend to clothe themselves at all, drape in statuesque folds about their brown limbs and bodies a few yards of white or crimson cloth, which adorns rather than conceals....The lower class of working people are black, shining, and polished as Indian idols. At work they wear only a breechcloth, but when evening comes they catch up a square of creamy transparent stuff, and by a twist or two of the wrist fold it beautifully and loosely about themselves, and with erect heads tread silently away through the dusk—slender, proud, and mysterious-eyed. The Malays are of an exquisite bronze, gleaming in the sun like burnished gold. They have full silken inky hair, very white teeth, and dress much in draperies of dull-red cotton, which makes them delicious to contemplate. Mingled with all these is the ubiquitous Chinaman in a pair of short loose blue breeches, his handsome muscular body shining as yellow satin.

Miss Bisland would doubtless have been deeply offended to be informed of her sensuality, which breathes through every line of that passage. It would not have been proper for her as a model Southern gentlewoman to admit to her healthy sexual urges. But she had them, and they made her seem to smolder with passion, whereas Nellie Bly's attitude toward men on the trip was playful. Nor did Nellie share her rival's need to be waited on royally in an ambiance of elegance. It is difficult to imagine Nellie reacting to luncheon at a hotel in Singapore the way Elizabeth Bisland did:

We are served by Hindoos in garments and turbans of white muslin, who have slender melancholy brown faces, and eyes that shine through wonderful lashes with the soft gleamings of black jewels. I can scarcely eat my tiffin for delight in the enchanting pathetic beauty, the passionate grace and sadness, of the face of the lad who brings me butter in a lordly dish, the yellow rolls laid upon banana leaves, and serves me curry with a spoon made of a big pink shell. Every one is in lily white from head to toe, like a bride or a debutante—white duck trousers and fatigue jacket, white helmet, and white shoes. This is the dress of two young sunbalterns with heads like canary birds, and the sappy red of English beef still in their cheeks, just out from home for their first experience of Eastern service.

Miss Bisland's accommodation in the hotel was a huge, dim apartment with a stone floor that opened directly upon the lawn and into the dining room. "It has only slight jalousies for doors," she reported, "but no one peers or intrudes." Her bed was an "iron frame"; the single hard mattress was spread with a sheet, but there were no covers. Even the pillow was of straw. Her bathroom, a lofty flagstoned chamber, contained a big earthenware jar, "which the coolies fill for me three times a day, and into which I plunge to rid me of the burning heat."

That night an intruder did steal into her bed-chamber, but not in human form. She had just gotten into bed and blown out the candle when she heard what sounded like "some great animal stalking about." She felt suddenly icy cold. That noise. What could it be? Her imagination leaped to a fearful surmise. They had told her that tigers came over from the mainland and carried off an average of one person a day. It must be a tiger! He could easily push open those blind doors and walk in! She heard him coming toward her bed with "heavy stealthy rustlings." There was not even a sheet for her to draw up over her. The room was hot, utterly black and still, "save for the sound of those feet and the loud banging of my heart against my ribs." The hotel was so horribly silent it seemed dead. Has the tiger, she wondered, eaten every one else already? She knew that tigers hunted by night:

> The darkness is of no use; he can see all the better for that; so that I will strike a match and at least perish in the light. As the blue flame on the wick's tip broadens I meet the gaze of a frightfully large, calm gray rat who is examining my shoes and stockings with care. He regards me with only very faint interest and goes on with his explorations through all my possessions. He climbs the dressing-table and smells critically at my hat and gloves. This is almost as bad as the tiger, but as I have no intention of attacking this terrible beast and my

notice appears to bore him, I blow out the candle and go to sleep, leaving him to continue those heavy rustlings which so alarmed me.

How courageous Elizabeth Bisland was to go back to sleep despite the presence of that giant rodent in her room! What previous experience, if any, with rats inured her to this one? In the 1880s in New York City, rats were so readily available that dog-versus-rat contests replaced dog-versus-raccoon ones as a popular diversion. Boys were paid to catch the rats, at a rate of five to twelve cents a head. The dogs were always fox terriers, and a good rat-dog could kill a hundred rats in thirty to forty-five minutes. Matches drew as many as a hundred betting spectators, from all walks of life, with purses starting at 125 dollars. It is doubtful that the refined Elizabeth Bisland had the stomach for witnessing these male rites of slaughter, but there is no question she was extremely brave in that hotel room in her private contest of woman-versus-terrifying rat.

During her two-day stay in Singapore, Miss Bisland went for a drive to the lush botanical gardens where swans and "rose-flushed" lotuses floated on glassy pools and "ghostly white, pallidly purple" blossoms writhed into "fantasticalities of scarlet." On the way back, she observed "a race of brown goddesses" singing along the road. They were Kling women who had been transplanted from Pondicherry, the last fragment of India still retained by France. Her heart went out to them as she admired their tall slender figures, their gracefulness of deportment, and their "fine, haughty, dark features." She seemed to identify with them, as if she shared with each the anguish of being an exile—a woman in a world ruled by men, torn from home and loved ones and sent to wander in strange lands. She reported:

> As we pass, they raise languid great eyes of unfathomable blackness with a gaze half mystical, half sensual, that stirs the heart with a vague sudden pain of yearning and sadness....It is a race famous throughout India for the astonishing beauty of women; but as they will not allow themselves to be photographed, I can get no record of their loveliness.

Elizabeth Bisland spent the afternoon browsing through

shops and visiting museums in Singapore, then returned to her hotel to freshen up. Time....Time. Half-past four! The ship was about to leave! She re-boarded the *Thames*. Little, almost-naked Malay children ages three to seven called shrilly for coins from the cluster of canoes in the bay below. Miss Bisland observed:

A few shillings changed into the native currency pro-cures a surprising number of small pieces of money, which we fling into the clear water. They plunge over after these with little splashings like frogs, and wiggle swiftly down to the bottom, growing strange and wavering of outline and ghostly green as they sink. They are wonderfully quick to seize the glinting coin before it touches the sands below, and come up, wet, shining, and showing their white teeth. We play at this game until the whistle blows, and then sail away, leaving the blond waving his handkerchief to us from the shore.

It was the tall blond who was grandson of one of the world-famous conquerors of the East and who had gone ashore with her at Singapore. She must have relished the moment although she knew she probably would not see him again. For what could be more poignant, more romantic than bidding farewell forever to a gallant gentleman?

CHAPTER THIRTEEN

WORRY IN PARADISE

After a six-day voyage across the Gulf of Aden and the Arabian Sea, the *Victoria* anchored in the bay at Colombo, Ceylon. The island of green trees and white arcaded buildings against the background of a high mountain was a welcome sight to the passengers after the heat they had endured on the ocean, and they were impatient to leave the ship. Some of them went ashore in the sturdy steam launch, but Nellie Bly opted for a strange-looking craft that she was told would be speedier. The natives called it a "catamaran," and the tourists, an "outrigger." It was, according to a gentleman of vast travel experience who offered to escort her on the boat and on the island as well, perfectly safe. Looking at one, she doubted his judgment but said nothing. She depicted:

> The boat was a rudely constructed thing. The boat proper was probably five feet in length and two feet in width across the top, narrowing down to the keel, so that it was not wide enough to allow one's feet to rest side by side in the bottom. There were two seats in the middle of the boat facing one another. They are shaded by a bit of coffee sack that must be removed to give room for passengers to get in. The two men sit at either end of this peculiar boat, and with one paddle each. The paddle is a straight pole, with a board the shape and size of a cheese-box tied to the end of it, and with both these paddles on the same side they row us ashore. The boat is balanced by a log the length of the boat and fastened out by two curved poles, probably three feet from the boat.

A catamaran may have looked primitive by Western standards, Nellie Bly indicated, but it proved marvelously efficient in practice:

> With but slight exertion the men sent the boat cutting through the water, and in a few moments, we had distanced the steam launch and had accommodations engaged at the hotel before the launch had landed its

passengers. It is said at Colombo that catamarans are used by the native fishermen, who go out to sea in them, and that they are so seaworthy and so secure against capsizing that no case of an accident to a catamaran has ever been reported.

It was the morning of December 8th and Nellie was out of New York twenty-four days. She must have felt good about her chances of beating Father Time and Phileas Fogg, for she was two days ahead of the schedule planned for her by the editors of the *World*. The gods of travel, she presumed, were on her side. She still had no idea that another woman had been sent out to race against her.

As if to make up for the barbarities Nellie Bly had suffered on the *Victoria*, the gods of travel smiled on her in Colombo. They provided the Grand Oriental Hotel, a fine, large establishment with tiled arcades and airy and comfortable corridors. It was furnished with easy chairs and "small, marble-topped tables which stood close to the broad arm-rests, for one to sip the cooling lime squashes or the exquisite native tea, or eat of the delicious fruit while resting in an attitude of ease and laziness." Nellie found, she reported, no place away from America where smoking was not socially acceptable; men smoked on the lovely hotel promenade. They also "consumed gallons of whiskey and perused the newspapers" while the women read novels or bargained with vendors for dainty hand-made lace or gems of remarkable beauty.

Phileas Fogg enjoyed no such respite from his enervating journey down the Suez Canal and Red Sea and across the Arabian Sea. His creator Jules Verne dispatched him not to comfortable Ceylon but to Bombay and thence across India to Calcutta in an arduous trip by rail, carriage, and jouncing elephant. When Nellie visited the celebrated novelist in Amiens, it will be recalled, he asked her why she was not going to Bombay as his fictional hero had done—and she replied it was because she wanted to save time. How seriously her editors at the *New York World* were concerned about her scrupulously duplicating Fogg's route is open to question. (They must have feared for the safety of a single woman traveling alone across the vast sub-continent of India.) No one but Verne appeared mindful of the discrepancy. Based upon his studies as a geographer and his experience as a world trav-

111

eler, he scheduled Phileas Fogg's itinerary as follows:

From London to Suez via Mt. Cenis and Brindisi,
by rail and steamboat...07 days
From Suez to Bombay,
by steamer ....13 days
From Bombay to Calcutta,
by rail ....03 days
From Calcutta to Hong Kong,
by steamer ....13 days
From Hong Kong to Yokohama (Japan),
by steamer ....06 days
From Yokohama to San Francisco,
by steamer ....22 days
From San Francisco to New York,
by rail ....07 days
From New York to London,
by steamer and rail ....09 days
Total...80 days

Nellie Bly knew the contents of *Around the World in Eighty Days* like the palm of her hand. She knew that she had taken one day less than Fogg to travel from London to Suez. She knew that she had taken two days less to travel from Suez to Ceylon than he had taken to go from Suez to Bombay but that the difference might be ascribed to Bombay's lying hundreds of miles apart from Ceylon. Thus far, her trip verified Verne's research on how long it would take to go around the world. The race between her and Fogg was nip-and-tuck. She may have wondered if the means of global transportation had speeded up all that much in the seventeen years since Verne's novel was first published. (It was not until she crossed the Pacific that Nellie Bly made sizeable inroads into Fogg's timetable; she voyaged from Yokohama to San Francisco in fourteen days whereas Fogg took twenty-one—a gain attributable to the superiority of Nellie's steamship, a four-masted-with-funnel vessel driven by screw propeller as opposed to Phileas Fogg's three-masted-with-funnel driven by paddle wheels.)

Nellie Bly kept waiting to hear that her ship for Hong Kong was ready to depart and that she should come aboard. Quite naturally, she was exasperated by what she took to be an unnecessary delay. But the charms of beguiling Ceylon lulled her into a state of euphoria. On the promenade of the Grand Oriental Hotel, she marveled at the quality of the jewelry that the vendors tried to sell her and her fellow travelers:

There were deeply-dark emeralds, fire-lit diamonds, exquisite pearls, rubies like pure drops of blood, the lucky cat's-eye with its moving line, and all set in such beautiful shapes that even the men, who would begin by saying, "I have been sold before by some of your kind," would end by laying down their cigars and papers and examining the glittering ornaments that tempt all alike. No woman who lands at Colombo ever leaves until she adds several rings to her jewel box, and these rings are so well known that the moment a traveler sees one, no difference in what part of the globe, he says to the wearer inquiringly: "Been to Colombo, eh?"

Nellie Bly's next brush with the ignorance abroad about America happened when she saw how the diamond merchants regarded U.S. currency. For the first time since leaving her country she saw American money. It was popular, all right, in Colombo—as jewelry! As money, it was close to worthless; when Nellie offered it in payment of her bills, she was told it would be taken at sixty-percent discount. The Colombo diamond merchants were happy to get American twenty-dollar gold pieces and paid a high premium on them. Nellie reported:

The only use they make of the money is to put a ring through it and hang it on their watch chains for ornaments. The wealth of the merchant can be estimated by his watch chain, they tell me; the richer the merchant the more American gold dangles from his chain. I saw some with as many as twenty pieces on one chain.

The blandishments of Colombo extended as well to the "picturesque stateliness" of the hotel dining room whose small tables were richly decorated daily with the native flowers of the town and whose cooling system was similar to the one Elizabeth Bisland enjoyed on the steamship *Oceanic*:

From the ceiling were suspended embroidered punkas, that invention of the East which brings comfort during the hottest part of the day. The punkas are long strips of cloth, fastened to bamboo poles that are suspended within a short distance of the tables. They are kept in motion by a rope pulley, worked by a man or boy. They send a lazy, cooling air through the building, contributing much to the ease and comfort of the guest. Punkas are also used on all the ships that travel in the East.

Nellie Bly was also pleased with the hotel's food and service, which came as a blessed relief after the past fortnight on the *S.S. Victoria*. The varied menu was particularly welcome after her marine siege of "eating the same kind of food under daily different names," and the courteous Singalese waiters—who spoke English very well—were a dramatic improvement over the *Victoria*'s careless and impertinent English stewards. At tiffin, Nellie had some "real" curry, the famous native dish of India. With her usual gift for clothing the trivial with human interest, she reported:

> I had been unable to eat it on the *Victoria*, but those who knew said it was a most delicious dish when prepared rightly and so I tested it on shore. First a divided dish containing shrimps and boiled rice was placed before me. I put two spoonfuls of rice on my plate, and on it put one spoonful of shrimps; there was also chicken and beef for the meat part of the curry, but I took shrimps only. There was handed me a much divided plate containing different preserved fruits, chuddah, and other things hot with pepper. As instructed, I partook of three of this variety and put it on top of what had been placed first on my plate. Last came little dried pieces of stuff that we heard before we saw, its odor was so loud and unmistakable. They called it Bombay duck: It is nothing more or less than a small fish, which is split open, and after being thoroughly dried is used with the curry. One can learn to eat it. After all this is on the plate it is thoroughly mixed, making a mess so very unsightly, but very palatable, as I found. I became so given to curry that I only stopped eating it when I found, after a hearty meal, curry threatened to give me palpitation of the heart.

In the melting pot that was New York City in 1889, a popular method of stereotyping nationalities was by the odor of their breath: The French smelled of garlic; the Germans of sauerkraut and beer; the English of roast beef and ale; the Americans of corn cakes and pork and beans; the Chinese of opium, cigars, and dried fish. "Real" Indian curry was a novelty to Nellie Bly's readers and so was its hot, spicy smell. Still, she recognized that her description of it and how it was served ran on too long. She seasoned the verbal meal with a pinch of humorous anecdote:

> A story is told concerning the Bombay duck that is very amusing. The Shah of Persia was notified that some high official in India intended to send him a lot of very fine Bombay duck. The Shah was very much pleased and, in anticipation of their arrival, had some expensive ponds built to put the Bombay ducks in! Imagine his consternation when he received those ill-smelling, dried fish!

Colombo reminded Nellie Bly of Newport, Rhode Island. The roads, made apparently of red asphalt and embowered by over-arching trees, were the smoothest she had ever seen. The beautiful homes were set back in tropical gardens, and the roar of the breakers along the beach that fronted Galle Face Drive was the most musical sound that she had ever heard waters make. A poetic yearning for something beyond the finite seized her:

> The road lies very close to the water's edge, and by the soft rays of the moon its red surface was turned to silver, the deep blue of the sea was black; and the foamy breakers were snow drifts. In the soft, pure light we would see silent couples strolling along arm and arm, apparently so near the breakers that I felt apprehensive lest one, stronger than the others, should catch them unawares and wash them out to that unknown land where we all travel to rest....One can see through the forest of tall palms where the ocean kisses the sandy beach, and while listening to the music of the wave, the deep, mellow roar, can drift—drift out on dreams that bring what life has failed to give; soothing pictures of the imagination that blot out for a moment the stern disappointment of reality.

Was there, one is led to wonder, some romantic misadventure in her own life? The beachfront after dark became a place where Nellie Bly tried to sort out her feelings:

> Lazily I sat there one sweet, dusky night, only half hearing my escort's words that came to me mingled with the sound of the ocean. A couple stood close together, face bending over a face up-turned, hand clasped in hand and held closely against a manly heart, standing, two dark figures, beneath an arch of the veranda, outlined against the gate lamp. I felt a little sympathy for them as wrapped in that delusion that makes life heaven or hell, that forms the foundation for every novel, play or story, they stood, until a noisy new arrival wakened her from blissful oblivion, and she rushed, scarcely waiting for him to kiss the hand he held, away into the darkness. I sighed again, and taking another sip of my lime squash, turned to answer my companion.

A longing suffuses this passage, a pathos and mystery. Did Nellie wish she was the girl with face upturned, hand clasped in her lover's hand, breast beating against his breast? Was it the couple, or herself, she sighed for? She made male friends easily, but racing around the world made getting to know any one man well an impossibility.

On the one hand, Nellie Bly wanted to leave Ceylon as soon as possible; on the other, she felt herself fall under the spell of that paradisiacal island: Toast and tea before arising...a morning excursion out past the lake where men, women, children, oxen, horses, buffalo and dogs disported...past where laundry folk beat, soaked, and wrung their clothes and spread them on the grass to dry...past the white people driving, riding bicycles, and walking. The curving roads were bordered and arched with magnificent trees burdened with brilliant blossoms. Around noon, the hotel guests took a rest, and after luncheon they took a nap. They slept during the hottest part of the day, and at four they were again ready for a drive or walk, from which they returned after sunset in time to dress for dinner. After dinner, there were "pleasant little rides in jinrickshas or visits to the native theatres."

Nellie Bly, of course, was a devotee of the theatre. She was, after all, a consummate actress, who in her job as investigative reporter had already starred in several roles—feigned insanity and uncovered the abuse of patients in an asylum, masqueraded as a shopgirl, servant girl, and factory girl and brought to light the inhumane practices of employers and employment agencies, posed as the wife of a manufacturer of quack medicines and inveigled a corrupt lobbyist into accepting her offer of a bribe. She had even been on the stage for one evening, playing the role of an Amazon complete with shield and spear in a spectacular pantomime featuring one hundred showgirls—and written a story for the *New York World* deprecating her clumsy debut. So, with her curiosity about acting technique, she took a special interest in the Parsee theatre in Colombo. Her escort—she never seemed to lack for a male escort—told her that all the actors were men because no native woman would think of going on the stage. To the beat of a tomtom and the playing of a "strange-looking organ," the actors sang, danced, gestured, and spoke their roles. Nellie reviewed the performance with lenity:

> The actors were amusing, at least. The story of the opera was not unlike those in other countries. The basis or plot of the play was a tale of love and tragedy. A tall young man, with his face painted a death-like white, sang shrilly through his very high-arched nose to another young man, dressed in the costume of a native woman. The latter was the lady and the heroine of the play, and he sang sharply through his nose like his, or her, lover. All the actors sang through their noses, and the thinner their voices and the more nasal sound they employed the more the audience applauded.

Nellie Bly went on to describe in intricate detail the opera: the twists and turns of the plot, the stage business of secret compartments (tea-chests), poisoned wine, and plunging dagger, and the melodramatic conflict between good and evil. The heroine of the play, maid-servant to a very wealthy tea-planter, thwarted the designs of the bold, bad robber to seduce her and kill her master and was rewarded for her noble bravery with the hand of the master's son in marriage. Nellie may well have been trying to capitalize on her readers' interest in grand opera, what with the opening in 1883 in New York of the Metropolitan Opera Company with

Gounod's *Faust*. A Parsee theatrical production might not have been an earth-shaking event, but Nellie's audience hungered for morsels about the exotic people and places she visited in her travels. She must have wondered if she would ever run into a big story on the trip—short of her day of homecoming. She must have wanted to shake loose from the drowsy Ceylon routine.

Nellie Bly thrived on flirting with danger. She got a whiff of it later that night, on the way back to the hotel. She and her companion were riding in a cart pulled by a bullock, "a strange modest-looking little animal with a hump on its back and crooked horns on its head." The driver was stopped by a policeman who informed them they were all under arrest for driving in a vehicle in one of whose lamps the candle had burned out. Nellie's escort made things right with the constable. ("We went," she reported, "to the hotel instead of the jail.")

One morning, as she watched the native snake charmers who haunted the hotel perform their tricks, the craving for peril returned with compelling urgency. "See the snake dance?" one of them urged her. Nellie said she would like to, but that she would pay to see the snake dance and for nothing else. She reported:

> Quite unwillingly the man lifted the lid out of the basket, and the cobra crawled slowly out, curling itself upon the ground. The "charmer" began to play on a little fife, meanwhile waving a red cloth which attracted the cobra's attention. It rose up steadily, darting angrily at the red cloth, and rose higher at every motion until it seemed to stand on the tip end of its tail. Then it saw the charmer and it darted for him, but he cunningly caught it by the head and with such a grip that I saw the blood gush from the snake's mouth. He worked for some time, still firmly holding the snake by the head before he could get it into the basket, the reptile meanwhile lashing the ground furiously with its tail. When at last it was covered from sight, I drew a long breath, and the charmer said to me sadly: "Cobra no dance, cobra too young, cobra fresh!" I thought quite right; the cobra was too fresh.

One can imagine Nellie Bly gazing in fascination as the reptile uncoiled. She must have felt a tremor at the sight of that darting venomous head, but her love of danger cooled her nerve; she did not miss the story. It was a young cobra, unschooled in the art of dance. The snake charmer, as a professional, would know that.

Time hung heavy now on Nellie in the island paradise. She took her first ricksha. She reported:

> The jinricksha is a small two-wheel wagon, much in shape like a sulky, except that it has a top that can be raised in rainy weather. It has long shafts joined at the end with a crossbar. The jinricksha men are black and wear little else than a sash. When the sun is hot they wear large hats that look like enormous mushrooms, but most of the time these hats are hanging to the back of the 'ricksha. There are stands at different places for these men as well as carriage stands. While waiting for patrons they let their 'rickshas rest on the shafts and they sit in the bottom, their feet on the ground. Besides dressing in a sash these men dress in an oil or grease, and when the day is hot and they run, one wishes they wore more clothing and less oil. The grease has an original odor that is entirely its own.

Whereas Elizabeth Bisland had felt unhappy about riding jinrickshas in Japan and had "humbled" herself before the chairbearers of Hong Kong, Nellie Bly soon was able to accept this sort of transport as part of the culture of the East; the men were simply doing their jobs:

> I had a shamed feeling about going around the town drawn by a man, but after I had gone a short way, I decided it was a great improvement on modern means of travel; it was so comforting to have a horse that was able to take care of itself! When we went into the shops it was so agreeable not to have the worry of fearing the horses were not blanketed, and when we made them run we did not have to fear we might urge them into a damaging speed. It is a great relief to have a horse whose tongue can protest.

She felt a rising irritation at being required to stay five days on Ceylon, however beautiful that island might be. She became impatient to get on the ship for Hong Kong. She began to chafe at the constraints of Paradise. Enjoying time was one thing, killing it was quite another. Nellie visited the two newspaper offices in Colombo, met with the famous high priest at the Buddhist college, and toured the world-renowned gardens at Kandy. The smoothness of the island roads, she concluded, was due to the absence either of beer wagons or of New York City street commissioners. The newspapers were run by two very kind, clever young Englishmen to whom she felt indebted for "a great deal of pleasure during my stay in Ceylon." The elderly priest, who spoke English fluently, told her that he received hundreds of letters from the United States every year and that he found more converts to the Buddhist religion in America than in any other land. The train to Kandy was crowded; it wound upward on a mountainside that looked down on a deep valley with terrace after terrace of "the softest, lightest green." After all she had heard about Kandy, Nellie Bly found it a disappointment. The old temple surrounded by a moat contained "several altars of little consequence, and a bit of ivory which they told us was the tooth of Buddha." Instead of being cool, Kandy was so hot that Nellie and her companions thought with regret of seaside Colombo. With her were the Spanish diplomat who was going to Peking and a "jolly Irish lad" who was bound for Hong Kong. Both had traveled with her from Brindisi and both, like her, felt cheated by what they had seen at Kandy. The gods of travel, however, are whimsical; what the trio of travelers came looking for in Kandy they found instead in the great botanical garden at Parathenia.

That evening, they returned by train to Colombo. Nellie Bly was feeling tired and hungry and the extreme heat had given her a sick headache. Nellie reported the following incident:

On the way down, the Spanish gentleman endeavored to keep our falling spirits up, but every word he said only helped to increase my bad temper, much to the amusement of the Irish boy. He was very polite and kind, the Spaniard, I mean, but he had an unhappy way of flatly contradicting one, that, to say the least, was very exasperating. It was to me, but it only made the Irish boy laugh. When we were going down the mountain side the Spaniard got up, and standing, put his head through the open window in the door to get a view of the country. "We are going over," he said, with positive conviction, turning around to us. I was leaning up in a corner trying to sleep and the Irish boy, with his feet braced against the end of the compartment, was trying to do the same.

The Spanish diplomat was terrified and well he should have been. Even the redoubtable Nellie Bly caught her breath at their precipitous descent. When he told her "We are going over," she eked out a reply:

"We won't go over," I managed to say, while the Irish boy smiled. "Yes, we will," the Spaniard shouted back, "Make your prayers!" The Irish boy screamed with laughter, and I forgot my sickness as I held my sides and laughed. It was a little thing, but it is often little things that raise the loudest laughs. After that all I needed to say to upset the dignity of the Irish boy was: "Make your prayers!"

That hysterical laughter of hers was more than a means by which she broke the tension of playing "Hurry-up-and-Wait" on Ceylon. She was laughing not simply at the diplomat's use of English in the Spanish idiom, she was laughing in the face of Death.

The trip to Kandy and return made Nellie too sick to go to dinner. Instead she went right to bed. The next morning, she quit her plan to visit the pearl market, she didn't feel up to it. When her acquaintances returned and told her a man bought some leftover oysters for one rupee and found five hundred dollars worth of pearls in them, she felt her zest for living dangerously revive. "I felt sorry that I had not gone," she reported, "although there was great danger of cholera."

One night, after she had been five days in Colombo, Nellie Bly learned from the blackboard in the hotel corridor that the *Oriental* would sail for China the following morning, at eight o'clock. The next day she was awakened at 5 a.m. Later, the Spanish gentleman wanted her to join him while he shopped for some jewelry, but she was nervous and anxious to get on the ship that would take her to Penang, Singapore, and Hong Kong. When she boarded the *Oriental* she found it was deserted except for a couple of passengers. "When will we sail?" she asked.

"As soon as the *Nepaul* comes in," the handsome elderly man replied. "She was to have been here at daybreak, but she hasn't been sighted yet. Waiting for the *Nepaul* has given us this five days' delay. She's a slow old boat."

"May she go to the bottom of the bay when she does get in!" Nellie said savagely. "The old tub! I think this is an outrage to be kept waiting five days for a tub like that."

"Colombo is a pleasant place to stay," the elderly man said with a twinkle in his eye.

"It may be if staying there does not mean more than life to one. Really, it would afford me the most intense delight to see the *Nepaul* go to the bottom of the sea."

Nellie's ill-humor startled them. Their look of surprise amused her, for she knew something they did not know:

> ...I thought how little anyone could realize what this delay meant to me, and the mental picture of a forlorn little self creeping back to New York ten days behind time, with a shamed look on her face and afraid to hear her name spoken, made me laugh outright. They gazed at me in astonishment, while I laughed immoderately at my own unenviable position. My better nature surged up with the laugh, and I was able to say, once again: "Everything happens for the best."

Nellie Bly was the first to spot it.

"There is the *Nepaul*," she said, pointing out a line of smoke just visible above the horizon. At first they doubted her, but in a few minutes she was proven correct. "I am very ill-natured," Nellie said by way of apology. She glanced from the kindly blue eyes of the elderly man to the laughing blue eyes of the younger man. "But I could not help it." After being delayed for five days, she explained, she was called at five in the morning because they said the ship was to sail at eight, and here it was nine o'clock and there was no sign of the ship sailing and—she was simply famished!

The two men laughed commiseratively at her woes and when the gong sounded for breakfast on the ship they took her down. The *Oriental*, although much smaller than the *Victoria*, was "very much better in every way." The cabins were more comfortable, Nellie Bly reported, the ship was better ventilated, the food was "vastly superior," and the officers were "polite and good-natured." At one o'clock that afternoon, the ship sailed. It was December 13th and Nellie had been out of New York twenty-nine days. The shores of seductive Ceylon faded from view. Nellie spent the next three days lounging lazily on deck. She woolgathered:

> I found it a great relief to be again on the sweet, blue sea, out of sight of land, and free from the tussle and worry and bustle for life which we are daily, hourly even, forced to gaze upon on land. Although the East is, in a very great measure, free from the dreadful crowding for life, still one is bound to see signs of it even among the most indolent of people. Only on the bounding blue, the grand, great sea, is one rocked into a peaceful rest at noon of day, at dusk of night, feeling that one is drifting, drifting, not seeing, or knowing, or caring, about fool mortals striving for life. True, the sailors do this and that, but it has an air far from that of elbowing each other for a living.

Nellie Bly was happy to be on the ship and leave Ceylon far behind; she was pleased to be moving forward again. How could she know that when she arrived in Hong Kong the trip would jolt her into an alarming new dimension? The challenge was to be more than just Time and fictional Phileas Fogg;—it was to take on human form.

CHAPTER FOURTEEN

CHRISTMAS CRACKERS IN THE TOPICS

The *Thames* was steaming through the Straits of Malacca and along the palm-fringed Malaysian coast when Miss Bisland heard a cry and saw "a naked yellow body with man-acled hands" shoot from the ship's side and vanish in a boiling circle of foam. A Chinese prisoner being transported to Penang had knocked down his guards and jumped into the ocean. The engines were reversed and a lifebuoy thrown overboard but he did not appear. Elizabeth Bisland reported:

> After what seemed a great lapse of time, a head shows a long distance away and moves rapidly toward the shore. Evidently he has slipped his handcuffs and can swim. A boat is lowered full of Lascars very much excited, commanded by the third officer, a ruddy young fellow—calm and dominant. They pursue the head, but it has covered more than half the distance, some two miles between us and the shore before it is overtaken. There is some doubling back and forth, an oar is raised in menace, and the fugitive submits to being pulled into the boat. I am standing by the gangway when he returns. He is a fine, well-built young fellow. His crime is forgery, and he is to be turned over to the native author-ities against whom he has offended. Their punishments are terrible: prisoners receive no food and must depend upon the memories and mercies of the charitable. One of the Lascars holds him by the queue as he mounts the steps. He is wet and chilled, and has a face of stolid despair. They take him forward, and I see him no more.

In that graphic burst of narrative, Miss Bisland saw the human being inside that "naked yellow body" and movingly conveyed his plight.

It was Christmas Day—still very hot. Off to her right, she could see from time to time, were the purple outlines of Sumatra. The *Thames* was decorated with bunting; the "ser-vants," Miss Bisland reported, "assume an air of languid festivity; but most of us suffer from plaintive reminiscences of home and nostalgia." There was a splendid plum cake for dinner with a Santa Claus on top, "huddled in sugar furs despite the burning heat." Just as during the holidays back home, the ship's passengers each had his or her own Christmas cracker. Elizabeth Bisland's made a sharp popping sound when she tore the paper strip from the decorated cardboard cylinder. Her cracker was filled with paste jewels and was "profusely provided with poetry in brief segments and of an enthusiastically amatory nature," The sentiments were apparently addressed to the stunning Miss Bisland by the males aboard the *Thames*.

The peaks of Penang shot sharply up two thousand feet into the blue air. They were "wrapped in a tangle of prodigious verdure to their tops, enormous palm forests fringing all the shore." The ship anchored some distance from the docks and would remain but a few hours. Miss Bisland and the other passengers went ashore by a means of transport new to her:

> We are ferried to land in crazy sampans, the only alternative from out-rigger canoes—a narrow trough set on a round log and kept upright by a smaller floating log connected with the boat by bent poles. Only a native, a tight-rope walker, or a bicyclist would trust himself to these.

She stepped onto the dock to find "the same crowd of Hindoos, Malays, and Chinese." Among them, were little girls of twelve or thirteen "with their own children in their arms. They have been wives for a year or two. Very pretty, they are, miniature women fully formed; the babies fat and brown and nearly as large as the mothers."

A gharry drawn by "another pitiful little horse" bore Miss Bisland toward the gardens and the famous waterfall of Penang. The road skirted the town and intersected lagoons where Malay houses of cocoanut thatch stood on piles in what was probably the slums. The Romantic in her concluded that despite the stagnant water, the natives "preferred" (as if they had a choice!) to live there and that they "apparently suffer no harm." Farther on, as the ground rose, she passed the huge stone bungalows of the English officials and rich

Chinese merchants. The entrances to the grounds of the latter were adorned with ornate doors and guarded by carved monsters, curiously colored.

The gharry overtook a Chinese funeral winding toward the cemetery, all the mourners clad in white. The coffin, of unpainted wood, was so heavy and so large, Elizabeth Bisland reported, that twenty pall-bearers were required to carry it. It was a "most cheerful cortege," she observed, with no one seeming in the least depressed by the bereavement, inasmuch as "death is accepted by that race with the same stolid philosophy as are the checkered incidents of life." Her mood turned religious as the road swept into a palm forest, but it was Nature she worshipped, not God:

> Innumerable slender, silver-gray columns soar to an astonishing height—a hundred feet or more—bearing at the top a wide feathery crown where the big globes of the cocoanuts hang, green and golden. Up there, in the tops of the palms, flows a dazzling flood of light, and as the faint warm wind waves the huge drooping fans we catch glimpses of flaming blue; but below we are in shadow and cannot feel the wind's breath. A profound green twilight reigns here, with something, I know not what, of holy sadness and amid these silent gray aisles— delicate, lofty, still—such as might move the heart in an ancient minster's calm pillared silences.

Like Nellie Bly facing the beach that night on Ceylon, Elizabeth Bisland had experienced a longing for the ineffable. The arboreal refuge stirred her heart to the depths. Miss Bisland and the other passengers from the *Thames* visited the garden, a well-kept expanse of tropical plants and flowers that lay between two lofty cone-shaped peaks with green terraces down their sides. They could hear the sound of rushing waters in the hills. Their guide, a nine-year-old boy who was "inordinately vain" about his fluency with English, scampered ahead of them up a steep path with a speed and agility that left them panting for breath. Penang was a "steambath," the sweat pouring down their faces as they sprang from stone to stone and spiraled back and forth. They were deafened now by the roar of the falls but could catch no glimpse of them:

126

Exhausted, gasping, streaming with perspiration, we finally emerge upon a plateau high on the peak's side and are suddenly laved in that warm wind that stirred the palm fronds....At our feet is a wide, quivering green pool, crossed by a frail bridge; from far above leaps down to us a flood of glittering silver that dashes the emerald pool into powdery foam, races away under the bridge, and springs again with a shout into the thickets below. We lose sight of it amid the leaves, but can hear its voice as it leaps from ledge to ledge down to the valley and is silenced at last in the river.

Beside the pool, they visited a tiny shrine. A "thin melancholy-eyed young priest" lived alone at this great height and wore a spot of dried clay upon his forehead—a "token of humility." Miss Bisland lay a piece of money on the altar of the little black elephant-headed god. In return, she was given a handful of pale, perfumed pink bells that grew upon the mountainside. The priest asked her to remove her hat and decorate her hair with the flowers in the fashion in which his countrywomen wore them. Miss Bisland complied. The priest was pleased. He thus linked himself across the oceans with that kindly gentleman who more than a month ago had handed up to her from the wharf the great nosegay of white chrysanthemums and roses.

The passengers went back down to their ship through the steaming woods and the aisles of palms.

* * *

The voyage from Penang to the heavenly island of Ceylon lasted five days. To while away the time on the *Thames*—which Elizabeth Bisland described as being more like a beautiful yacht than a steamship—she and the remaining handful of other passengers (the rest had stayed on Penang) took a consuming interest in the ship's menagerie. She reported:

The pretty little fifth officer has a monkey—a surreptitious monkey—not allowed to members of the staff—and at such time as the stern officers are on duty, we amuse ourselves fearfully and secretly with his antics. A tiny Methuselah-faced simian, regarding all his human cousins with loathing suspicion, but to be placated with raisins. A small, shivering, chattering captive, dancing to amuse his jailers, with a grin of hate on his sorrowful weazened countenance. At other times, while the powers that be look on, the Fifth and I sport ostentatiously with two gorgeous and permissible cockatoos, whom we find, like most things permissible, dull and uninteresting.

What particularly interested her were the cats. The consul to Bangkok was taking home a family of Siamese; white, with tawny legs and fierce blue eyes, they were "uncanny beasts with tigerish ways." They lived in the fo'castle with "an impulsive Chinese puppy of slobberingly affectionate disposition." Miss Bisland was intrigued by the nobility of the dog:

....their prowling long-legged behavior gets upon his nerves most terribly. He is too manly a little person to hurt them, and his only refuge is an elaborate pretense of not seeing; even when they rub against his nose he gazes abstractedly into space and firmly refuses to be aware of their existence.

In a gaudy attribution of human qualities to an animal, she saw herself in the physician's Persian cat:

The doctor has two families of felines—one a respectable tortoise-shell British matron, absorbed with the cares of a profuse maternity, and the other a splendid Persian lady, madly jealous of the division in her owner's affections. He purchased her from a native on the wharves of Bombay—smelling of violet powder and with a gold thread around her neck—a theft from some zenana, and wild with several days' starvation and bad treatment. She has not, however, forgotten the ways of her odalisque mistress, and is greedy, luxurious, indolent, and bad-tempered. If the doctor dares, after touching the kittens, to caress her without having previously washed his hands, her keen nose detects his perfidy; she flies into a fury, claws, spits, rages, and finally rushes up into the rigging to sulk until he grovels with apologies and hold out seductive visions of dinner.

There was something catlike about Elizabeth Bisland, just as the frustrated suitor in New York had suggested to Lafcadio Hearn.

The *Thames* anchored off the coast of Ceylon at eight o'clock in the morning on December 30th. The following night, it sailed into the harbor of Colombo "by the light of great tropical stars" and the gleams of a "pharos" shining from the tall clock-tower. (Pharos, an island in the bay of Alexandria, Egypt, was the site of the famous ancient lighthouse.) Many ships, Miss Bisland reported, already lay in the narrow roadstead, and "It required the fine art of navigation to slip our boat's huge hulk into her berth between two of these and make her fast to her own particular buoy."

Like Nellie Bly, Elizabeth Bisland became instantly enchanted with Colombo. She inhaled the aromatic scent of the lemon grass wafted to her from the mountain forests by the warm sweet winds. The "Spice Island" looked to her just as it had to Nellie—like Paradise. She savored the white beaches frilled with foam and the sea of green mother-of-pearl under a sky of pale warm violet. Inland, the purple distances rose into lofty outlines "deliciously softened and rounded by their enormous garment of verdure." Eden beckoned to her. (Legend has it that the weeping Adam had been banished from here; the seven thousand-foot-high peak that dominated the island was named after him.) The prospect of a sojourn on Ceylon was so pleasing, Elizabeth Bisland reported, that "One is prepared to condone any possible vileness of the inhabitants." She thrilled to the vividness of the color: The soil was bright red, the color of ground cinnabar —deep-tinted as if "soaked with dragon's blood, of which antiquity believed cinnabar to be made." She doubted the evidence of her senses—doubted that the earth could be so red, the sea and sky so blue. Miss Bisland was in her element. She exulted:

> It is a miracle wrought by the ineffable luminosity of the Eastern day! One's very flesh tingles with an ecstasy of pleasure in this giant effulgence of color, as might a musician's who should hear the prodigious vibrations of some undreamably colossal harp.

CHAPTER FIFTEEN

NELLIE BLY AND THE MOO-MOO COW FAMILY

The five-day voyage across the Bay of Bengal was sooth-ing and serene, as Nellie Bly lazed in her deck chair dream-ing a young woman's sweet waking dreams about the meaning of life. Winning was not everything.

The *Oriental* anchored off Penang, or Prince of Wales Island, on December 16th at seven o'clock in the morning. The passengers were told that because of the long delay at Colombo, they would have but six hours to spend ashore. With "an acquaintance as escort," she was introduced to the sampan. Whereas Elizabeth Bisland had described this exot-ic means of transportation as crazily untrustworthy, Nellie's reportage was coolly factual:

> We went ashore in a sampan, an oddly shaped flat boat with the oars, or rather paddles, fastened near the stern. The Malay oarsman rowed hand over hand, standing upright in the stern, his back turned towards us as well as the way we were going. Frequently, he turned his head to see if the way was clear, plying his oars industriously all the while. Once landed he chased us to the end of the pier demanding more money, although we had paid him thirty cents, just twenty cents over and above the legal fare.

Just as Elizabeth Bisland had done, Nellie Bly hired a car-riage and visited Penang's famous waterfall that came tum-bling down the mountainside. Nellie's reaction to the experience seems sour compared to the intensely imaginative Miss Bisland's:

> The picturesque waterfall is nothing marvelous. It only made me wonder from whence it procured its water supply, but after walking until I was much heated, and finding myself apparently just as far from the fount, I concluded the waterfall's secret was not worth the fatigue it would cost.

Nellie's skepticism also extended to the hygiene in the Hindu temple that she and the other passengers next visited:

Scarcely had we entered when a number of half-clad bare-footed priests rushed frantically upon us, demanding that we remove our shoes. The temple being built open, its curved roof and rafters had long been utilized by birds and pigeons as a bedroom. Doubtless ages had passed over the stone floor, but I could swear nothing else had, so I refused emphatically and unconditionally to un-boot myself. I saw enough of their idols to satisfy me. One was a black god in a gay dress, the other was a shapeless black stone hung with garlands of flowers, the filthy stone at its base being buried 'neath a profusion of rich blossoms.

English, Nellie Bly reported, was spoken less on Penang than in any port she had visited. When she asked him why, a native photographer replied, "The Malays are proud, Miss. They have a language of their own and they are too proud to speak any other."

The photographer, Nellie noted, knew how to use his English to advantage. He showed her cabinet-size proofs for which he asked one dollar each.

"One dollar!" she cried. "That is very high for a proof!"

"If Miss thinks it is too high she does not need to buy. She is the best judge of how much she can afford to spend."

"Why are they so expensive?" she demanded to know.

"I presume because Penang is so far from England," he casually rejoined.

Nellie Bly took offense at what seems to have been a perfectly reasonable response. She was pleased, she reported, to be told afterwards that a passenger from the *Oriental* "pulled the photographer's long, thin black nose for his impudence." She was glad to hear that he had been punished for what she, too, felt was his impertinence. One is hard put to believe that Nellie Bly could unravel, but she did on Penang. Nothing pleased her: The famous waterfall was a disappointment, the temple a haven for pigeon-droppings, and the photographer a smart aleck. Her mood of dissatisfaction persisted when she visited a Chinese joss-house or temple before whose idol (joss), the custom was, worshippers burned sticks of incense.

Chinese lanterns and gilt ornaments decorated the dark interior; little shrines, with the usual rations of rice, roast pig, and smoldering joss-sticks gave off a "strangely sweet perfume." Nellie Bly found the shrines "no more interesting" than a dark corner in the temple where "the superstitious were trying their luck, a larger crowd of dusky people than were about the altar." Nellie apparently placed little trust in the power of the idol to reward them for their belief in it. The only devotee at the altar, she observed, was a "waxen-haired Chinese woman, with a slit-eyed brown baby tied on her back, bowing meekly and lowly" before a painted, be-bangled image. At the invitation of the shaven-headed priests, Nellie Bly and the other passengers from the *Oriental* drank tea with them from china cups refilled so often with the milkless and sugarless beverage that she felt thankful the cups were like play-dishes. "We were unable to exchange words," Nellie reported, "but we smiled liberal smiles, at one another."

If the English language had little currency on Penang, American gold and paper currency possessed virtually none at all! Nellie Bly reported that Mexican silver was used almost exclusively on the island; American silver was accepted at the same value, but American gold and paper were looked on with contempt. Yet another shock awaited Nellie and her escort when they started back to the ship. Huge waves had sprung up in their absence and now threatened to engulf their small boat. Her escort, ashen-pale, hung his head over the side; if Nellie Bly was afraid, she did not let on. She reported:

> I could not help likening the sea to a coquette, so indifferent and heedless is it to the strange emotions in the breast.

A coal barge was busy fueling the steamship *Oriental*. The rolling of the barge increased the swell, which pitched Nellie and her escort onto the ship's ladder. Hardly had they climbed on deck when the barge was ordered to cut loose; simultaneously, the ship hoisted anchor and started on its way. The coolies left aboard the ship were terrified:

> About fifty ragged black men rushed frantically on deck to find that while depositing their last sacks of coal in the regions below, their barge and companions had

cast off and were rapidly nearing the shore. Then followed dire chattering, wringing of hands, pulling of locks, and crying after the receding barge, all to no avail. The tide was coming in, a very strong tide it was, too, and despite the efforts of those on it the barge was steadily swept inward.

Danger—whether to herself or to others—seems to have exhilarated Nellie Bly. The antics of the coolies struggling to get onto the coal barge struck her as comical, just as had the behavior of the Spanish diplomat going down the mountainside in the train in Ceylon and crying "Make your prayers!" Together with the other passengers on the deck of the *Oriental* she watched the coolies the same way a spectator in the city might watch the victim of an automobile accident being lowered onto a stretcher—not only with curiosity but with a feeling of superiority and of being entertained:

> The captain appeased the coolies' fears by stating that they should go off in the pilot's boat. We all gathered to see the sight and a funny one it was! The tug being lashed to the ship they first tried to take the men off without slowing down but after one man got a dangerous plunge bath and the sea threatened to bury the tug, then the ship was forced to slow down. Some coolies slid down a cable, their comrades grabbing and pulling them wet and frightened white on to the tug. Others went down the ladder which lacked five feet of touching the pilot boat. Those already on board would clutch the hanging man's bare legs, he meanwhile clinging despairingly to the ladder, fearing to loosen his grasp and only doing so when the ship officers would threaten to knock him off. The pilot, a native, was the last to go down. Then the cable was cast off and we sailed away seeing the tug, so overloaded that the men were afraid to move even to bail it out, swept back by the tide towards the place where we had last seen the land.

That word "funny" and the exclamation point that follows it sound a discordant note in Nellie Bly's engrossing narrative of the coolies' efforts to avoid drowning. Which was she expressing—her detachment as a journalist, or a perturbing immaturity? Certainly, the coolies did not regard their plight as comical; her reaction to it was cruel, mean, without discretion.

Several mornings at daybreak, Nellie was awakened in her cabin down below by the squabbling of the children in the cabin next to hers. They were cared for by a nurse, she reported, because the parents had "wisely" removed themselves to a cabin on the other side of the ship where they could rest in peace. The noisiness of the children made Nellie Bly bear a grudge against their parents. She described the mother as vain and domineering: "She made some show of being a beauty. She had a fine nose, everybody confessed that, and she had reduced her husband to such a state of servitude and subjection that she needed no maids." There wasn't much news on the *Oriental* headed for the Straits of Malacca; once again, Nellie Bly found herself in the position of having to invest the inconsequential with human interest. To her readers back in New York eager for juicy anecdotes Nellie narrated:

I have always confessed that I like to sleep in the morning as well as I like to stay up at night, and to have my sleep disturbed makes me as ill-natured as a bad dinner makes a man. The fond father of these children had a habit of coming over early in the morning to see his cherubs, before he went to his bath. I know this from hearing him tell them so. He would open their cabin door and in the loudest, coldest, most unsympathetic voice in the world would thoroughly arouse me from my slumbers by screaming: "Good morning. How is papa's family this morning?" A confused conglomeration of voices sounded in reply; then he would shout: "What does baby say to mamma? Say what does baby say to mamma?" "Mamma!" baby would at length shout back in a coarse, unnatural baby voice. "What does baby say to papa? Tell me, baby, what does baby say to papa?" "Papa!" would answer back the shrill treble. "What does the moo-moo cow say, my treasure, tell papa what the moo-moo cow says?" To this the baby would make no reply and again he would shout: "What does the moo-moo cow say, darling; tell papa what the moo-moo cow says?" If it had been once, or twice even, I might have endured it with civilized forbearance, but after it had been repeated, the very same identical words every morning for six long weary mornings, my temper gave way and when he said: "Tell papa what the moo-moo cow says?" I shouted frantically: "For heaven's sake, baby, tell papa what the moo-moo cow says and let me go to sleep." A heavy silence, a silence that was heavy with indignation and surprise, followed and I went off to sleep to dream of being chased down a muddy hill by babies sitting astride cows with crumpled horns, and straight horns, and no horns at all, all singing in a melodious cow-like voice—moo! moo! moo!

After that, Nellie Bly reported, the fond parents did not speak to her; they gazed upon her with disdain. Nellie felt guilty. When the mother became seasick, Nellie persuaded an acquaintance of the afflicted that it was her "Christian duty" to go see her. Nellie had smelled something fishy when she learned that the mother would not allow the ship's doctor to visit her; rather, she dispatched her husband to relate her ills to the physician so that he could prescribe for them. Nellie cattily disclosed:

I knew there was something she wished to keep secret. The woman, true to my counsel, knocked on the door; hearing no voice and thinking it lost in the roar of the ocean (she) opened the door. The fond mother looked up, saw, and screaming buried her face in the pillows. She was toothless and hairless! The frightened Samaritan did not wait to see if she had a cork limb! I felt repentant afterwards and went to a deck cabin where I soon forgot the moo-moo cows and the fond parents. But that woman's fame as a beauty was irrevocably ruined on that ship.

Nellie Bly probably thought this gossipy item would entertain her readers back in New York. Instead of covering up this petty incident she reported it, exposing the family to ridicule from those who knew them. To what end her spiteful disclosure? It only proved that she was not the kind of journalist you would want to get on the wrong side of. Curdling with resentment, she had mislaid her vaunted objectivity—her sense of fairness—and her reporting in this instance was malicious. One might attribute her irritability to the headaches, the heat, the boredom at sea...the pressing need to comprehend new peoples and new cultures quickly...the grinding pressure of getting the story and getting it right and getting it to New York before the deadline...the ghost of fictional Phileas Fogg haunting her at every turn and making any delay in her schedule seem a tormenting eternity. The *Oriental* steamed through the Straits of Malacca. The weather, Nellie reported, was unbearable:

> It was so damply warm in the Straits of Malacca that for the first time during my trip I confessed myself uncomfortably hot. It was sultry and foggy and so damp that everything rusted, even the keys in one's pockets, and the mirrors were so sweaty that they ceased to reflect. The second day out from Penang we passed some beautiful green islands. There were many stories told about the Straits being once infested with pirates and I regretted to hear that they had ceased to exist, I so longed for some new experience.

The experience that awaited Nellie was not one she could have hoped for. The *Oriental* was scheduled to reach Singapore that night. Nellie was anxious that it should, for the sooner they got in the sooner they would leave.

> ...and every hour lost meant so much to me. The pilot came on at six o'clock. I waited tremblingly for his verdict. A wave of despair swept over me when I heard that we should anchor outside until morning, because it was too dangerous to try to make the port after dark. And this was the result of slowing down to leave off the coolies at Penang. The mail contract made it compulsory for the ship to stay in port twenty-four hours, and while we might have been consuming our stay and so helping me on in my race against time I was wasting precious hours lying outside the gates of hope, as it were, merely because some black men had been too slow. Those few hours might mean the loss of my ship at Hong Kong; they might mean days added to my record. What agony of suspense and impatience I suffered that night!

The key word, of course, is "black." According to Nellie

Bly, the slowness not of some *men*, but of some *black* men, had jeopardized her chances of winning the race. In the throes of emotional crisis, she made manifest that as a Northerner, she was no freer of the prejudice prevalent in her day than was her Southern counterpart.

When Nellie Bly came on deck the next morning, the ship lay alongside the wharf. (It had arrived there at 5 a.m.) She did not report that she received assurances the *Oriental* would leave port that same day, but apparently she did receive them. Her reaction to Singapore suggests that she felt much less worried than she had the night before. She and her new escort, a young Welsh doctor, hired a gharry. She described this latest novel means of transportation as follows:

> ...a light wagon with latticed windows and comfortable seating room for four with the driver's seat on the same level on the outside. They are drawn by a pretty spotted Malay pony whose speed is marvelous compared with the diminutive size, and whose endurance is of such quality that the law confines their working hours to a certain limit.

Nellie and Dr. Brown drove through Singapore and into the countryside. Her reportorial eye shrewdly caught the passing scene: The road "smooth as a ballroom floor," shaded by large trees and "made picturesque" by native houses built on pins in marshy land on either side...the great number of graveyards and "the generous way in which they were filled"...the utter absence of sidewalks in Singapore...the predominantly blue-and-white-painted houses in which families seemed to occupy the second story, the lower generally being devoted to business...the occasional glimpses through latticed windows of "peeping Chinese women in gay gowns" and Chinese babies "bundled in shapeless, wadded garments"...while down below, in widely opened fronts, people pursued their trades, the principal one being tonsorial:

> A chair, a comb, a basin and a knife are all the tools a man needs to open a shop, and he finds as many patrons if he sets up shop in the open street as he would under shelter. Sitting doubled over, Chinamen have their heads shaven back almost to the crown, when a spot about the size of a tiny saucer is left to bear the crop of

hair which forms the pig-tail. When braided and finished with a silk tassel the Chinaman's hair is "done" for the next fortnight.

Nellie Bly captured this series of fleeting impressions with cogent insight from her speeding gharry. In that part of the world, the betel-nut habit was ubiquitous:

> The people here, as at other ports where I stopped, constantly chew betel nut, and when they laugh one would suppose they had been drinking blood. The betel nut stains their teeth and mouths blood-red. Many of the natives also fancy tinting their finger-nails with it.

So that betel was more than just a narcotic stimulant;—it gratified the user's vanity! Nellie's rapid grasp of those singular details that illuminate an experience shone forth in the monkey-house in Singapore:

> There was besides a number of small monkeys one enormous orangutan. It was as large as a man and was covered with long red hair. While seeming to be very clever he had a way of gazing off in the distance with wide, unseeing eyes, meanwhile puffing his long red hair up over his head in an aimless, insane way that was very fetching. The doctor wanted to give him a nut, but feared to put his hand through the bars. The grating was too small for the old fellow to get his hand through, but he did not intend to be cheated of his rights, so he merely stuck his lips through the gratings until they extended fully four inches. I burst into laughter at the comical sight. I heard of mouths, but that beat anything I ever saw, and I actually laughed until the old fellow actually smiled in sympathy. He got the nut! The doctor offered him a cigar. He did not take it but touched it with the back of his hand, and then subsided into that dreamy state, aimlessly pulling his hair up over the back of his head.

Nellie Bly's description of the orangutan's behavior including his "dreamy state" indicated that the nut was a betel.

After her brush with the insularity of the Malays on Penang, Nellie felt relieved to be in cosmopolitan Singapore. The agents in the cable office in that international port were conversant with English and accepted American silver at par (although they did not care to handle other U.S. money). Nellie dined splendidly on the verandah of the Hotel de L'Europe, a long low white building fronting the sea and set back from it by a wide green lawn and beautiful esplanade. Afterwards, she and Dr. Brown set forth again in their gharry. They heard a weird din and discord of many instruments that sounded to Nellie like "a political procession after the presidential election." Their Malay driver announced, "That's a funeral."

"Indeed! If that is the way you have funerals here, I'll see one," Nellie said. As was the case with the Chinese funeral Elizabeth Bisland witnessed on Penang, the mourners outside Singapore seemed happy rather than sorrowful. What differed were the reactions of the two journalists.

The serious, intellectual Miss Bisland waxed philosophical, ascribing the carefree spirit of the mourners to the general fatalistic attitude toward death in Eastern cultures. The mirthful, prankish Nellie Bly saw it all as a sort of Mardi Gras event:

> So he pulled the gharry to one side where we waited eagerly for a funeral that was heralded by a blast of trumpets. First came a number of Chinamen with black and white satin flags which, being flourished energetically, resulted in clearing the roads of vehicles and pedestrians. They were followed by musicians on Malay ponies, blowing fifes, striking cymbals, beating tomtoms, hammering gongs, and pounding long pieces of iron, with all their might and main. Men followed carrying on long poles roast pigs and Chinese lanterns, great and small, while in their rear came banner-bearers. The men on foot wore white trousers and sandals, with blue top dress, while the pall-bearers wore black garments bound with blue braid. There were probably forty pall-bearers. The casket, which rested on long poles suspended on the shoulders of the men, was hidden beneath a white-spotted cloth with decorations of Chinese lanterns or inflated bladders on arches above it. The mourners followed in a long string of gharries. They were dressed in white satin from head to toe and were the happiest looking people at the funeral. We watched

until the din died away in the distance when we returned to town as delighted as if we had seen a circus parade.

"I would not have missed that for anything," Dr. Brown said to Nellie.

"You could not," she replied, laughing, "I know they got it up for our special benefit."

And so laughing and jesting "about what had to us no suggestion of death," they drove back to see the temples. One feels inclined to join them in their hilarity, Nellie Bly's depiction of the pageantry that permeated the funeral procession is so glorious! She and Dr. Brown were not permitted to pass beneath the gate of the Mohammedan temple so they went on to the Hindu. Here Nellie's feminism clashed with native religious belief. Just as she had refused to "un-boot" in the Buddhist temple en route to Kandy, she refused now to remove her shoes in the Hindu temple in Singapore. Now as then, she objected to the "filth." But now, she felt she had especial reason to protest. She reported:

> It was a long stone building, enclosed by a high wall. At the gateway leading to it were a superfluity of beggars, large and small, lame and blind, who asked for alms, touching their foreheads respectfully. The temple was closed, but some priests rushed forth to warn us not to step on the sacred old dirty stone-passage leading to it with our shoes on. Its filth would have made it sacred to me with my shoes off! My comrades were told that removing their shoes would give them admission but I should be denied that privilege because I was a woman. "Why?" I demanded, curious to know why my sex in heathen lands should exclude me from a temple, as in America it confines me to the side entrances of hotels and other strange and incommodious things. "No Senora, no mudder," the priest said with a positive shake of the head. "I'm not a mother!" I cried so indignantly that my companions burst into laughter, which I joined after a while, but my denials had no effect on the priest. He would not allow me to enter.

Nellie Bly's vehemence reflected the growth of the rights-for-women movement in her own country. Wives still called their husbands "Mister" in America, for he was the monarch of the family. But women now wanted the right to vote (they had already been granted it in the Wyoming Territory, in 1869); husbands no longer owned the clothing and jewelry they gave their wives; divorce from intolerable males, about eleven thousand nationwide in 1870, was to rise to more than 55,000 by 1900. But while Nellie's feminism was a breath of fresh air in the United States, it was a gross intrusion upon the sanctified precinct of the Hindu priests. In her zealousness to be treated as equal to a man, she failed to recognize that the monks were sworn by their faith to celibacy and prohibited any contact with a woman. She was also oblivious to the fact that the priest who called her "Mudder" was not intimating that she looked maternal but was employing an Eastern honorific;—to be called "Mother" was to be regarded as worthy of respect and veneration.

With a journalist's fascination for the grotesque, Nellie Bly felt drawn to the idols in the temple. Her description of them was rather cavalier:

In some sheds which lined the inner part of the high wall we saw a number of fantastically shaped carts of heavy build. Probably they were juggernauts. Near by we saw through the bars a wooden image of a woman. Her shape was neither fairy-like nor girlish; her features were fiendish in expression and from her mouth fell a long string of beads. As the mother of a poor man's family she would have been a great success. Instead of one pair of arms she had four. One pair was employed in holding a stiff wooden baby before her and the other three pairs were taking care of themselves much like the legs of a crab. They showed us a white wooden horse mounted on wheels, images of most horrible devils, in short, we saw so many images of such horrible shapes that it would be impossible to recall them all. I remember one head that I was very much interested in and the limited English of the priest failed to satisfy my curiosity as to who, what, and for what purpose the thing was invented. It was only a head but it must have been twelve feet high and wide in proportion. The face was a fiery scarlet and the eyes were tightly closed.

Nellie's mocking of the heathen deities reached its climactic expression when she and Dr. Brown confronted what appeared to be a sacred cow:

On the lawn, fastened to a slight pin, was a white cow, the only presentable cow I saw during my trip. I noticed the doctor gave her wide range keeping his eye on her as she playfully tossed her head. "Be careful," he said nervously to me. "I believe that's the sacred white cow." "She looks old enough— and tough enough—to make her sacred in the eye of a butcher!" I replied, "If she is the sacred cow," he continued, despite my levity, "and went for us they would consider it their duty to let the old beast kill an infidel. That pin does not look very strong." So to quiet the fears of the doctor we left the old cow and the gods behind.

Nellie Bly seems to have made no effort to understand the Hindu religion; rather, she treated its gods with disrespect. But her insight on the caste system was compelling:

The people in Singapore have ranks as have people in other lands. There they don't wait for one neighbor to tell another or for the newspapers to inform the public as to their standing but every man, woman, and child carries his mark in gray powder on the forehead so that all the world may look and read and know their caste.

The driver of their gharry took Nellie and Dr. Brown to his humble home and introduced them to his pretty little Malay wife and her several little brown naked babies. Dressed in a single wrapping of linen, she had, Nellie reported, a large gold ring in her nose, rings on her toes and around the rim of her ears, and gold ornaments on her ankles. At the door of the home Nellie saw a monkey. Freed from having to grapple with what seemed to her the incomprehensibilities of Hinduism, her natural buoyancy returned:

I did resist the temptation to buy a boy at Port Said and also smothered the desire to buy a Singalese girl at Colombo, but when I saw the monkey my will-power melted and I began straightway to bargain for it. "Will the monkey bite?" I asked the driver, and he took it by the throat, holding it up for me to admire as he replied: "Monkey no bite," but he could not under the circumstances.

142

CHAPTER SIXTEEN

A LETTER FROM HOME

Like Nellie Bly, Miss Bisland stayed in the Grand Oriental Hotel near the water. Much to her delight, the arcade was full of British folk including Australians and Anglo-Indians, passing to and from the dining room, to the stairs, to the front entrance. Her admiration for Albion knew no bounds:

> Handsome, as an Anglo-Saxon crowd of the well-to-do is apt to be—tall florid men in crisp white linen and white Indian helmets; tall, slim, well-poised girls in white muslin, with a delicious fruit-like pink in their cheeks, brought there by the heat, which curls their blond hair in damp rings about their brows and white necks. And tall, imposing British matrons, with something of the haughtiness of old Rome in their bearing—the mothers and wives of conquerors.

Miss Bisland's preoccupation with physique included her servant, who sat outside her hotel door seemingly at all hours waiting to gratify her needs. A "curious creature" whose sex was "not easy to determine," he was "woman-eyed" and the "femininities" of his face disappeared at the chin in a short close-curled black beard. His long rippling black hair was knotted at the back with a tortoise-shell hand comb; he was "full-chested as a budding girl, but clothed himself to the waist in shirt, coat, and waistcoat, the slender male hips being wrapped in a white skirt that falls to his ankles." Miss Bisland forgave what appeared to her his androgynous tendencies when she saw what a devoted servant he was:

> He is, however, an eminently agreeable person. The gentle and confiding affection of his manner leaves me speechless with amazement the humbled victim of the harsh and haughty tyranny of the American servant-girl. He not only executes orders with noiseless dispatch, but receives them with a little reverence of the slim fingers to the brow, and a look in his eyes of such sweet eagerness to serve that my heart is melted within me. I

find myself asking for hot water with the coo of a sucking dove; I demand butter at table in the mild tones of a wind-harp, and converse with the guide in a manner I might naturally assume to a beloved younger sister. This atmosphere of loving-kindness is that of Paradise. It expands the heart with unreflecting happiness, and makes man, even servant-man, my brother.

If Elizabeth Bisland was benignly indulgent toward her servant, she felt among her equals at tiffin. The "remarkable assemblage" at her table in the hotel dining room included: The poet William Wordsworth's grandson; Lord Chelmsford "in whose African campaign the Prince Imperial was killed and the English suffered a hideous butchery, surprised by savages"; Dom Leopoldo Agostino, with news that his grandfather Dom Pedro, ruler of Brazil, had been dethroned and exiled; Sir William Robinson (looking "lean and bold as the head of Caesar") an Irishman, a well-known composer, and a colonial governor; Sir Henry Wrenfordsly, a colonial chief justice; Lady Broome ("A tall handsome woman with a noble outline of brow and head") who under the title of Lady Barker, was the author of "many well-known and delightful books on life in the Antipodes," and her husband Sir Napier Broome, who was "also tall and handsome," on his way home from an Australian governorship. Also at the table were two Americans who seemed to Miss Bisland out of place in this glittering company:

> Near us is a man with a bulging forehead and a badly-fitting frock-coat of black broadcloth—a noted mesmerist from America, with a little Texan wife fantastically gowned; she, poor soul, having a picturesque instinct, but no technique.

Elizabeth Bisland's expressed willingness to "condone any possible vileness" of the inhabitants of Ceylon dissipated when she visited the native shops in Colombo. The merchandise, she reported—the basketwork, wrought brass, jewels, carvings in ivory, ebony, and tortoise-shell, India shawls and silks, and Cingalese silver-work—was vastly overpriced, and the merchants themselves were detestable:

> Most of these shops are kept by Moormen—large, yel-

low, unpleasant-looking persons in freckled calico petticoats, heads shaven quite clean and covered with a little red basket too small for the purpose. They inspire carking disgust and suspicion by their craven oiliness; their wares for the most part not worth a tenth of the sums asked.

Like Nellie Bly before her, she watched the tourists bargain with the vendors over Colombo's famous jewels. Like Nellie, too, she watched a snake-charmer perform in front of the hotel. His tricks included making a coconut and an egg seem to disappear. Miss Bisland reported:

Simple feats that are surprising, because he is quite naked save for a turban and a loin-cloth, and has no aids to this art but the brown cotton bag in which he carries his few properties, and a small flat basket where a cobra is coiled. But his hands are marvelously deft and supple—the hands of an old race, slim, pliant, well modelled, and exquisitely dexterous.

Unlike the snake Nellie had watched, this one was not "fresh" and "too young" and disobedient; rather, he "danced" to the tune of his lord:

He takes off the cover of the same basket, the reptile within lying sullenly sluggish until a rap over the head induces him to lift himself angrily, puff out his head, and make ready to strike. But his master is playing a low, monotonous tune on a tiny bamboo flute, with his eyes fastened upon the snake's eyes, and swaying his nude body slowly from side to side.

And like Nellie Bly, Elizabeth Bisland did not flinch. With the same presence of mind, she noted every nuance of behavior by the charmer and his poisonous reptile:

The serpent stirs restlessly, and flickers his wicked, thin red tongue; but the sleepy tune drones on and on, and the brown body moves to and fro—to and fro. Presently the serpent begins to wave, softly, following the movements of the man's body and with his eyes fixed on the man's eyes, and so in time sinks slowly in a languid heap of relaxed folds...the music grows fainter,

fainter; dies away to a breath—a whisper—ceases. The man hangs the helpless serpent—drunk with the insistent low whine of the flute—about his bare neck and breast, and comes forward to beg a rupee for his pains.

And what if this snake, like the one Nellie had witnessed perform, had "darted" at the charmer and the charmer had "cunningly caught it by the head" and made "the blood gush from the snake's mouth" and held him by the head before he could get him into the basket as the reptile meanwhile was "lashing the ground furiously with its tail"? Would Miss Bisland *then* have *blenched* and lost her powers of concentration? Not likely. Neither of these strong-minded women normally was intimidated or given to hysterical response. Nellie Bly had no monopoly on aplomb.

Together with the Lady from Boston, her son, and the Ceylon tea-planter, Elizabeth Bisland hired a carriage and drove past the clock-tower whose pharos had lit their path last night...past the banks and the haunts of the money-changers with their "fat yellow hook-nosed faces" and "great circles of gold wire in their ears"...past the beautiful sickle-shaped beach of Galle Face where Nellie Bly had grappled with love's mysteries. They journeyed inland through the multitudinous palms. Miss Bisland reported:

> ...cocoanut palms (forty millions of these, the guide says), Palmyra palms, from which the heady palm-wine is made; Kitu palms that yield sugar and sago; talipot palms, upon whose papyrus-like leaves were inscribed the sacred writings—Mahawanso—five hundred years years before Christ, and preserved twenty-two centuries at Wihares; and the areca palm, that gives the nuts the natives chew with their betel leaves. We pass banyan-trees with roots like huge pythons coiling through the grass, and down-dropped stems from the far-spreading branches, making dim, leafy cloisters; breadfruit trees, monster ferns, full of lotus plants, and orchids growing almost as freely as weeds.

Sago was the powdery starch obtained from the trunk of the palm tree and used in Asia as a food thickener and textile softener. At Elizabeth Bisland's request, the gentlemanly guide with the usual mane of hair bound in a knot at the nape untwisted it and let it fall "far below his waist in silky black waves—restoring it in a moment by a quick turn of the wrist to its former neat compactness." When Miss Bisland packed her hasty wardrobe in New York, she couldn't have dreamed that her hairpins would prove useful to a male:

> He has never seen a hair-pin, and the gift of one of mine childishly delights and amuses him. He thrusts it in and out of his hair, and finally fastens it upon a string of queer charms and fetishes worn in his bosom.

Everywhere the beauteous Elizabeth Bisland went on her trip around the world she found men who were gallantly attentive. She was, in fact, to write when her extraordinary peregrinations were completed:

> I was a young woman, quite alone, and doing a somewhat conspicuous and eccentric thing, yet throughout the entire journey I never met with other than the most exquisite and unfailing courtesy and consideration; and if I had been a princess with a suite of half a hundred people I could have felt no safer or happier. It seems this speaks very highly for the civilization existing in all travelled parts of the globe, when a woman's strongest protection is the fact that she is unprotected.

Although Miss Bisland was no princess, she was accustomed to being treated like one. The solicitous guide introduced her to the native custom; he wrapped for her a bit of areca nut with a paste of wet lime in a leaf of the betel pepper and bade her chew. She reported:

> Instantly my mouth is full of a liquid red as blood, and tongue and lips are shriveled with a sharp aromatic astringent resembling cloves. I hasten to spit it out, but all day my lips are still hot and acrid from the brief experiment. The entire population of Ceylon are wedded to the betel habit, save the servants of Europeans who object to the unpleasant vampire red of the stained mouth and corroded teeth. It harms no more than tobacco, and the natives prefer it even to food. From time to time along the road we come upon old women sitting upon the earth with little stores of nuts, lime, and betel leaves spread before them for the refreshment of the wayfarer.

One senses that Elizabeth Bisland opened up to experience on Ceylon, as if this sultry Eden freed her to express the sultriness deep within her. The guide responded to her openness:

"Mem Sahib," says the guide, touching his brow with his fingers, and giving me one of those smiling black glances—"You are my father and my mother. Will you that we go to the cinnamon gardens?"....And on the way he feeds upon ripe mangoes that have a reddish custard-like pulp, sweetly musky in flavor.

The cinnamon bushes growing in the white sand breathed faint odors in the steaming heat. Out jumped a lean, naked youth asking for alms:

He is not to be shaken off, following in a leaping dance with flying hair and a white-toothed smile, clapping his elbows against his ribs with a noise like castanets, and rattling his bones together loudly and merrily as though a skeleton pranced after us through the dust; so that we are fain to end the exhibition of his unique powers with a few coins.

Was the youth starving? The fanciful Miss Bisland pictured him as engaged in a grotesquely comic ballet. What she regarded as "the reverse side of this island paradise" she found in the museum in the cinnamon garden:

The dull, venomous cobra in his spotted cowl; clammy, strangling folds of long pythons; twenty-foot sharks with horrid semi-circular hedges of teeth—the wolves of these pearl-sown seas—and endless stinging, biting, poisoning creatures wrought into wanton bizarreries by nature in some mood of cynical humorousness. Here are also the uncouthly hideous masks of the old devil dancers; great gold ornaments, splendid robes, and the ingeniously murderous weapons of this mild-mannered race, who count in their history twenty-six kings done treacherously to death.

Her hothouse imagination ran rampant as she and her companions wandered through the museum:

In other rooms are the stuffed skins of beautiful birds,

huge mammals, and collections of rich-colored butter-flies and moths—all very hardly defended from the rav-enous tropical disintegration, as fierce and implacable as the productiveness is profuse. It is a nature that devours her own children; creating with a furious fecun-dity, and consuming all her creations with insatiable, relentless voracity.

Was it Nature, one is led to inquire, that had slaughtered the birds and mammals, caught and killed the insects, per-formed the taxidermy on them and put their lifeless shells on display? Miss Bisland was in love with the English language; the sound of words, their melodiousness, intoxicated her.

She and her companions drove past palm-thatched hats and "idle brown folk, half naked, dreaming in the heat." The betel had put these natives into a state of lethargy and reduced their incentive to explore beyond their immediate circumstances. Miss Bisland visited a temple where Lord Buddha reclined on his elbow, drowsing in the hot semi-dark-ness among the stifling scents of pink jasmine blossoms. She reported:

> He is forty feet long, painted a coarse vivid crimson and yellow, but his flat wooden face is fixed in the same passive low-lidded calm that we saw upon it when he sat on his lotus among the Japanese roses, or listened to his tiny mountain shrine at Penang to loud voices of the waters. A Nirvana peace, undisturbed by passions or pity ...dreaming eternal dreams in the hot, perfumed gloom. About the walls are painted in archaic frescoes the pains and toils of his fifty incarnations of Buddhahood, through which he attained at last to this immortal peace.

As they emerged from the temple, Elizabeth Bisland, the Lady from Boston, her son, and the Ceylon tea-planter were besieged by swarms of people demanding alms:

> They have roused themselves from their lethargy in the simmering gloom of the palm-shaded huts, and throng clamorous and insistent for the charity Lord Buddha has enjoined, impeding our footsteps and cling-ing to the carriage. Old women hold out the little soft

hands of the dimpled naked babies they carry on their hips. They themselves are hideous repulsive hags— mere wrinkled, disgusting rags of humanity with red-stained toothless mouths; and this at forty years. The young women are plump and pretty, with a discontented knot in their brows, and hopeless, peevish mouths— femininity being a perplexing and bitter burden in the East. Small brown imps, naked as Adam, save for a heavy silver necklace hung about their fat little stomachs, cling to our knees and use their fine eyes with a coquette's conscious power, smilingly seducing the coin out of our pockets.

Her acute concern over the dilemma of the native woman in the Far East suggests that Elizabeth Bisland was already a feminist. She was later to become vitally involved in promoting a better life for women—in the United States.

It was the last night of 1889. The passengers from the steamship *Thames* prepared to ring out the old year and ring in the new on equatorial Ceylon. The dining hall in the Grand Oriental Hotel had been converted into a ballroom for the occasion. The men, all in white and sporting cummerbunds, circled languidly with the pretty English girls in their arms while a warm wind whirled through the veranda and fluttered the draperies of the onlookers. Elizabeth Bisland observed the social scene:

The woman from Texas, in a fearful and wonderful costume, that casts a slight but comprehensive glance at the modes of three centuries and muddles them all, is tossing her powdered head and flirting shrilly with the soft-voiced governor with the Caesar face. A handsome ruddy old soldier with gray hair is moodily mounting guard over his three lank-elbowed partnerless daughters, whose plump and pleasing mama is frolicking jovially about, clasped to the bosom of all Ceylon's military ornaments. Wordsworth's grandson, who looks as if designed to an order by Du Maurier, is waltzing, lazily graceful, with one of the smartly gowned blond girls.

George Du Maurier (1834—1896) was a British caricaturist for *Punch* who satirized mainly the growing *nouveau-riche* class and the aesthetes led by Oscar Wilde. A mood of melancholy seized Miss Bisland as she watched the dancers float across the improvised ballroom:

> Faint rhythmic breathings of the music come to my chamber window. The night is hot and silent—full of musky perfumes, of vague ghostly stirrings of "old unhappy far-off things," that move one with poignant mysterious memories of the dense tropical darkness with its silent, flitting figures—full of the glimmering, bewildered phantoms of passions and pains that perished centuries ago.

Elizabeth Bisland retired to her bedchamber. She awoke on January 1, 1890, to find that she had received a letter from home. She rejoiced:

> ...Morning! The new year is coming in a beautiful green dawn. A chrysoberl sky, translucent golden green, a misty green sea, and an ocean of feathery green plumes tossing noiselessly, as with a great silent joy, in the morning wind. I have sprung out of bed to receive a letter—my first one from home. A few lines, scrawled on the other side of the world, that I lean from the window to read in the faint early light. How beautiful they make the new year seem!—Whatever this coming year will contain of grief and rebuffs, at least it has begun with one good moment, and for that it is well to be grateful.

With her distinctive need for privacy, Elizabeth Bisland did not indicate from whom the letter came. One would like to think it was from her fiancé Charles W. Wetmore who anxiously awaited her return.

At four o'clock on the afternoon of New Year's Day, Miss Bisland left Ceylon on the Australian mail ship *Britannia* bound for Aden and the Suez Canal. She had been away from home forty-eight days.

CHAPTER SEVENTEEN

NELLIE LEARNS OF THE OTHER WOMAN

Time.

Flowing like the ocean all around her.

Time.

Boundless as the sky above her and the Dream that drove her.

Time.

There was never enough time.

And sometimes, there was too much of it.

Time.

From her vantage point on the deck of the *Oriental* steaming toward Hong Kong, Nellie Bly gazed at the South China Sea. The descending sun dazzled the expanse of blue with a road of silver. The moon was already a pale crescent in the sky. What a grand and glorious spectacle! Too much for any mere mortal to comprehend....

Time was the *enemy*.

Nellie Bly had two self-winding watches: the one in her pocket which was set to New York time, and the other which she wore on her wrist to record local time. Nellie eyed the watch on her wrist: 19:05 hours. Another hour and she would be sitting down to dinner with the English in their crisp white linens and white muslins on an English ship headed for another English port. The English owned everything—even time! It was no accident that the prime meridian cut through Greenwich, England, and that the world's twenty-four time zones were reckoned based upon Greenwich Time. Nellie watched the small hand tick away the seconds. Time was remorseless. If somebody could invent a device to stop time, he or she would become a millionaire! 19:08 hours. It was 7:08 p.m. now in Hong Kong. It was 6:08 a.m. that same day— December 19th—in New York City. Nellie could hear the rattle of the trolley cars in the streets. At the *World* office on Park Row, the city room was empty; outside, the newsboys were hawking the morning edition with, perhaps, her latest story on her travels in it. Good old New York. It was the only place to be. Nellie felt suddenly faint. Seasick? How could she be seasick when the ocean was calm as glass?

To confirm that she was right about the time in New York, Nellie Bly drew from the pocket of her blue broadcloth dress from Ghormley's her other watch. It—the dress—was holding up pretty well; she wished she could say the same about Yours Truly! There were times (she couldn't get that word "time" out of her head) during the trip when she thought she would go crazy at how *slowly* everything went—time, people, transportation. The modern world liked to believe it was out of the horse-and-buggy age, but travel was still an unpredictable business. Especially if you were in a hurry to get somewhere! Nellie was still trying to forget that delay on Ceylon. The *Nepaul*, that old tub! Steaming at long last onto the horizon like a drunk after a night's debauch! Nellie laughed now at how she had raged at the slow boat from India for which the *Oriental* had had to wait. The calm of the ocean augured well for making up the lost time. Not a cloud in the sky. Nellie glanced fondly at the watch from her pocket. 6:09 a.m. in New York—another minute in time's precious hoard had just slipped away. It was a handsome timepiece, gold-plated, the Arabic numerals on its face ranging from "1" to "24." It made her feel more at home to know what the time was in New York. She returned the watch to her pocket.

Time.

Time was her best friend!

She was having the time of her life! She was going around the world not to race against time but to enjoy a much-needed vacation. She had headaches; the best doctors in New York said she was suffering from overwork and needed rest and recreation.

She could be forgiven that little white lie. She knew very well she wanted to win so bad she could almost taste them— the sweets of victory. Who could blame her for that charming exercise in self-delusion if it helped to ease the strain on her. Racing against time and the wily Phileas Fogg was no joke; neither was coming home a loser and the object of universal pity. The whole world was either rooting for sassy Nellie Bly or hoping she fell flat on her face. She might have had nightmares about the possible headline emblazoned across the front pages: "NELLIE BLY LOSES TO FATHER

TIME!" Losing was not Nellie's style. And if telling herself she was on a vacation took some of the heat off her, well, that was her prerogative.

Nellie Bly became aware of somebody watching her from the after-deck. It was that idiot who kept following her all around the ship asking her to marry him. Hell would freeze over before she tied the nuptial knot with the likes of him! Tease him a little and he loved it—they all did! Nellie turned toward the poor guy and flashed that radiant grin that had melted the mighty Pulitzer when she came looking for a job at the *World* and had seduced a wide assortment of male crooks and criminals into yielding up their darkest secrets. Her suitor visibly trembled; the next moment, he was rushing down to throw himself at her feet, so to speak, and tell her he adored her. He meant well;—he was just a bit of a nit.

The *Oriental* plowed her watery furrow toward Hong Kong. The sun went down and Nellie Bly joined her fellow passengers for dinner. Afterwards, back on deck, she watched the sky redden in the West. The moon rose and hung aloft like a ripe fruit waiting to be plucked. For someone so often in the public eye, Nellie treasured these moments of seclusion when she could be alone with her inner voices. They told her that Fame was full of empty promises and that she must not forget who she was—Nellie Bly, investigative reporter, whose job was to give her readers the truth. With that knowledge as her sedative, she slept soundly that night. She awoke next morning to that by-now-familiar feeling of faintness. Was her body trying to tell her something? You had to hand it to the English;—they sure knew how to build ships. It was not until Nellie went up on deck that she discovered the vessel was running into a monsoon. Blustery headwinds whipped the ocean into foaming whitecaps. Nellie mastered her faintness. Throughout the morning, the good ship *Oriental* bucked the headwinds, which kept growing in intensity and churned the waters into a maelstrom. Nellie could feel the ship slow in its grinding battle against wind and sea. Would she get to Hong Kong on time? There was that word again! Time. What made her feel so queasy—seasickness, or worry about losing time? Again, Nellie fought down the faintness. She sat on deck marveling at the horrendous swell of the sea—rise and fall, rise and fall, one moment the bow of the *Oriental* standing upright

154

on a gigantic wave, the next plunging straight down as if to carry them all to the bottom. Danger! Nellie loved it!

By noon, almost all the passengers had disappeared below. The monsoon raged unabated and the ship's cook enjoyed a holiday. Those few hardy wayfarers who remained on deck engaged in good-natured banter. Getting seasick was worse than falling victim to Montezuma's curse, an affliction Nellie (but not her Mother, whom she sent home) managed to avoid during her six months in Mexico exposing the tyranny of the rich and powerful there.

Time—Phileas Fogg—a monsoon. If the *Oriental* was unsinkable, so was Nellie Bly. Not even that December 19th night on the rolling ocean, when her avid, panting swain— that nit—made her a proposal so weird it could have made the sensationalizing *World*'s most jaded readers blink in astonishment. The heave of the sea was dreadful, the atmosphere thick and close; some of the men made no secret of being seasick and came on deck for a breath of air.

And there he was. The NIT. Stretched out on a deck chair, his gills quivering, like a fish out of water. Seasick again! She had ignored his previous pleas for sympathy. She knew it was cruel of her, but she felt unmoved by the sight of a seasick man. Was it because men had teased women aboard ship when they became seasick and now the shoe was on the other foot? Her lover spotted her; she didn't let on she saw him. She wasn't about to let him sweet-talk her again. All that guff about how she might never believe it but he was enjoying a vacation. How she didn't know how nice he could look. And how if she would only stay over with him in Hong Kong a week she would see what a terrific lover he could be. He got to be such a pest that one of her pals told him she was engaged to the Chief Officer who did not approve of her talking to other men.

One stormy evening, finding Nellie Bly alone on deck, her wooer curled up at her feet and gripped the arm of her chair. There was a wild look in his eyes. Here is Nellie's account of their conversation:

"Do you think life is worth living?" he asked.

"Yes, life is very sweet. The thought of death is the only thing that causes me unhappiness," I answered truthfully.

"You cannot understand it or you would feel different. I

could take you in my arms and jump overboard, and before they would know it, we would be at rest," he said passionately.

"You can't tell. It might not be rest—" I began and he broke in hotly.

"I know, I know, I can show you. I will prove it to you. Death by drowning is a peaceful slumber, a quiet drifting away."

"Is it?" I said with a pretense of eagerness. I feared to get up for I felt that the first move might result in my burial beneath the angry sea.

"You know, tell me about it. Explain it to me," I gasped, a feeling of coldness creeping over me as I realized that I was alone with what for the time was a mad man.

So much for Nellie Bly's flirtation with death! Talk about the perils of Pauline! Thank goodness, the Chief Officer happened upon her and her frenzied suitor and rescued her from his clutches. The ship's captain wanted to clap the poor fellow into irons but Nellie prevailed upon him to show mercy. Thereafter, she was careful not to spend time on deck alone and unprotected. Time....Time...in what strange ways one was forced to pass the time aboard a ship at sea! Time finite and time infinite. Those few terrifying moments when Nellie Bly was in mortal danger, she caught a fleeting glimpse of eternity.

Anyone who has ever taken an ocean cruise knows how misleading the travel brochures can be. They do not tell how monotonous and confining life aboard a passenger ship can be. Every effort, of course, is made nowadays to divert the traveler: lavish meals and entertainments, casino gambling and the latest movies, dozens of daytime activities and dancing on deck under the stars. Life aboard an ocean liner in 1889 presented the traveler with a truer test of his ingenuity for combatting boredom. There were no program directors then to pamper the passengers. Left to their own devices, they created charades, staged tableaux, organized group songfests, played shuffleboard, or simply lounged on deck. But several days of this routine must have been enough to drive the more discerning wayfarer bonkers. When that happened, the men, as befitted their status as the privileged sex, were more daring than the women. They made love to willing females in dark nooks and corners of the ship; they bet staggering sums of money on games of chance of their own devising; or they got stupefyingly drunk. Nellie Bly was amazed at how much whiskey and soda the Englishmen on the *Oriental* consumed. And who could blame them? Life aboard the *Oriental* was not like a cruise to the Bahamas! It was more like being in a war—days and days of lulling routine then all hell broke loose (in this case, a monsoon, not cannon shot and bullets). Nellie could empathize: nobody at the *World* had warned her that in her purported race against time, one of her main problems would be not how to save time—but how to spend it. Nellie spent hers wisely; others aboard the *Oriental* squandered it on either their passion for excess or their need to complain. As a reporter cabling stories back to New York, she occupied her time ingratiating herself with those passengers who were not bent on marrying her. A particular asset to her as a professional journalist was her ability to make friends quickly. Nellie put the five-day journey from Singapore to Hong Kong to good use, by observing and noting down for the delectation of her readers the foibles and follies of her fellow inmates on the *Oriental*.

There was the woman who told the Chief Officer she wanted a cabin over the ship's screw (she got it and was miserably seasick); there was the passenger who protested that the berths had spring rather than horsehair mattresses; there was the bridal couple who slept in their life preservers because they thought it was the thing to do aboard a ship; there was that gallant Spanish diplomat who told Nellie that on another boat he had fallen in love with a beautiful woman and been loved by her, but upon learning she was married—albeit to a beast of a husband—urged her, "Go; be a good woman." All this and more Nellie Bly reported with charm and good humor. Danger sharpened her eye for the absurd: When the plunging *Oriental* flung her across the deck and a young man rushed to save her from injury but turned upside down and landed on his face, Nellie was convulsed with laughter at the ludicrousness of his position. She ran for the ship's doctor; the man's nose was broken. While Nellie pitied him, she was seized by an irresistible need to guffaw whenever she tried to tell him how much she appreciated his effort to help her. This incident, too, she reported.

How well Nellie knew that a reporter was only as good as his or her sources. Most of that stuff about the passengers, she must have realized, was soft, chit-chatty, more like gossip than solid news. No wonder she sometimes felt she was on vacation—there were no challenges! Oh, for those good old days when she was nailing thieves and charlatans to the wall and crusading against society's cruel injustices! Her words sang then, oh, how they sang! What would it take to bring back that Nellie Bly, whose power as a reporter thrilled the masses and made her Joseph Pulitzer's pride and joy? Phileas Fogg was not the answer...and certainly not shuffle-board.

Despite the monsoon, the *Oriental*—which was a mail ship or built for speed—reached Hong Kong on December 22nd or two days ahead of time. It was a record-setting performance for the ship. Nellie Bly was thrilled. She had not only made up for the time lost on Ceylon, she arrived at Hong Kong two days ahead of her own schedule. She was thirty-eight days out of New York. She had to laugh when she learned that another passenger on the *Oriental* was suing the Occidental and Oriental steamship line for getting him to Hong Kong two days ahead of time! His ticket, he said, covered a certain length of time, and the company was responsible for his expenses—including his hotel bills—during the unexpired time-period.

Nellie marveled at the setting: Mountains looming on all sides to form the harbor basin...mansions gleaming white on the slopes in the early morning light...outlets between the mountains so narrow that ships navigated them with extreme care on their passage to the sea...a host of vessels from many nations thronging the sun-dazzled bay—from heavy iron-clads, torpedo boats, and mail steamers to Chinese junks and sampans and Portuguese *lorchas* with their European hulls and Chinese lugsails. As was the custom with mail ships, the *Oriental* fired a cannon as it entered the bay. Nellie Bly went ashore with her friend Dr. Brown. On the pier they were besieged by carriers with an urgency that reminded her of hackmen around railway stations in America. She and the good doctor each selected a sedan chair. Wherever Nellie happened to visit she made her readers feel they were there right along with her. There was a knack, she reported, to getting properly into a sedan chair: The chair was placed upon the ground...the carriers tilted the shafts downward...the patron stepped inside, back towards the chair, and eased into it backward. Once the patron was seated, the carriers hoisted the chair to their shoulders and started off "with a monotonous trot, which gives the chair a motion not unlike that of a pacing saddle horse." Nellie's practiced reportorial eye picked out the passing details: the continuous line of warehouses...the buildings from which the Chinese families hung out their laundry, balcony to balcony, on clotheslines in a "washing jubilee"...the masses of "dirty" natives who blocked the passage of the sedan chairs... the trotting carriers who snorted and grunted to clear a way through the crowds of people whose pigtails straggled round their shaven heads. As her chair wound upward on a mountain from tier to tier, Nellie Bly seethed with impatience. Time. Pitiless Time. It always went too fast, and never nearly fast enough. She could hardly wait to get to the office of the Occidental and Oriental steamship company and learn the earliest possible time she could leave for Japan. She felt good about her present situation. Thirty-nine days out of New York and here she was in British China two days ahead of schedule. Luck was riding with her in that sedan chair. Nellie Bly luck. It had never failed her before, it would not fail her now. If her luck held, she would be able to leave Hong Kong in advance of the date originally planned for her departure.

Now that Nellie began to see she might beat Time to the finish line, she stopped telling herself she was on a vacation. Her job was to win the race. She began to feel she was being tested by smirking Time. Could she capitalize on the advantage handed her by the *S.S. Oriental* and the seamanship of her captain and crew?

Nellie Bly and Dr. Brown entered the O. and O. office on a high tide of cheerful expectation. She asked the man behind the desk the date of the next sailing for Japan.

"In one moment," he said. The air of mystery grew as he retreated to an inner room. He returned with a Mr. Harmon who looked at her inquiringly. When she repeated her question he asked her what her name was.

"Nellie Bly."

The name seemed to mean nothing to them. That staggered Nellie. Perhaps she had grown accustomed to believing that wherever she traveled on her celebrated quest her fame preceded her. Or maybe she wondered just how firm her originally scheduled Hong Kong—Yokohama connection was. (As for the agent, if "Nellie Bly" truly meant nothing to him, that was probably because Elizabeth Bisland had never mentioned her rival's name to him!)

Harmon ushered Nellie into his room and motioned her to sit down, as if alerting her to brace herself. He told her: "You are going to be beaten."

Nellie Bly caught her breath. Was she hearing aright? No, No, she insisted, that was impossible, she had made up the delay suffered on Ceylon.

"You are going to lose it." The agent's voice rang with conviction.

"Lose it? I don't understand. What do you mean?" Nellie Bly's imagination leaped to insanely comical surmises. Had the Pacific Ocean dried up? Had all the ships of the O. and O. been destroyed? It never occurred to supremely confident Nellie that the agent might be right, but she felt trapped now in the disturbing position of being unable to prove that he was wrong. Nellie was visibly shaken; she had not come half way around the world to hear these cruel tidings, and yet she was hearing them.

"Aren't you having a race around the world?" Harmon seemed to pick up on her bewilderment and, to some degree, share it.

"Yes, quite right. I am running a race with Time."

"Time? I don't think that's her name."

"Her! Her!" Nellie cried. Nothing that Pulitzer and his editors had told her before she left New York prepared her for this nightmare twist of events. Who was crazy, she or the travel agent? It had to be him, it sure wasn't going to be her! She told herself that he was mentally unbalanced. How else could she preserve her sanity? What was he driving at?

"Yes, the other woman," the agent was saying. "She is going to win. She left here three days ago."

Nellie stared at him. He was not the sort of man you would look at twice in the street;—but he was the man in her life now, the prophet who had stopped her on her fateful journey to warn her of some dire outcome. She tried to tell herself that this must be a dream from which she would shortly awake. But this was no dream. Perhaps for the first time during her trip on which almost everything had been arranged for her in advance, she appreciated how big and strange and unknowable the world was. The illusion that she was in control of events had been ripped from her grasp. Nellie forced herself to laugh and put on an air of uncaring:

"The other woman?"

"Yes." The agent spoke with the brisk efficiency of a surgeon who meant to save the patient's life by cutting her heart out. Didn't she know? The same day Miss Bly left New York another woman started out to beat her time, and she was going to do it. They probably met, in fact, somewhere near the Straits of Malacca.

Nellie Bly listened in frozen disbelief. The other woman, the agent went on, had the authority to pay any amount to get ships to leave in advance of their scheduled departure time. Indeed, her editor had offered one or two thousand dollars to the O. and O. if it would have the *Oceanic* leave San Francisco two days ahead of time. The steamship's officials refused to push ahead the ship's date of departure, but they did do their best to get her here in time to catch the English mail for Ceylon. Harmon poured it on: "If they had not arrived long before they were due, she would have missed that boat, and so have been delayed ten days. But she caught the boat and left three days ago, and you will be delayed here five days." It would certainly seem that John Brisben Walker was on top of Nellie Bly's itinerary.

"That is rather hard, isn't it?" Nellie said, masking her desperation. But worse was yet to come.

"I'm astonished you did not know anything about it," the agent said. "She led us to suppose that it was an arranged race."

An arranged race! Incredible! Nellie, stung, retorted that her editor would not arrange a race without advising her he was doing so. "Have you no cables or messages for me from New York?"

"Nothing."

"Probably they do not know about her." What choice did she have but to trust her employers?

"Yes, they do," Harmon said. "She worked for the same

newspaper you do until the day she started."

Nellie Bly must have felt like a child whose parents have abandoned her;—but she tried to tough it out. Either the man was misinformed regarding the *World* or he was a very good liar. She knew from her experience as an investigative reporter that people could look you straight in the eye and lie, lie, lie. But what reason would the agent have to lie to her? Who was this other woman? What possessed her? Was she good-looking? One could understand Nellie's angst. She tried to put the Other Woman out of mind. But this other woman's entry onto the scene gave the race a poignancy, a wounding edge it had not had before. Time, a mere concept and abstract entity, could not crow about his victory if he won and made her feel envious or humiliated; the other woman, a sentient human being, could.

"I do not understand it," Nellie said, ashamed to admit her ignorance regarding a matter that had grown more important to her than life itself. "You say I cannot leave here for five days?"

"No."

Harmon reiterated his belief that Nellie was doomed to lose. The relentlessness with which he shredded her hopes must have made her wonder if he had found the other woman particularly attractive and was rooting for her to win. Nellie knew that she herself got by on her charm; she was no raving beauty.

"And I don't think you can get to New York in eighty days." The man made Cassandra sound like an eternal optimist! "She intends to do it in seventy. She has letters to steamship officials at every point requesting them to do all they can to get her on. Have you any letters?"

Nellie Bly had but one letter of introduction—from an agent of the Peninsular and Oriental steamship line requesting the captains of their boats to be good to her because she was traveling alone. If she felt the *World* might have done a better job arranging the details of her trip, she didn't let on.

"Well, it's too bad," Harmon commiserated in his own uncompromising way, "but I think you have lost it; there is no chance for you. You will lose five days here and five days in Yokohama, and you are sure to have a slow trip this season."

Nellie gave a little smile. How brave she was to hide her

heartache! This was a kind of courage different from braving storms at sea, for as Pascal observed, There is pleasure in being in a ship beaten about by a storm, when we are sure it will not founder. Despite her reporter's natural skepticism toward any information received from a source that she had not learned to trust, Nellie Bly must have felt for a moment that her Dream was foundering on the rocks of reality. But she was too proud to admit even the possibility of defeat.

The purser of the steamship *Oceanic*, which would take Nellie to Japan and America, came into the O. and O. office. His eyes warm with sympathy, he told her that Mr. Harmon had urged him to go down to the ship and meet her. They both, Mr. Fuhrmann said, wanted to take good care of her now that she was in their charge. When he missed her at the ship, he looked for her at the hotel but nobody there knew anything about her. He became afraid she was lost, so he came here looking for her.

That balanced judgment of Nellie Bly's rushed to the fore. She was quick to recognize that the agent who had so zealously burdened her with bad news was trying to help—not hurt—her.

"I have found kind friends everywhere," Nellie softened, motioning toward Dr. Brown, who was clearly distressed by the turn of events.

The purser strove to comfort her. "You are," he assured her, "with your own people now, and we are only too happy to be of service." Who, then, it must be asked, were *not* Nellie's own people? Apparently the well-meaning Mr. Fuhrmann, like the well-meaning Mr. Harmon, was caught up in the universal need to view life as a competition in which the winner takes all. There were heroes, and there were goats, and we all identify with the heroes! In his own subtly undermining way, the purser consoled her: She must not feel bad if someone got around the world faster than she did, or if someone stole the idea that had originated with her. After all, she had suffered the worst travel connections it was possible to make, and if someone did purloin the work of her brain, well, everybody *knew* it was Nellie Bly's idea and would credit her for it.

It would be hard to imagine advice to Nellie in those circumstances that could have been more damaging than the purser's to her morale. Harmon devastated her with the bluntness of his revelations, Fuhrmann killed her with kindness! Couldn't they see the rage in her? She told them:

"I promised my editor that I would go around the world in seventy-five days, and if I accomplish that I shall be satisfied. I am not racing with anyone. I would not race. If someone else wants to do the trip in less time, that is their concern. If they take it upon themselves to race *against* me, it is their lookout that they succeed. I am not racing. I promised to do the trip in seventy-five days, and I will do it; although had I been permitted to make the trip when I first proposed it over a year ago, I should then have done it in sixty days."

If she sounded defensive, Nellie Bly's outburst of—what? nobility? bravado? being the good sport?—was a cunning camouflage of her true feelings. *Not* racing? Whom was she kidding? The same inner fire that had compelled her to outcompete men in the male-dominated newspaper business now drove her to vanquish the Other Woman. Her show of feeling virtuous was her way of catching her emotional breath before grappling with the new challenge. She was no longer racing just against Time;—she was pitted against a living person who was, she must presume, like her, driven by a ferocious determination to win. Nellie Bly wanted to win;—winning meant being First.

The two men returned with Nellie Bly to the hotel where a room had already been secured for her. They arranged the transfer of her luggage from the *Oriental* to the *Oceanic*, which was not scheduled to leave for another five days.

CHAPTER EIGHTEEN

THE KORAN ON THE BARE MALE BREAST

The *Britannia*, Elizabeth Bisland reported, was the height of luxury. It was one of those enormous Peninsular and Oriental vessels built in the Jubilee year (celebrating the 50th anniversary of the birth of Queen Victoria) and was "on her way home to England." Miss Bisland was very much impressed by the accommodations for first-class travelers; the spaciousness of the handsome salons, decks, and bedrooms was made possible by an absence of provision for steerage travel. Although the main function of the *Britannia* was to transport mail, the passengers fell into making the ship their home. They hung their rooms with photographs and decorated them with bric-a-brac; on deck, each had his or her long bamboo lounging chair, a little table, and "a tea-service for that beautiful ceremony of five o'clock tea—all being made possible by the fact that the sea is smooth as glass and the decks level as a drawing-room floor." Elizabeth Bisland, now forty-seven days out of New York, was in the position of marking time on the *S.S. Britannia* bound for Aden, the Suez Canal, and Italy. Time was always a factor, but she had no choice but to succumb to the amenities of the ship: The courtesies exchanged in the form of invitations to afternoon tea; the dancing on deck for which the band played three times a week; the tableaux, private theatricals, and fancy balls that filled the evenings; and the afternoons of watching the men play a lively game of cricket on the after-deck. There were other attractions, among them a seductive infant who held everyone in her thrall. Miss Bisland reported:

> The principal personage on board is Miss Ethel Roma Detmold, age two and a half years, and familiarly known as Baby Detmold. There are other infants aboard, but merely the common or "garden" baby, not to be mentioned with this blue-and-gold girl child who sparkles out upon us a morning vision in a white frock and an enigmatic smile. The entire male force of the ship is her slave, and trailing about after her, humbly suing

for favors she is most chary in granting, she possessing already the secret of power over her kind in an airy, joyous indifference to any one's attentions and services, which we therefore—with the curious perversity of human nature—persist in thrusting upon her.

Elizabeth Bisland seems to identify with the beautiful little girl who is the cynosure of all eyes and who balks and frustrates in the same moment that she bewitches and invites. Clearly she placed herself and the child in the magic circle of those whose magnetism, pulchritude and sex appeal make them uniquely desirable. She observed:

All women are not born free and equal. There is some subtle force in this tiny turquoise-eyed coquette which will secure for her without effort, her life through, devotion other women may not win with endless sacrifices or oceans of tears. Even the cook's pet chicken, who flies from everyone else, allows himself to be hauled about by one leg or squeezed violently to her youthful bosom, and, far from protesting, looks foolishly flattered by the notice of this imperious cherub.

As the *Britannia* steamed across the Arabian Sea, all was intense blue sky, tropical heat, and calm waters. Flights of fishes sported in the wake of the ship, and an occasional whale blew up a column of spray. Miss Bisland felt lulled into a reverie that made time stand still:

...nothing marks the passage of the hours save the coming and going of light. When the azure blossom of the day dies in irised splendors, rosy clouds float up over the horizon's edge like wandering fairy islands drifting at will in a golden world—vanishing when the moon appears. Magical white nights of ineffable stillness and purity fade into the blaze of daffodil dawns....Time goes by in lotus dreams that have no memory or reckoning of a future till we wake suddenly, and find anchor cast in the gulf of Aden.

Elizabeth Bisland was now fifty-two days out of New York. Certainly she knew that if she was to beat the time Nellie Bly had promised to achieve she would have to accomplish the balance (more than 6,900 miles) of her journey in no more

166

than twenty-two days. But all she could do for the time being was surrender to the flow of experience. She gazed at the terrain surrounding the strategic port of Aden: Red barren masses of jagged stone, arid dusty hills, rocks seamed and withered—a "dead land" where not a drop of rain had fallen in three years. Whereas Nellie Bly saw the English as subjecting the East, Elizabeth Bisland marveled at their mastery:

As a coaling station and harbor from which war-ships may guard the entrance of the Red Sea; Aden is valuable; and therefore, like Hong Kong, Singapore, Penang, Ceylon—like everything else much worth having in this part of the world—it is an English possession.

Miss Bisland hired a carriage to convey her to the Tanks, the only bit of sightseeing to be done at Aden. She reported:

These Tanks are of unknown antiquity and are variously attributed to Solomon, the Queen of Sheba, the Arabs, and—as a last guess—to the Phoenicians. Historians, when in doubt, always accuse the Phoenicians. In this rainless region, where water falls only at intervals of years, it was necessary to collect and preserve it all, and *some one* built among the hills huge stone basins with capacity of hundreds of thousands of gallons. These basins are quite perfect still, though the name of the faithful builder thereof has long ago perished.

Just as Nellie Bly had done before her, Miss Bisland rode past the English fortress high on the mountain and down into Aden. While Nellie found the town dirty and "nothing extraordinary," her journalistic counterpart perceived romance there:

There is no evening mistiness of vision; the flat little white town, the shore, the turbaned figures moving to and fro in the streets, the ships afloat on the glassy sea, the tawny outline of the rocks—all standing out with keen clearness through the deepening of the twilight. So might have looked some Syrian evening of long ago; and as if to answer the thought, there slowly lifts itself above the crest of the hills, in the green dusk, a huge white planet—the Star in the East! The dusk has van-

167

ished when we reach the wharf—"At one stride comes the dark"—and suddenly, in an instant, innumerable glittering hosts rush into the heavens with a wild, astonishing splendor, startling as the blare of trumpets... unimaginable myriads, unreckonable millions.

By the light of the moon, Elizabeth Bisland and the other passengers from the *Britannia* revisited the Tanks. They passed a loaded train of camels lurching away to the desert; stepping beside them were "lean, swarthy Arabs, draped statelily in white—such a caravan as might have gone down into Egypt to buy corn from Pharaoh four thousand years ago—nothing in the interval changed in any way." Despite her predilection for a higher Pantheism, Miss Bisland showed an acquaintance with the Bible. The haunting silence of the Tombs inspired veiled references to the prophet Jeremiah and the young King David:

We should feel no surprise to come suddenly among the rocks upon a gaunt Hebrew with wild eyes, clothed in skins, and wrestling in the desert with the old unsolvable riddles of existence—a prophet whose scorching words should wither away in one instant all the falsities and frivolities of our lives, leaving us gaping aghast in the awful verge of Truth....Nor should we start to hear the thin high voice of a wandering lad with the shadow of a crown above his brow, who should come chanting psalms of longing for green pastures and still waters.

The complexity of Elizabeth Bisland makes Nellie Bly seem transparent by comparison. Soon she was to exhibit a startling metamorphosis from the sacred to the profane. It began innocently enough with a description of the townspeople enjoying their leisure:

The population is gathered in the square playing dominoes and games of chance at little tables and drinking coffee—liquor being forbidden in these Mahometans. Bearded Arabs with delicate features and grave, sad eyes, who fold their white bornouses about them with a wonderful effect of dignity; and more jovial and half-naked negroes of every tint and race —from Zanzibar, the Soudan, Abyssinia.

Miss Bisland felt benevolent toward the Muslims in the square, so that what she did next seems a bewildering transformation. She behaved toward one of them with a brazenness far out of keeping with her self-image as an exemplar of propriety. She reported:

> The Soudanese are fine, stalwart animals—fighting-men all—stripped to the waist, shining like polished ebony, with beardless mouths full of ivory teeth, and long wool combed straight out and vividly red—made so by being plastered down for a week under a coat of lime. Egypt and England know how well these men can fight; yet when I lean forward and take into my hand the little case of camel-skin containing verses from the Koran, hanging on the muscular black breast of one of these gigantic Africans, he laughs the same mellow, amiable laugh I should hear from a Negro at home on the plantation, did I show a like familiarity and interest.

The African must have smarted at the effrontery of the regal lady, but he simply laughed. When she rode back to port to board the *Britannia*, she was delighted to see a British man-of-war steaming out of the harbor on its way to the lower coast "to over-awe the Portuguese making futile protests against English domination in the neighborhood of Delagoa Bay."

The next day—her last in the tropics—Miss Bisland went up on deck to pleasure in the "delicious moist warmth of the equatorial morning." She saw a young man lounging on one of the bamboo chairs in "a neglige of Indian silk" and drinking a tiny cup of coffee in the early freshness. He was, she reported, the only other person visible on deck. The same Miss Bisland who had clutched the little book of Koranic verses dangling upon the naked breast of the Soudanese was seized now with pangs of modesty:

> I hesitate for a moment, conscious of the dishevelment of locks beneath the lace scarf tied under my chin, but think better of the hesitation and remain. I may never see this again, this world where one is really for the first time "Lord of the senses five"—where the light of night and of day have a new meaning; where one is drenched and steeped in color and perfume; where the

169

husk of callous dullness falls away and every sense replies to impressions with a keenness as of new-born faculties.

What we remember from our travels are not the magnificent monuments and the marvels of nature but those chance encounters with strangers when something magical occurs. Just such a moment was now happening to Elizabeth Bisland:

> The young man's silky black head is ruffled too, and his yellow eyes still sleepy as he comes and leans over the rail. He is holding a little black pipe in a slim olive hand that is tipped with deep-tinted onyx-like nails, and with it he points to the first canoe putting out from shore. It is a long brown boat, very narrow, and filled with oranges heaped up in the centre. It is cutting a delicate furrow along the pearly lilac of the glass-like sea. A faint gray mist, scarcely more than a film, lies along the shore. Above it the red rocks stand up sharply against the white sky, which the coming sun is changing to gold. The young man turns and smiles, showing a row of white teeth through lips as red as pomegranate flowers.

If one gets out of a trip only as much as he or she puts into it, then it must be said that Elizabeth Bisland's journey around the world was already a triumph. She had brought to it not only a richness of historical and literary associations, but her fine-tuned sensibility to Nature. Perhaps her own evaluation of that unexpected meeting with the young man in the early-morning hours best describes what she had already accomplished. It came after she returned to New York and looked back on that experience on deck:

> Every moment I have spent in the tropics is to me just as vivid as this. I see everything. Not a beauty, not a touch escapes me. Every moment of the day means intense delight, beauty, life....And now, after six months, not a line has faded or grown dim. I can live back in it every emotion, every impression, as though not an hour divided me from it....It is well to have thus once really lived.

The epicurean Miss Bisland had enjoyed herself to the

fullest in the tropics. What better proof that—at least in the philosophical sense—she was already, in Aden, a success? She had lived well. The deck of the *Britannia*, she now reported, swarmed with merchants selling ostrich feathers, grass mats and baskets from Zanzibar; ornaments of shells, boxes of Turkish Delight, embroideries, photographs, and a three-months-old lion cub in a wooden cage. The Bombay mail, for which the ship was waiting, arrived, together with new passengers with mountains of luggage. Elizabeth Bisland noted with pride that the passengers included two prominent Britons: Charles Bradlaugh, the "famous atheist, who fought the whole House of Commons, and forced it to admit him without taking an oath," and his colleague, Sir William Wedderburn, a "Scotch baronet, a gentle enthusiast and theoretical radical, whose heart is overflowing with vague tenderness to mankind." There was a stir among the passengers because Henry Morton Stanley had just arrived on the coast from the interior of Africa; there was talk of his going home on the *Britannia*. The British- American explorer was famous for his rescue from "darkest Africa," in 1871, of Scottish missionary and explorer David Livingstone ("Dr. Livingstone, I presume?") and for his subsequent discovery and development of the Congo. Stanley's last of several expeditions into Africa, begun in 1887, was for the relief of Emin Pasa, governor of the Equatorial Province of Egypt, who had been cut off by the Mahdist revolt of 1882 in the neighborhood of Lake Albert. After a grueling march during which he lost one of his officers to murder and others to fever, he was astonished to find that Emin declined to leave his Province. Stanley forged onward, through wilderness and across mountainous terrain, correctly estimating the size of Lake Albert and its tributary the Semliki River, and reached the east coast of Africa. Elizabeth Bisland's hopes of meeting the great explorer were, however, doomed to disappointment. "The government," she reported, "sends down a special convoy to take him to Egypt, and we steam without him." Miss Bisland awoke one night missing the throbbing of the screw and found that the ship was moving "at a snail's pace in smooth water." She reported on her introduction to the Suez Canal:

> The moon is very dim behind the clouds, and from the port-hole it would appear that we are sailing across

endless expanses of sand: nothing else is to be seen. Morning shows a narrow ditch in a desert, half full of green water—so narrow and so shallow apparently that nothing would convince us our great ship could pass through save the actual proof of its doing so. At one of the wider parts made for this purpose we pass a French troop-ship which dips her colors and sends a ringing cheer from the throats of the red-trousered soldiers on their way to Tonquin.

Tonquin (Tonkin) was northern Vietnam, a French colony. (The term Tonquin was never officially used by the Vietnamese to describe their country). It must be presumed that the *Britannia* dipped her colors in return, for while the sun never set on the British Empire, France still ruled a goodly portion of the land. As if symbolic of how the wealth and power in the world was distributed, a dead Arab floated by in the green water but was, Miss Bisland reported, "regarded with indifference as a common episode, and merely suggestive of an imprudent quarrel overnight." Stones and sand stretched as far as her eye could see; day ended with "a dim and lurid sunset." That night, the Britannia anchored off Port Said. Light-hearted Nellie Bly had ridden a bouncing burro through the streets of the town and bet her English gold on the wheel in the local gambling house with reckless and laughing abandon. Dignified Elizabeth Bisland's reaction to Port Said was judgmental, sternly moralistic:

...a wretched little place, dusty, dirty, and flaring with cheap vice—all the flotsam of four nations whirling about in an eddy of coarse pleasures. The shopkeepers are wolfish-looking, and bargain vociferously. Almost every other door opens into a gambling-hall and concert-hall. One of these gambling places boasts an opera. At the tables stand amid the crowd two handsome young Germans—blond, but with none of the ruddy warmth of the English blond; pale and flaxen, with deep-blue eyes and haughty of manner. Not nice faces; high-bred, but cold and brutal. They are officers from Prince Henry of Prussia's ship, the *Irene*, lying now in the harbor.

In 1890, militaristic Prussia was the most powerful state in the Germany which had conquered France nineteen years earlier in the Franco-Prussian War and established itself as an empire. Miss Bisland's feelings were, apparently, that the French fared no better at opera than they did in battle:

> In the concert-hall, *"Traviata"* is being sung by a fourth-rate French troupe, and the audience sit about at little tables, drinking, and eating ices. I ask for something native—Turkish—to drink, and they bring me a stuff that to all the evidences of sight, taste, and smell, cries out that it is a mixture of paregoric and water, and one sip contents me. We are glad to go away.

It was the third week in January. The *Britannia* bound for the Italian port city of Brindisi sailed across the Mediterranean. The sea was cold and rough; if Elizabeth Bisland had a premonition of things to come, she did not reveal it. (Newspapers in New York were reporting some of the worst storms in the history of the North Atlantic.) The Mediterranean evoked in her a swell of cultural allusions:

> In India nature is so tremendous she swallows up all memory of man; in Aden, one remembers only the Bible; but nearing Greece the past takes shapes and meaning, and history begins to have a new vividness and significance. Here man has been "lord of the visible earth"; has dominated and adorned her. She has been but the stage and background against which he played out the tragedies and comedies of humanity.

The accommodating personnel of the *Britannia* understood Miss Bisland's need. One morning at sunrise the stewardess tapped on her door and said, "The first officer's compliments, Miss, and will you please get up and look out of the scuttle."

Elizabeth Bisland wrapped herself in her kimono—a "treasure-trove" from Japan—and thrust her head and shoulders through the wide porthole. The sight of Crete transported her back to classical antiquity:

> Directly before me is Candia—abrupt mountains rising sharply from the sea and crowned with snow. Among them are trailing clouds looping long scarfs of mist from peak to peak; at their feet Homer's "wine-dark sea," furrowed by a thousand keels: Greek galleys,

Roman triremes, fighting vessels from Carthage, merchant and battleships from Venice, Genoa and Turkey; the fleets of Spain; men-o'-war with the English lion at the peak; and lastly, the world's peaceful commerce sailing serenely over the bones and rotting hulls that lie below.

The sunrise put Miss Bisland into a rapture that transcended mundane reality. In a lyrical outburst of hope and apprehension, she reported:

> The sun comes up gloriously out of the sea, deepening it to a winy purple in its light. Suddenly the mountain-tops take fire; the snow flushes softly, deepens rosily in hue, grows crimson with splendor; the sleeping mists begin to stir and heave, to lighten into gold, to float and rise into the warming blue above. Once more the splendors of a new day—such a sunrise as Cervantes may have seen; as glad Greek eyes may have witnessed bowing in prayer to the sun-god; as the galley-slave may have watched dully as a signal for new labors, and admirals gazed upon with tightening lip, not knowing whether the new sun should look upon defeat or victory, glory or death.

The dressing-gong clanged noisily throughout the ship and the colors paled into "the common day." With her return to the Western world, Elizabeth Bisland re-focused on her trip. The time for dilly-dallying was over, the time for action was here. There were so many things to do: She had to pack her wardrobe...tip the ship's personnel...check for her passport and other documents...assemble her notes...bid farewell to fellow passengers. And she would have to move fast. There was bound to be a milling about at debarkation and she was determined to be among the first to get off. She just had to catch that train from Brindisi to France.

The next morning, the 16th of January, the *Britannia* made fast to the docks at Brindisi.

CHAPTER NINETEEN

NELLIE BLY EXPOSES CHINESE ATROCITIES

Just as Harmon the travel agent forewarned, Nellie Bly encountered a five-day delay in Hong Kong. But far from discouraging her, her unsettling confrontation with him strengthened her will to recover her touch as an investigative reporter. She vowed that whatever happened from now on, she would dig for hard news. Luck had always smiled on her before because she was good at what she did best. At the hotel, she met a number of people after lunch who were interested in her trip and "ready and anxious to do anything they could to contribute to my pleasure during my enforced stay." She received invitations for her to attend dinners or receptions in her honor. Nellie, however, was of a mind to toughen herself for the challenge ahead. When the wife of a prominent Hong Kong gentleman offered her the use of their home during her stay, she politely begged off:

> ...I told her I could not think of accepting her kindness, because I would wish to be out most of the time, and could not make my hours conform to the hours of the house, and still feel free to go, come and stay, as I pleased. Despite her pleadings I assured her I was not on pleasure bent, but business, and I considered it my duty to refrain from social pleasures, devoting myself to things that lay more in the line of work.

Learning about the Other Woman tore Nellie Bly from her gossipy reportage and revitalized her as a journalist. She knuckled down to serious work. But first, there was one social affair she didn't want to miss:

> I had dinner on the *Oriental*. As I bade the captain and his officers farewell, remembering their kindness to me, I had a wild desire to cling to them, knowing that with the morning light the *Oriental* would sail, and I would be once again alone in strange lands with strange people.

Nellie Bly took on the strange city of Hong Kong as if her reputation as a reporter were at stake. To say that her accounts on that town were trenchant and distinctive tells only half the story; the other half involves her gift for seizing so much of the life around her in such little time. Remarkably, Nellie was able to capture the essence of international Hong Kong and the nearby big city of Canton in five days; her learning of the Other Woman revived her competitive instinct as a professional. She seemed now to be everywhere, an observer upon whom nothing was lost. Hong Kong was, she noted, like other ports she had visited, filled with happy, handsome, well-to-do bachelors who made her wonder why women did not flock there. ("It was all very well some years ago to say, 'Go west, young man'; but I would say, 'Girls, go East!'") Rich and poor alike, she reported, thronged the local racetrack to bet on native-bred Mongolian ponies—since there were no horses. The graveyards in lovely, tropical "Happy Valley" accommodated all faiths, with the Fire Worshipper and Mahommedan dead lying in close proximity to the Presbyterian, Episcopalian, Methodist, and Catholic. In the crowded districts (1,600 souls to an acre) of the city, people huddled together in disease-breeding filth. The communications gap between the upper and the lower classes, Nellie found, was bridged through the use of *lingua franca*. She reported:

"Chin, chin," which means "good day," "good-bye," "good night," "How are you?" or anything one may take from it, is the greeting of Chinamen. They all speak mongrel English, called "pidgin" or "pigeon" English. It is impossible to make them understand pure English, consequently Europeans, even house-keepers, use pidgin English when addressing the servants. The servants are men, with the exception of the nurses, and possibly the cooks. To the uninitiated it sounds absurd to hear men and women addressing servants and merchants in the same idiotic language with which fond parents usually cuddle their offspring; but even more laughable is it to hear men swear in "pigeon English," at an unkind or unruly servant. Picture a man with an expression of frenzied rage upon his countenance, saying "Go to hellee, savvy?" Pidgin, or pigeon, is applied to everything. One will hear people say, "Hab got pigeon," which means they have business to look after; or if a Chinaman is requested to do some work which he thinks is the duty of another, he will say: "No belongee boy pigeon."

Nellie strolled the Chinese districts of the town, absorbing impressions. In an eating house, diners perched round a table on a circular bench "like chickens on a fence," not letting their feet touch the floor but sitting with "their knees drawn up until knees and chin met," and holding large bowls against their chins, "pushing the rice energetically with their chopsticks into their mouths," At all hours of the day, Nellie noted, they consumed cup after cup of tea—always minus sugar and cream and in cups that were quite small and saucerless. In nooks and recesses of prominent thoroughfares professional scribes doubled in brass, not only writing letters for people but telling their fortunes. Merchants invariably weighed the money, and they put their private stamp upon the silver dollar as an assurance of its legality and worth. Much silver, Nellie Bly reported, was "beaten into such strange shapes by this queer practice that at first I was afraid to accept it as exchange." She watched a Chinese marriage procession pass, complete with band of musicians, elegant lanterns and banners, and coolies carrying "curious-looking objects in blue and gilt which, I was told, represent mythical and historical scenes." She also learned that while participants in such processions brought roast pig to the temple of the josses, they afterwards very sensibly took it home to eat.

Nellie Bly soaked up information like a sponge in Hong Kong. She ascertained that the chances of a man out of work getting a job there were hopeless. She explained why:

The banking and shipping houses, controlled by Europeans, certainly employ numbers of men, but they are brought from England under three and five years' contracts. When a vacancy occurs from a death, or a transfer, the business house immediately consults its representatives in London, where another man signs an agreement, and comes out to Hong Kong.

During her five-day sojourn, Nellie Bly turned herself into not only a walking encyclopedia of Hong Kong but a riding one as well. One day she went up Victoria Peak, named in honor of the Queen and said to be 1,800 feet high, the highest point on the island. An elevated tramway, built in 1887, ran from the town to Victoria Gap, 1,100 feet above the sea. Before that time, people were carried up in sedan chairs exclusively.

The first year after its completion, the tram bore 148,344 persons up the mountain side. Victoria Peak was not a place where the poor were likely to reside:

> During the summer months Hong Kong is so hot that those who are in a position to do so seek the mountain top, where a breeze lives all the year round. Level places for buildings are obtained by blasting, and every brick, stone, and bit of household furniture is carried by coolies from the town up to the height of one-thousand, six-hundred feet.

Nellie Bly rode up the mountain side in a sedan borne by three coolies. It paused at the Umbrella Seat—a mere bench with a pinnacled roof—where all the bearers were customarily allowed to rest, then resumed its steep climb, passing sightseers and nurses with children along the way. The sedan stopped again; Nellie got off, and traveled by foot to the signal station. She gazed down at Hong Kong and the harbor:

> The view is superb. The bay, in a breastwork of mountains, lies calm and serene, dotted with hundreds of ships that seem like tiny toys. The palatial white houses come half way up the mountain side, beginning at the edge of the glassy bay. Every house we notice has a tennis-court blasted out of the mountain side. They say that after night the view from the peak is unsurpassed. One seems to be suspended between two heavens. Every one of the several thousand boats and sampans carries a light after dark. This, with the lights on the roads and in the houses, seems to be a sky more filled with stars than the one above.

One morning a gentleman who was the proud possessor of a team of ponies, "the finest in Hong Kong," called at Nellie Bly's hotel to take her for a ride. The small but powerful animals and the low, easy phaeton whirled her through the town and out to the bay where she viewed "the beautiful dry- dock on the other side, which is constructed entirely of granite and is said to be of such size that it can take in the largest vessels afloat." Elizabeth Bisland had admired the same drydock a little more than a week earlier (no indication, of course, who was ahead in the race, since the two women were traveling in opposite directions).

Nellie and her companion saw some shrines which incited the same disrespect from her as had the ones in Penang and Singapore. But finally, her even-handedness as a reporter won out:

> During our drive we visited two quaint and dirty temples. One was a plain little affair with a gaudy altar. The stone steps leading to it were filled with beggars of all sizes, shapes, diseases and conditions of filth. They were so repulsive that instead of appealing to one's sympathy they only succeed in arousing one's disgust. At another temple, near by a public laundry where the washers stood in a shallow stream slapping the clothes on flat stones, was a quaint temple hewed, cave-like, in the side of an enormous rock. A selvage of rock formed the altar, and to that humble but picturesque temple Chinese women flock to pray for sons to be born unto them that they may have someone to support them in their old age.

Nellie Bly felt that she had covered everything of interest in Hong Kong; now she wanted to see a "real Simon-pure Chinese city." Like Elizabeth Bisland, she was a product of her time; both were acutely aware of the problem of Chinese immigration in America. But whereas Miss Bisland feared "the pigtails" would engulf the United States, Nellie saw them as being excluded from it. She asserted: "I knew we were trying to keep the Chinese out of America, so I decided to see all of them I could while in their land. Pay them a farewell visit, as it were. So on Christmas Eve, I started for the City of Canton."

If Hong Kong marked a resurgence of Nellie Bly's reportorial powers, Canton was to test them in the refiner's fire.

* * *

An agent of the Occidental and Oriental steamship line escorted Nellie Bly to the *Powan*, the vessel that was to take her to Canton. She was given into the charge of Captain Grogan, an American who had lived for years in China. His corpulence evoked in Nellie that same streak of cruelty she had shown toward the Spanish diplomat and the "moo-moo cow" family. In the next breath, however, she tempered her brashness of youth with mature self-appraisal:

A very bashful man he was, but a most kindly, pleasant one. I never saw a fatter man, or a man so comically fattened, a wild inclination to laugh crept over me every time I caught a glimpse of his roly-poly body, his round red face embedded as it were, in the fat of his shoulders and breast. The thoughts of how sensitive I am concerning remarks about my personal appearance, in a measure subdued my impulse to laugh. I have always said to critics, who mercilessly write about the shape of my chin, or the cut of my nose or the size of my mouth and such personal attributes, that can no more be changed than death can be escaped: "Criticize the style of my hat or gown, I can change them, but spare my nose, it was born to me." Remembering this, and how nonsensical it is to blame or criticize people for what they are powerless to change, I pocketed my merriment, letting a kindly feeling of sympathy take its place.

Whatever Nellie Bly felt about herself, men were attracted to her by her vivacious personality.

That night on the *Powan* steaming toward the Pearl River, Nellie Bly went on deck to listen to her inner voices:

They can talk of the companionship of men, the splendor of the sun, the softness of moonlight, the beauty of music, but give me a willow chair on a quiet deck, the world with its worries and noise and prejudices lost in distance, the glare of the sun, the cold light of the moon blotted out by the dense blackness of the night. Let me rest, rocked gently by the rolling sea, in a nest of velvety darkness, my only light the soft twinkling of the myriads of stars in the quiet sky above; my music, the sound of the kissing waters, cooling the brain and easing the pulse; my companionship, dreaming my own

dreams. Give me that and I have happiness in its per-
fection. But away with dreams. This is a work-a-day
world and I am racing Time around it.

After dinner, the *Powan* anchored outside Canton, then
waited for the tide which was to carry the ship safely over
the bar. Nellie Bly went below to see the Chinese in steerage.
All huddled together in one large room, they were gambling,
smoking opium, sleeping, cooking, eating, reading and talking. They carried "their own beds, a bit of matting, and their
own food, little else than rice and tea." Before daybreak, the
Powan arrived at Canton. The Chinese went ashore immediately; the other passengers stayed on board for breakfast, at
which Captain Grogan introduced Nellie Bly to Ah Cum, the
English-speaking guide he had secured for her. First, Ah Cum
thoughtfully wished Nellie and the others in the tour group a
Merry Christmas (it had slipped their minds it was
Christmas!). A clever Mongolian, he had been educated in an
American mission in Canton; so had his son. English, he
assured Nellie with great earnestness, was all he learned
there;—he would have none of the Christian religion. He was,
Nellie averred, a shrewd businessman:

> Besides being paid as guide, Ah Cum collects a per-
> centage from merchants for all the goods bought by
> tourists. Of course the tourists pay higher prices than
> they would otherwise, and Ah Cum sees they visit no
> shops where he is not paid his little fee.

Ah Cum, Nellie Bly reported, was "more comely in features than most Mongolians, his nose being more shapely and
his eyes less slit-like than those of most of his race." Over the
blue, stiffly-starched garment that reached his heels he wore
a short padded and quilt silk jacket, "somewhat similar to a
smoking jacket." His tight-fitting navy-blue trousers were tied
around the ankle, and he had on his feet beaded black shoes
with white soles. The crowning touch, so to speak, in Nellie's
physical description of the guide was his long, coal-black
queue. Finished with a tassel of black silk, it touched his
heels, and "on the spot where the queue began rested a round
black turban."

Ah Cum had chairs ready for the tourists. Once he was in
his own chair—an elegant arrangement of black silk hang-

ings, tassels, and fringe, with black wood-poles finished with brass knobs—he closed it and was "hidden from the gaze of the public." Nellie's and the others' were plain willow chairs with "ordinary covers, which, to my mind, rather interfere with sightseeing."

Nellie's first stop on her tour of Canton was green and picturesque Shameen or Sandy Face, a small island inhabited exclusively by Europeans. (The latter were so hated in Canton that the law forbade Celestials to cross onto the island.) Here, for the first time since leaving New York, Nellie saw the Stars and Stripes. The sight of her country's flag floating over the gateway to the American Consulate filled her with a pugnacious pride:

> It is a strange fact that the further one goes from home the more loyal one becomes. I felt I was a long ways off from my own dear land; it was Christmas Day, and I had seen many different flags since last I gazed upon our own. The moment I saw it floating there in the soft, lazy breeze I took off my cap and said: "That is the most beautiful flag in the world, and I am ready to whip anyone who says it isn't."

> No one said a word. Everybody was afraid; I saw an Englishman in the party glance furtively towards the Union Jack, which was floating over the English Consulate, but in a hesitating manner, as if he feared to let me see.

She was finally getting even with the English who ruled the world wherever she went and regarded America as a cultural backwater. She may even have felt she was making up for all those rudenesses she suffered aboard the British ship *Victoria*.

Nellie Bly and the others in her little party were welcomed at the American Consulate by the affable Mr. Seymour, an editor before he went to China with his wife and daughter to be consul. He was interested in embroideries and carved ivories and would steer visiting tourists to the best buys in them.

In her chair borne by three coolies, Nellie Bly rode from pastoral Shameen into crowded Canton. On streets no more than a yard wide, she passed the wide-open gaily colored shops crammed with buyers, sellers, and rich enticing wares...past the bookkeepers who wore enormous tortoise-shell-rimmed glasses and whose desks fronted the shops. Ah Cum had cautioned Nellie to be ready for anything in this city of millions of people. He had warned her not to be surprised if Chinamen stoned her while she was in Canton; he told her that Chinese women usually spat in the face of female tourists when the opportunity offered. But Nellie Bly was not intimidated. She reported:

> However, I had no trouble. The Chinese are not pleasant-appearing people; they usually look as if life had given them nothing but trouble; but as we were carried along, the men in the stores would rush out to look at me. They did not take any interest in the men with me, but gazed at me as if I was something new. They showed no sign of animosity, but the few women I met looked as curiously at me, and less kindly. The thing that seemed to interest the people the most about me were my gloves. Sometimes they would make bold enough to touch them, and they would always gaze upon them with looks of wonder.

The streets of Canton were more like lanes—so narrow that she thought she was being carried through "the aisles of some great market." It was impossible to see the sky owing to the signs and other decorations and the compactness of the buildings, and the open shops were "just like stands in a market," except that they were not cut off from the passing crowd by a counter. Nellie was astonished when Ah Cum told her that she was not in a market-house but in the streets of Canton. From time to time, her train of chairs would meet another train of chairs and hers would stop; a great deal of yelling and fussing would then ensue until both had safely passed, the way being "too narrow for both trains to move at once in safety." As the hours wore on, Nellie grew anxious about the health of her bearers:

> Coolie number two of my chair was a source of great discomfort to me all the day. He had a strap spanning the poles by which he upheld his share of the chair. This band, or strap, crossed his shoulders, touching the neck just where the prominent bone is. The skin was worn

white and hard-looking from the rubbing of the band; but still it worried me, and I watched all the day expecting to see it blister. His long pig-tail was twisted around his head, so I had an unobstructed view of the spot. He was not an easy traveler, this coolie, there being as much difference in the gait of carriers as there is in the gait of horses. Many times he shifted the strap, much to my misery, and then he would turn and, by motions, convey to me that I was sitting more to one side than to the other.

Nellie's consideration for coolie number two constrained her to contort her body into an unnatural position. She made such an effort to sit straight and not to move that when she alighted at the shops she felt "cramped almost into a paralytic state." The result was that before the end of the day, she had another of her sick headaches—all, she reported, from "thinking too much about the comfort of Chinamen." Compassion gave way to querulousness; she concluded:

> A disagreeable thing about the coolies is that they grunt like pigs when carrying one. I can't say whether the grunt has any special significance to them or not, but they will grunt one after the other along the train, and it is anything but pleasant.

Nellie Bly was eager to see the execution ground, so she and Ah Cum were carried there. As they walked down a crooked back alley and past rows of half-dried pottery outside a shed, Nellie noticed that the ground in one place was very red. When she asked the guide about it, he said indifferently, kicking the red-stained earth with his white-soled shoe: "It's blood. Eleven men were beheaded here yesterday." What a glorious Christmas present for an investigative reporter! After traveling forty-one days and more than 10,600 miles around the globe, Nellie Bly had finally run into horrifying hard news— a story that, because of its consequence, must be printed as soon as possible. But according to Ah Cum, she reported, it was an ordinary thing for ten to twenty criminals to be executed at one time. The average number annually, he told her, was something like four hundred, and in the year 1855, over fifty-thousand rebels were beheaded in this narrow alley.

184

Ah Cum was indispensable to Nellie Bly during the Canton experience, but it was she who pursued the story. While the guide was talking, Nellie noticed some crudely fashioned wooden crosses leaning against the high stone wall. Supposing they were used for religious purposes before and after the executions, she asked Ah Cum about them.

"When women are condemned to death in China," he said, "they are bound to wooden crosses and cut to pieces."

His words sent shivers down Nellie's spine. Men died right away, he went on, if their crime was a lesser one—they were beheaded with one stroke. If it was the worst kind, they were meted out the same slow, agonizing death the women were given—to indicate how discreditable the offense was.

"When they are cut to bits, it is done so deftly that they are entirely dismembered and disemboweled before they are dead. Would you like to see some heads?"

Nellie Bly's inborn skepticism rushed to the fore. A Chinese guide, she thought, could tell a whopper just as readily as any other guide, and who could beat a guide for "highly colored and exaggerated tales"? So she said coldly:

"Certainly, bring on your heads!"

Nellie tipped a man as Ah Cum told her to do; with the clay of the pottery still on his hands, the man went to some barrels which stood near the wooden crosses, put in his hand and pulled out a head! Nellie Bly trembled, but was able to report:

> These barrels are filled with lime, and as the criminals are beheaded their heads are thrown into the barrels, and when the barrels become full they empty them out and get a fresh supply. If a man of wealth is condemned to death in China he can, with little effort, buy a substitute. Chinamen are very indifferent about death; it seems to have no terror for them.

Nellie was experienced at probing beyond surface impressions. She went next to the jail and was surprised to see all the doors open. The doors were rather narrow; when she squeezed inside she learned why there was no maximum security in this prison—all the prisoners had thick, heavy boards fastened around their necks. "I no longer felt surprised at the doors being unbarred," Nellie reported. "There was no need of locking them."

Nellie Bly's introduction to the Chinese system of criminal justice took her to the court. At the entrance to the massive, square, stone-paved building was a large gambling establishment. She was presented to some judges whom she found lounging about in small side-rooms smoking opium and playing fan-tan (a Chinese betting game). They took her to see the instruments of torture, which included "such pleasant things as thumb screws, split bamboo to whip with, and pulleys on which people were hanged by their thumbs." While Nellie was there they brought in two men who had been caught stealing. She reported:

> The thieves were chained with their knees meeting their chins, and in that distressing position were carried in baskets suspended on a pole between two coolies. The judge explained to me that as these offenders had been caught in the very act of taking what did not belong to them, their hands would be spread out on flat stones and with smaller stones every bone in their hands would be broken. Afterwards they would be sent to the hospital to be cured. Prisoners dying in jail are always beheaded before burial.

While a reporter depends greatly upon his or her sources, there is no substitute for eye-witness testimony or for "being there." An American who had lived many years near Canton told Nellie there was a small bridge spanning a stream in the city where it was customary to hang criminals in a fine wire hammock, first removing all their clothing. A number of sharp knives, he told her, were laid at the end of the bridge, and every one crossing while the man was there was "compelled to take a knife and give a slash to the wire-imprisoned wretch." Nellie Bly reacted to this source's account the way she had to Ah Cum's mention of the heads—with wary disbelief. "I saw none of this," she reported to her readers in New York, "I only give these stories as they were given to me."

Whatever her reservations about the reports, Nellie was not squeamish. She wanted to know more. Her subsequent description of the Chinese bamboo torture showed how intrigued she was by the atrocities inflicted upon those who fell afoul of the law. Once again, she was careful to point out to her readers that her information was second-hand. That, however, it should be noted, did not stop her from relaying it to them in spellbindingly clinical detail:

> They tell me a bamboo punishment (I cannot now recall the name they gave it) is not as uncommon in China as one would naturally suppose from its extreme brutality. For some crimes offenders are pinioned in standing position with their legs astride, fastened to stakes in the earth. This is done directly above a bamboo sprout. To realize this punishment it is necessary to give a little explanation of the bamboo. A bamboo sprout looks not unlike the delicious asparagus, but is of a hardness and strength not equaled by iron. When it starts to come up, nothing can stop its progress. It is so hard that it will go through anything on its way up; let that anything be asphalt or what it will, the bamboo goes through it as readily as though the obstruction didn't exist. The bamboo grows with marvelous rapidity straight up into the air for thirty days, and then it stops.

Nellie was very conscious of her readers; to tantalize them, she departed briefly from the gruesome and struck a note of the enticing:

> When its growth is finished it throws off a shell-like bark, its branches slowly unfolding and falling into place. They are covered with a soft airy foliage finer than the leafage of a willow. From a distance a bamboo forest is a most beautiful thing, exquisitely soft and fine in appearance, but adamant is not harder in reality.

The tone of melodrama returned, a touch of wonderment in it:

> As I have said, nothing ever equaled the rapidity of its growth, it being affirmed that it can really be seen growing! In the thirty days that it grows it may reach a height of seventy-five feet.

The narrative voice became manipulative, a trifle too familiar given the circumstances, then shifted into excruciating high gear:

Picture then the convict above a bamboo sprout and in such a position that he cannot get away from it. It starts on its upward course never caring for what is in its way; on it goes through the man who stands there dying, dying, worse than by inches, conscious for a while, then fever mercifully kills knowledge, and at last, after days of suffering, his head drops forward, and he is dead.

Nellie poured it on, transposing to other fiendish forms of Chinese torture:

But that is not any worse than tying a man in the boiling sun to a stake, covering him with quick-lime and giving him nothing but water to quench hunger and thirst. He holds out and out, for it means life, but at last he takes the water that is always within his reach. He drinks, he perspires, and the lime begins to eat. They also have a habit of suspending a criminal by his arms, twisting them back of him. As long as a man keeps muscles tense he can live, but the moment he relaxes and falls, it ruptures blood vessels and his life floats out on a crimson stream. The unfortunate is always suspended in a public place, where magistrates watch so that no one may release him.

Nellie exposed the heinous hypocrisy and corruption of the Chinese regime:

Friends of the condemned flock around the man of authority, bargaining for the man's life; if they can pay the price extorted by him, the man is taken down and set free; if not, he merely hangs until the muscles give out and he drops to death. They also have a way of burying the whole of criminals except their heads. The eyelids are fastened back so that they cannot close them, and so facing the sun they are left to die. Sticking bamboo splints under the fingernails and then setting fire to them is another happy way of punishing wrong-doers.

It was hard news, the kind of news Nellie Bly was accustomed to writing. This was a Pulitzer-prize-winning performance; all the horrors she was subjected to in one morning she reported in luminous prose. Nellie, like her publisher, knew what sold newspapers. Joseph Pulitzer's formula for success was a peculiar mix of high-minded crusading for social reform and of pandering to his mass audience with stories about sex, violence, and bizarre exotic customs. But that took nothing away from Nellie Bly's achievement in uncovering for her readers in America the murderous, legalized insanity of the Chinese criminal-justice system.

The frightfulness must have seemed never-ending to Nellie. She didn't know what to expect when she mounted the filthy stone steps to the Temple of Horrors; she guessed it must be an exhibition of "human monstrosities." It was that; it was also an expression of the agony and desperation of the maimed and the indigent:

> The steps were filled with dirty Mongolians of all sizes, ages, shapes, and afflictions. When they heard our steps, those who could see and walk, rushed up to us, crying for alms, and those who were blind and powerless raised their voices the louder because they could not move. Inside, a filthy stone court was crowded with a mass of humanity. There were lepers, peddlers, monstrosities, fortune tellers, gamblers, quacks, dentists with strings of horrid teeth, and even pastry cooks! It is said the Chinese worship here occasionally and consult idols. In little, dirty cells were dirty figures, representing the punishment of the Buddhists' hell. They were being whipped, ground to death, boiled in oil, beheaded, put under red hot bells, being sawed in twain, and undergoing similar agreeable things.

A welcome respite from the hellishness took Nellie Bly to the Temple of the Five Hundred Gods (there were over eight-hundred temples in Canton) where Ah Cum asked her if she was superstitious. When she said Yes, he said he would show her how to try her luck. Apparently the sagacious guide knew that she was racing around the world and that she would need every ounce of luck the deities could grant. Nellie watched him place some joss sticks in a copper jar before the luck-god, then take from the table two pieces of wood worn smooth and dirty from frequent use, and which, fitted together, were like the shape of a pear. One can well imagine Nellie Bly held her breath while she awaited the fateful omen. She reported:

> With this wood—he called it the "luck pigeon"—held with the flat sides together, he made circling motions over the smouldering joss sticks, once, twice, thrice, and dropped the luck pigeon to the floor. He explained if one side of the luck pigeon turned up and the other turned down it meant good luck, while if they both fell in the same position it meant bad luck. When he dropped it they both turned the one way, and he knew he would have bad luck.
>
> I took the luck pigeon then, and I was so superstitious that my arm trembled and my heart beat in little palpitating jumps as I made the motions over the burning joss sticks. I dropped the wood to the floor, and one piece turned one way and one the other; and I was perfectly happy. I knew I was going to have good luck.

Thus the luck-god frowned on Ah Cum, but he smiled on Nellie Bly, thereby confirming what she had always felt in her bones—that she would win the race.

Ah Cum's group then visited yet another torture chamber—this one, Confucian style—the Examination Hall, where there were accommodations for "the simultaneous examination of eleven-thousand, six-hundred, sixteen celestial students, all male." Thin, black pigs rooted hungrily in the grimy park-like space before the entrance. Followed by crowds of children clamoring for alms, the tourists pressed onward—past a few women who, aided by canes, hobbled about on their small, cramped feet and stopped to look after them with "grins of curiosity and amusement." There was nothing amusing, however, about the Examination Hall. Nellie and the others entered through the Gate of Equity and the Dragon Gate and walked down the great avenue toward the watch tower, which contained a god of literature in the second story. On either side of the open green space were rows of whitewashed buildings; they were, she reported, not unlike railway cattle cars in appearance. Their interiors were rigorously constrictive:

In these ranges of cells, cells that measure 5 1/2 feet by 3 2/3 feet, eleven-thousand, six-hundred, sixteen pig-tailed students undergo their written examination. On the sides facing the avenues are Chinese descriptions showing what study is examined in that range. In each cell is a board to sit on, and one a little higher for a desk. This roughly improvised desk must be slid out to allow the student to enter or depart unless he crawls under or jumps over. The same texts are given to all at daylight, and when essays are not finished at night the students are kept overnight in their cells. The Hall is about one-thousand, three-hundred and eighty feet long by six-hundred, fifty feet wide, and is really a strangely interesting place well worth a visit. It is said the examinations are very severe, and from the large number of candidates examined, sometimes only one hundred and fifty will be passed. The place in which the essays are examined is called the Hall of Auspicious Stars, and the Chinese description over the avenue translated reads, "The opening heavens circulate literature."

The Examination Hall reflected the best and the worst practices developed over the centuries by the followers of Confucius (551-479 B.C.) China's most famous teacher, philosopher, and political theorist. Confucianism taught obedience to authority (family, employer, state) and virtuous conduct, but it also established a civil service system whose arrogance stunted the growth of modern China, creating a chasm between the educated elite and the illiterate laboring classes. Imagine wanting a job nowadays with the Civil Service and finding that one of the requirements is to memorize Tolstoy's *Anna Karenina*! Those 11,616 pigtailed exam-takers who sought to rise into the Chinese bureaucracy were expected to know by heart Confucius' *Analects* (the collection of his sayings and short dialogues) as well as other Chinese classics. The imperial civil-service examination system was not abolished until the early 1900s.

Nellie Bly expressed to Ah Cum her great curiosity to see the leper village. Nellie was appalled by the squalor and filth of the village, an assemblage of bamboo huts that emanated a stench so odious that Ah Cum advised the group to smoke cigarettes while they were there. She was aghast at the misery of the lepers, who endeavored to hide their nakedness with their few, filthy rags. There was no furniture—little else than a few old rags and some dried grass on the dirt floors. Nellie Bly reported that many of the lepers were featureless, some were blind, some had lost fingers, others a foot, some a leg, but all of the hundreds of them were "equally dirty, disgusting, and miserable." Nellie regarded the lepers unflinchingly, her need to see them as human beings warring with her loathing and her concern about contagion. She reported:

> Those able to work cultivate a really prosperous-looking garden, which is near their village. Ah Cum assured me they sold their vegetables in the city market! I felt glad to know we had brought our luncheon from the ship. Those lepers able to walk spend the day in Canton begging, but are always compelled to sleep in their village, still I could not help wondering what was the benefit of a leper village if the lepers are allowed to mingle with the other people. On my return to the city I met several lepers begging in the market. The sight of them among the food was enough to make me vow never to eat anything in Canton. The lepers are also permitted to marry, and a surprising number of diseased children are brought into a cursed and unhappy existence.

Ah Cum led the tour group away from the leper village. Nellie Bly felt a gnawing emptiness; it was Christmas Day, and she thought with regret of dinner at home—although one of the men said it was midnight in New York. Picking up their homesickness, the guide took them for luncheon to a pretty place within a high wall, where some long-legged storks (made so familiar to them by pictures on Chinese fans) stood in still water against a background of low, overhanging trees. Ah Cum conducted them to a room which was shut off from the court by a large carved gate; inside were hard wood chairs and tables. While Nellie ate, she heard chanting to the mournful sound of a tomtom and a shrill pipe. When asked where they were, the guide replied:

"In the Temple of the Dead."

Nellie Bly was eating her Christmas luncheon in the Temple of the Dead! A number of Chinamen crowded around the gate and looked curiously at her, and held up several of their well-clad, clean children for her to see. Reported Nellie:

> Thinking to be agreeable, I went forward to shake hands with them, but they kicked and screamed, and getting down, rushed back in great fright, which amused us intensely. Their companions succeeded after awhile in quieting them, and they were persuaded to take my hand. The ice once broken, they became so interested in me, my gloves, my bracelets and my dress, that I soon regretted my friendliness in the outset.

The dolorous chanting continued. Nellie Bly learned that it was customary at the death of a person to build a bonfire and cast into it the deceased's household articles such as money boxes and ladies' dressing cases, while the priests played upon shrill pipes. They claimed, she reported, that the devil which inhabits all humans leaves the body to save the property of the dead, and that "once they play him out he can never re-enter, so souls are saved."

Bloodshed, torture, beheadings, death—it was a Christmas Day Nellie Bly would always remember. Almost as if to purge the dreadfulness from her consciousness and that of her readers, she closed with a coda exquisite for its precision:

> I climbed high and dirty stone steps to the water-clock, which, they say, is over five hundred years old, and has never run down or been repaired. In little niches in the stone walls were small gods, before them the smouldering joss sticks. The water-clock consists of four copper jars, about the size of wooden pails, placed on steps, one above the other. Each one has a spout from which comes a steady drop-drop. In the last and bottom jar is an indicator, very much like a foot rule, which rises with the water, showing the hour. On a blackboard hanging outside, they mark the time for the benefit of the town people. The upper jar is filled once every twenty-four hours, and that is all the attention the clock requires.

Time. Time.

Nellie Bly returned to the *Powan* where she found some beautiful presents from Consul Seymour and the cards of a number of Europeans who had called to see her. Word obviously had spread she was racing around the world; she was no longer an anonymity. Suffering from a pounding headache, she retired to her cabin. Shortly, the *Powan* was on the way back to Hong Kong; Nellie's visit to Canton on Christmas Day was history.

CHAPTER TWENTY

ELIZABETH BISLAND MISSES THE BOAT

From Brindisi, the steamer *Britannia* would have taken Elizabeth Bisland the long way—out through the Strait of Gibraltar on up to Portsmouth. But while in Ceylon, she had taken the precaution of securing a berth on the special passenger coach of a British government mail train which ran down through France and Italy to meet the Peninsular and Oriental steamships and thus gained five days in the arrival of mails from India and Australia. The arrangement hung, however, on Miss Bisland's being able to get her luggage through customs on time. She went ashore at Brindisi only to discover that ten minutes before the departure of the train, her luggage was missing. She rushed back to the ship and found her possessions in the hands of a "pig-headed Italian" customs inspector who insisted they had not been properly examined and who demanded the keys. When he strewed her garments about the deck she was furious and berated him in un-ladylike terms that made him turn pale and waver. She stuffed her belongings into her trunk and rushed to catch her train. Happily, like most trains in Italy, it wasn't bound by "narrow interpretations of time-table." Although she arrived late, it had not yet left the station.

The incident involving the customs inspector greatly upset Miss Bisland. She prized her dignity as a gentlewoman, and she hoped she had not sacrificed it when she lost her temper. But more significantly, this was the first time during her journey around the world that the Southern belle gave any very strong indication she felt she was in a race. The same woman who had started out abhorring the trip and regarding it as "a ridiculous wild-goose chase" now began to see herself as in a competition. Now sixty-three days out of New York, she was nearing the homestretch, so to speak, with a very real chance of winning. She knew that she had gained time on her rival by getting that fast government boat from Yokohama to Hong Kong and that Nellie Bly had suffered delay in both cities. She knew also that Miss Bly's ship to San Francisco was now

running into bad weather on the Pacific. She must have pleasured quietly in the thought that she stood a good chance of
beating that sensationalizer with the hunger for the limelight
who had turned her, Elizabeth Bisland's, life upside down,
forcing her to leave her home and her friends and go gadding
nonsensically about the globe. That officious bureaucrat at
customs with his cocked hat and air of imperial importance!
Who did he think he was? King Umberto? An hour passed
before Miss Bisland regained her composure. The images
flowing past her train window soothed her: The "lapis-lazuli"
of the Adriatic dotted with frolicsome sails, the haunting
strangeness of the gnarled olive groves, the "little snow-white
towns" along the shore—all this made her "fain to forgive the
Italians because of Italy."

The train began climbing into the Alps; the air grew very
cold. Villages tucked into the clefts of mountainsides flashed
past, and the outlines of a ruined castle crowning a crag.
Patches of snow appeared here and there; the cold intensi-
fied; suddenly she caught a glimpse of white heights against
the blue; they were in the Alps now. The train thundered
through the darkness of the Mt. Cenis tunnel and into a
France where, unlike in Italy, the customs officer was smartly
uniformed and a model of politeness and dispatch, the railroad station large and in a good state of repair, and the atmosphere one generally of "prosperity, thrift, and alertness."
Telegrams had been following Elizabeth Bisland along the
route concerning the possibility of catching a ship to New
York at Le Havre. As the race between her and Nellie Bly
entered its climactic stages, *Cosmopolitan* was in continual contact with steamship-line officials in that port. Miss Bisland,
who had begun to smell pay-dirt (a bonus, perhaps, depend-
ing on how well she finished?),now agonized that her train
northward bound from Marseilles was running behind
schedule. If only she could connect with the *S.S.
Transatlantique*...if only. (She called the ship by the name of
the company—actually it was the Compagnie Générale
Transatlantique's *Le Champagne*.) Her rival had promised to
go around the world in seventy-five days but now there was
every likelihood that she, Elizabeth Bisland, could—as Walker
felt she could—do it in less than that.

The questions clamored in Miss Bisland's feverish brain as

the wheels clicked across the tracks: Would the train make up for lost time? If the train could not, would the CGT steamer consent to wait for her? Would the captain be willing to delay its departure for at least another hour or two? She wondered this even though *Cosmopolitan* assured her the ship would wait. She recalled the magazine's bold ploy in San Francisco when it pressured to no avail that other steamship line, asking them to advance the date of sailing for her ship to the Orient. And then she remembered the $8,000 *Cosmopolitan* offered to get her on the fast government boat from Yokohama to Hong Kong. She couldn't have asked for a stronger demonstration of support from her bosses in New York! Surely *now*, at this critical point in the game, they would be able to persuade officials in Le Havre to have the ship wait for her! She felt sure that it *would* wait for her.

Some two hours after midnight, on the morning of January 17th, Elizabeth Bisland was roused out of bed by a train guard and was handed a telegram which said she must be ready at 4 a.m. to change cars for Paris. This meant that the elegant Miss Bisland must leave her trunk—under seal for London—and cross the ocean with a few belongings in a traveling bag. She arose, dressed quietly so as not to disturb the sleep of her fellow passengers, then with traditional Southern graciousness, scribbled a few notes of farewell to those who had been "especially courteous" to her. When the train stopped at Villeneuve, a suburb of Paris, Miss Bisland was prepared to change cars. What happened next must have made her wonder whether there was such a thing as Nellie Bly luck and whether the breaks were against her. She was met in the railroad station by a young Frenchman who introduced himself as an agent from the Thomas Cook and Son tourist bureau in Paris. In 1890, Cook's already enjoyed an international reputation as a travel agency. Thomas Cook was believed to have been the first to advertise publicly excursions by train in England. Cook went on to invent the guided tour, an innovation that became enormously popular. During the Paris Exhibition of 1855, he conducted excursions from Leicester to Paris; the following year, he led his first Grand Tour of Europe. Ten years later, Cook ceased to conduct personal tours and became an agent for the sale of domestic and overseas travel tickets. Later, together with his son Thomas

Mason Cook, a partner in the business, he broadened the firm's activities to include military transport and postal services for England and Egypt. His most spectacular achievement was the transportation, in 1884, of an entire expeditionary force (18,000 men) up the Nile for the attempted relief of General Charles George Gordon at Khartoum. So that when Elizabeth Bisland was met by the young Frenchman in the station at Villeneuve, she must have felt double reason to be confident that everything was going as planned: First was *Cosmopolitan*'s assurances, second was Cook's reputation as a reliable travel agency. The agent's face was long and his voice tense: He regretted to inform her that he was the bearer of bad news. The CGT vessel, he told her, had refused to wait for her past its scheduled time of departure—at seven this morning. It was already past 4 a.m. There was, he said, no chance of catching the ship now. None. Miss Bisland listened with growing horror. Was it possible? Was the train that far behind time? How could *Cosmopolitan* have failed to persuade the steamship line in Le Havre to hold the ship for her? Didn't they realize that if she missed this final connection all might be lost? She felt abandoned, cut off, out of touch with the real world and her own feelings. Missed. Missed the boat. The man from Cook's departed. On the train, Miss Bisland threw herself onto her berth, her body aching, her nerves jangled. She lay wide awake in her clothes, unable to focus her mind on her next course of action—for she must act, and soon, to counter the setback. All she could do now was wait through the dawn for day to arrive. She watched the faint rime of clouds tinge her train window then vanish as if dispelled by a breath. Waxing poetic was perhaps a means by which she mastered her distress. Outside, the "lovely Corot-like visions—pale, shadowy, gray—(are) worth the lost sleep to have seen. Here and there a thin plume of smoke curls up against the dull frosty sky from the chimney of a thatched, lime-washed cottage set amid barns and stacks." Miss Bisland narcotized her pain with the drug of creativity. Her mind's eye delighted, as the day grew, in perceiving the peasants, like figures in a Millet painting, emerge from their cottages and walk the road, carrying bundles of branches or baskets of potatoes and turnips. Two legs and a pair of sabots appeared under a "perambulating heap of hay!" A big dog dragged a small cart full of milkcans, and a woman with a cap and tucked-up skirts, trudged along beside, "blowing on her fingers to warm them." The scene beyond Elizabeth Bisland's train window, just as had the scenes in Italy, looked familiar to her. It reminded her of pictures she had viewed and books she had read, in which "the little details of daily life" were reproduced with vivid realism.

Elizabeth Bisland stayed on the train through to Calais, arriving there at 10 a.m. that same morning. The English Channel boat for Dover had left and she would have to wait for the next one. But that at least gave her time for a bath and breakfast. She must have continued to brood about missing the *Le Champagne*. That unfortunate occurrence was bound to cost her precious days. She was now in the unenviable position of having to scramble to make up for lost time. What Elizabeth Bisland didn't know was that she had been given erroneous information by the travel agent in Villeneuve. The captain of the *Le Champagne* had, in fact, been instructed by steamship-line officials to wait for her well past the scheduled time of departure. The ship not only waited for Miss Bisland several hours in the harbor at Le Havre, but when the ebbing of the tide made crossing the bar a necessity, it lingered outside another half-hour in the hope that she might still come. How was *Cosmopolitan* able to persuade the officials of the Compagnie Générale Transatlantique to lay over the *Le Champagne* for several hours to the inconvenience of the other passengers? Why would a steamship wait several hours for a woman? What was John Brisben Walker's ultimate weapon? The whole affair smacked of bribery. But more disturbing is the role played by the travel agent. Was he, too, tampered with? And if so, by whom? Why, if he was from Cook's, would he give Elizabeth Bisland erroneous information? Did he knowingly and willfully mislead her? Or was he an unwitting accomplice, passing on to her information that was either false or the result of miscommunication but that he believed to be true? Who told him that the *Le Champagne* would not wait for her? And if he was lying to her, who prevailed upon him to do so? Who got to him? After all, if the man was working in cooperation with *Cosmopolitan*, wouldn't he have rushed Miss Bisland on to Le Havre and tried to get her on the ship? There was still time.

All Elizabeth Bisland knew on that cold morning of January 17, 1890 was that the vessel would leave without her. She took everything the man from Cook's told her —if indeed he was from Cook's—at face value. Skepticism was not her strong suit, as a writer of feature stories or what hardened journalists disdain as "soft news." If Nellie Bly had been in Elizabeth Bisland's situation, would she have detected something odd and pressed for clarification?

Miss Bisland believed the travel agent when he told her that the ship would not wait for her past its scheduled departure time. She believed him when he told her that her train was now so far behind time there was no way it could make Le Havre by 7 a.m. Why didn't she tell him that he could be wrong and that she would take her chances and go through to Le Havre? Would Nellie Bly have stopped at nothing to catch that boat? Elizabeth Bisland gave up on the *Le Champagne*. She did not switch at Villeneuve for travel through Paris to Le Havre. Instead she stayed on the train through to Calais. She felt cheated. She was on the verge of nervous collapse; she would have to hustle now to make up for lost time, and she was not sure she was up to it. But there was a hope to cling to—the back-up or contingency plan that *Cosmopolitan*'s business manager A.D. Wilson had arranged for her shortly after she left New York. It provided that in the event she missed the connection at Le Havre she would go on to Southampton, England, and would—the next day—sail home from there. Had her bosses foreseen that she might miss the *Le Champagne*? Hers was not to reason why! Tomorrow was January 18th; she would be sixty-five days out of New York and still WELL AHEAD—FOUR DAYS—OF HER PLANNED SCHEDULE! Through the haze of pain and confusion and anxiety she discerned that she COULD STILL WIN! For if she caught the North-German Lloyd steamer at Southampton and the Atlantic passage went as hoped, she would reach New York on January 25th—or three days before Nellie Bly expected to arrive there!

When the train rumbled into Calais and Elizabeth Bisland found that she had missed the Channel boat to Dover and would have to wait for the next one, she tried to calm her nerves by focusing on Southampton. Imagine her consternation when she got to England and was told that her ship out of that port had been suddenly "withdrawn" and would not sail until late in the week. Withdrawn! Miss Bisland had double reason now to feel defrauded. She became as one possessed; she was, in fact, to damned near kill herself to beat Nellie Bly. It was not until she got home that she learned she had been given false information at Villeneuve.

CHAPTER TWENTY-ONE

NELLIE BLY AND THE CLEVER JAPANESE

A number of the friends Nellie Bly had made in British China came down to the *S.S. Oceanic* to say farewell. They had been very kind to her and she regretted having to take leave of them. Together with Captain Smith in his cabin, they touched glasses and wished one another success and happiness. Most certainly, they, like Jules Verne—although Nellie does not mention it—toasted the success of her race around the world.

There was quite a story behind the ship that would take Nellie Bly to Yokohama, Japan, then across the Pacific to San Francisco. The Occidental and Oriental steamship line's *Oceanic*, upon which she now placed her hopes for a safe and speedy voyage, was no ordinary vessel. She reported:

> When it was designed and launched twenty years ago by Mr. Harland of Belfast, it startled the shipping world. The designer was the first to introduce improvements for the comfort of passengers, such as the saloon amidships, avoiding the noise of the engines and especially the racing of the screw in rough weather. Before that time ships were gloomy and sombre in appearance and constructed without a thought to the happiness of the passengers. Harland, in the *Oceanic*, was the first to provide a promenade deck and to give the saloon and staterooms a light and cheerful appearance. In fact, the *Oceanic* was such a departure that it aroused the jealousy of other ship companies, and was actually condemned by them as unseaworthy. It is said that so great was the outcry against the ship that sailors and firemen were given extra prices to induce them to make the first trip.

Nellie's description suggests that the evolution of the steamship *Oceanic* was free of difficulties and setbacks. She failed to mention that on its maiden voyage, in 1871, from Liverpool to New York via Queenstown, the ship encountered machinery trouble and had to be returned for repairs...or that a year later, it was returned to Belfast for alterations that included the addition of two boilers and a turtle-backed fo'c'sle, an enlargement of bunker (fuel storage) capacity, and shortening of the masts. Nellie went on puffing:

> Instead of being the predicted failure, the *Oceanic* proved a great success. She became the greyhound of the Atlantic, afterwards being transferred to the Pacific in 1875. She is the favorite of the O. and O. line, making her voyages with speed and regularity. She retains a look of positive newness and seems to grow younger with years.

In 1875, the *Oceanic* departed from Liverpool and voyaged eastward to Hong Kong and thence across the Pacific to San Francisco. This shift to the Orient was marked by a major accomplishment—the Hong Kong-to-San Francisco leg of the journey was achieved in the record time of twenty-five days. What Nellie Bly did not know was that the development of the *Oceanic* was a trial-and-error process. In 1879, the vessel was returned to Liverpool for modernization and new boilers, and on August 22, 1882, it collided off Lime Point, Golden Gate, with the American coastal steamer *City of Chester*, as the result of which accident the latter sank with a loss of fifteen lives. On November 11, 1889, three days before Nellie set out on her trip around the world, the *Oceanic* recouped its reputation, arriving in San Francisco after a record voyage of thirteen days, fourteen hours, and six minutes from Yokohama. As Nellie Bly put it:

> In November, 1889, she made the fastest trip on record between Yokohama and San Francisco. No expense is spared to make this ship comfortable for the passengers. The catering would be hard to excel by even a first-class hotel. Passengers are accorded every liberty, and the officers do their utmost to make their guests feel at home, so that in the Orient the *Oceanic* is the very favorite ship, and people wait for months so as to travel on her.

Nellie wound down from the tensions of her stay in British China. "What children we all become aboard a ship!" she reported. She swapped laughs and stories with her fellow passengers in the Social Hall, listened to the Captain grind out music on his organette, dined on oysters with punch and champagne—a rare treat which the purser had prepared in America just for this occasion. She participated in an uproarious word game and in a chorus that sang a song whose lyrics consisted of but one line, "Sweetly sings the donkey when he goes to grass—Sweetly sings the donkey when he goes to grass, Ee-ho! Ee-ho! Ee-ho!" Nellie was probably the life of the party.

When eight bells rang (it was now 7 a.m., December 31st, in New York), they all rose and sang *Auld Lang Syne* with glass in hand, toasting the death of the old year and the birth of the new. Nellie Bly reported:

> We shook hands around, each wishing the other a Happy New Year. 1889 was ended, and 1890 with its pleasures and pains began. Shortly after, the women passengers retired. I went to sleep lulled by the familiar negro melodies sung by the men in the smoking-room beneath my cabin.

Among the songs, surely, was the popular Stephen Foster spiritual, "Nellie Bly."

It should be noted at this point that Nellie's monkey (purchased in Singapore), too, celebrated the New Year aboard the *Oceanic*. He had been transferred from the *Oriental* and when Nellie asked the stewardess how the monkey was, she replied dryly:

"We have met." She had her arm bandaged from the wrist to the shoulder!

"What did you do?" Nellie asked in alarm.

"I did nothing but scream; the monkey did the rest," the stewardess replied.

Nellie's monkey was to play a meaningful role when the *Oceanic* bound for San Francisco ran into storms and headwinds on the Pacific.

* * *

Just as the travel agent Harmon predicted she would be, Nellie Bly was delayed five days in Japan. But she was in a reportorial groove now; her stay in Nippon was every bit as productive as the one in British China had been. Like Elizabeth Bisland before her, she went ashore in the busy harbor of Yokohama, a city in existence only since 1859 when Japan opened a few ports to foreign trade. Like Miss Bisland, Nellie stayed at the comfortable Grand Hotel, and like her was delighted by the Country of the Chrysanthemums:

> If I loved and married, I would say to my mate: "Come, I know where Eden is," and like Edwin Arnold, desert the land of my birth for Japan, the land of love — beauty—poetry—cleanliness. I somehow always connected Japan and its people with China and its people, believing the one no improvement on the other. I could not have made a greater mistake. Japan is beautiful.

Sir Edwin Arnold (1832—1904), English poet, scholar, and inveterate traveler, was famous in Nellie Bly's day for his *The Light of Asia*, an epic poem on the life and teachings of Buddha. Nellie, however, unlike Elizabeth Bisland, was not prone to literary allusions. And while both women fell in love with Japan, they viewed it through contrasting lenses. Miss Bisland's reaction to the country was scholarly, lyrical, romantic, whereas Nellie's was practical, down-to-earth, realistic. Miss Bisland saw the Japanese as children living in a fairyland; Nellie Bly, as adults coping with social and economic change. Nellie was familiar with the history: The arrival of U.S. Naval Commodore Matthew Perry and his "black ships" in 1853 on a trade-opening mission shocked the Japanese into a new awareness. His show of American power included a scale-model locomotive, a telegraph set, and cannon and revolvers which, they realized, would demolish their elegant armor and Samurai swords. Nearly three hundred years of isolation from foreign contact ended with the fear that unless Japan accommodated to Western technology and weaponry it would be destroyed. Other countries in Asia—Java, Vietnam, even China (the mother of civilizations)—were yielding to the march of Western progress. Insecure about their "proper place" among the nations of the Far East, the Japanese initiated what came to be known as the Meiji or "Enlightenment" era (1868—1911), during which the nation miraculously transformed itself from a feudal society into a modern industrial state. The Meiji leaders, paradoxically, sought to avoid foreign domination by adopting foreign techniques. They dispatched Japanese scholars around the world to study Western cultures; they welcomed American missionaries and encouraged them to Christianize the country; they invited in foreign experts—the English to advise on the navy, the French on the army, the Dutch on construction, and the Germans on medicine. When Elizabeth Bisland and Nellie Bly set foot in Japan, the nation already had its own Constitution, a parliament, and a court system modeled after the European. But the nation still retained the autocratic system developed by the shoguns during the Tokugawa dynasty (1603—1867). The secret of Japan's remarkable growth lay then—as it has in recent decades —not only in incorporating foreign technology but in adhering to Japanese values from the time of the shoguns: Energy, efficiency, skill, patriotism, devotion, group loyalty. Nellie Bly and Elizabeth Bisland both admired the character of the Japanese; where they differed was in their regard for the Japanese as human beings. Miss Bisland indulged them as children ("The very faults of the Japanese are such as are misdemeanors in adults but quite forgivable in children."); Nellie Bly perceived them as adults who adjusted shrewdly to their situation as citizens of a proud nation dependent upon Western know-how:

> The Japanese are very progressive people. They cling to their religion and their modes of life which in many ways are superior to ours, but they readily adopt any trade or habit that is an improvement upon their own. Finding the European male attire more serviceable than their native dress for some trades they promptly adopted it. The women tested the European dress, and finding it barbarously uncomfortable and inartistic went back to their underwear, which they found more comfortable than the absence of it, to which they had been accustomed. The best proof of the comfort of kimonos lies in the fact that the European residents have adopted them entirely for indoor wear. Only their long subjection to fashion prevents their wearing them in public.

Nellie Bly was greatly impressed by the intelligence and resourcefulness of the Japanese. Her analysis of them reads as if it were written yesterday; what she described foreshadows, uncannily, the tendencies that after World War II enabled

Japan to compete so successfully with the United States in trade, industry, and world markets. She affirmed:

Japanese patriotism should serve as a model for us careless Americans. No foreigner can go to Japan and monopolize a trade. It is true that a little while ago they were totally ignorant of modern conveniences. They knew nothing of railroads, or street cars, or engines, or electric lighting. They were too clever though to waste their wits in efforts to rediscover inventions known to other nations, but they had to have them. Straightway they sent to other countries for men who understood the secret of such things, and at fabulous prices and under contracts of three, five, and occasionally ten years duration, brought them to their land. They were set to work, the work they had been hired to do, and with them toiled steadily and watchfully the cleverest of Japanese. When the contract is up it is no longer necessary to fill the coffers of a foreigner. The employe was released, and their own man, fully qualified for the work, stepped into the position. And so in this way they command all business in their country.

Far from being elfin children, the Japanese were ingenious protectors of their national identity, holding the foreigner in check while taking from him the best he had to offer. In the same vein, during the late twentieth century, while Japan borrowed freely from American technology, it erected powerful barriers against goods from America. For Nellie Bly, the key word about the Japanese was "clever"; the Japanese men she met during her five days in Japan were, she reported, "far from prepossessing" but they had "the reputation of being very clever." The Japanese women, on the other hand, she found to be sweet and charming. Nellie was fascinated by the *geisha* girls about whom she had heard and read so much and whose performance she now eagerly awaited:

In the tiny maidens glided at last, clad in exquisite trailing, angel-sleeved kimonos. The girls bow gracefully, bending down until their heads touch their knees, then kneeling before us murmur gently a greeting which sounds like *"Kombanwa!"* drawing in their breath with a long, hissing suction, which is a token of great honor.

207

The musicians sat down on the floor and began an alarming din upon *samisens*, drums and gongs, singing meanwhile through their pretty noses. If the noses were not so pretty I am sure the music would be unbearable to one who has ever heard a chest note.

The *geishas* evoked in Nellie Bly a warmth that must have made the inhumanity in Canton seem even more terrible. Her depiction of them and their art was replete with endearing touches:

They are very short with the slenderest of slender waists. Their soft and tender eyes are made blacker by painted lashes and brows; their midnight hair, stiffened with a gummy wash, is most wonderfully dressed in large coils and ornamented with gold and silver flowers and gilt paper pom-poms. The younger the girl the more gay is her hair. Their kimonos, of the most exquisite material, trail all around them, and are loosely held together at the waist with an obi-sash; their long flowing sleeves fall back, showing their dimpled arms and baby hands. When they go out they wear wooden sandals.

The Japanese were the only women, Nellie asserted, who could rouge and powder without making themselves appear repulsive; they had a way of reddening their underlip at the tip that made their lips look like "two luxurious cherries." So it was with the *geishas*. Nellie Bly, entranced, watched them perform:

The musicians begin a long chanting strain, and these bits of beauty begin the dance. With a grace simply enchanting, they twirl their little fans, sway their dainty bodies in a hundred different poses, each one more intoxicating than the other, all the while looking so childish and shy, with an innocent smile lurking about their lips, dimpling their soft cheeks, and their black eyes twinkling with the pleasure of the dance.

The *geishas*, apparently, picked up in Nellie Bly a kindred spirit—someone who appreciated their artistry and knew how much went into achieving it. Afterwards, they came over to her. Nellie reported:

After the dance, the *geisha* girls made friends with me, examining, with surprised delight, my dress, my bracelets, my rings, my boots—to them the most wonderful and extraordinary things—my hair, my gloves, indeed they missed very little, and they approved. They said I was very sweet, and urged me to come again, and in honor of the custom of my land—the Japanese never kiss—they pressed their soft, pouting lips to mine in parting.

Geishas nowadays are members of a vanishing breed. They are highly specialized professional entertainers tipped exorbitantly by important Japanese businessmen and politicians to sing and dance for them, serve them drinks with consummate etiquette, and remain the essence of discretion regarding what they overhear. As they grow older, they may get married or become the mistress of a *geisha* establishment, but many—particularly those in the big cities—are not that fortunate. They are condemned to a life of soiling bondage unless some wealthy patron buys them out.

As a *gaijin* (foreigner) visiting Japan, Nellie Bly was attracted to pretty much the same things as today's tourist, for New Japan clings to the old customs and traditions. Japanese women still wear the kimono, though it is expensive (it may cost as many as ten thousand American dollars) and much more uncomfortable than Nellie reported (putting on the multi-layered kimono cannot be done without help, and women take special courses in the art). The wide-sleeved robes of the Japanese women fascinated Nellie in that January of 1890:

On a cold day one would imagine the Japanese were a nation of armless people. They fold their arms up in their long loose sleeves. A Japanese woman's sleeves are to her what a boy's pockets are to him. Her cards, money, combs, hair pins, ornaments, and rice paper are carried in her sleeves. Her rice paper is her handkerchief and she notes with horror and disgust that after using we return our handkerchief to our pockets. I think the Japanese women carry everything in their sleeves, even their hearts. Not that they are fickle—none are more true, more devoted, more loyal, more constant, than

209

Japanese women—but they are so guileless and artless that almost anyone, if opportunity offers, can pick at their trusting hearts.

Fourteen years later, an Italian opera with a Japanese setting echoed Nellie Bly's sentiments. Gay and affectionate Cho-Cho-San, the heroine of Giacomo Puccini's *Madama Butterfly*, with whom U.S. Naval Lieutenant Pinkerton contracted a temporary "Japanese marriage," believed that their union was a permanent one. Trustingly, she cut herself off from her religion and her people, only to see him recalled to America and later return with an American wife. Heartbroken but brave, she agreed to give her child into Mrs. Pinkerton's care, then, upon the latter's departure, killed herself with her father's sword.

If Nellie was charmed by what the Japanese women wore, she regarded the native dress of the men as comical:

Their legs are small and their trousers are skin-tight. The upper garment, with its great wide sleeves, is as loose as the lower is tight. When they finish their "get up" by placing their dish-pan shaped hat upon their heads, the wonder grows how such small legs can carry it all! Stick two straws in one end of a potato, a mushroom in the other, set it up on the straws and you have a Japanese in outline. Talk about French heels! The Japanese sandal is a small board elevated on two pieces of thin wood fully five inches in height. They make the people look exactly as if they were on stilts. These queer shoes are fastened to the foot by a single strap running between toes one and two, the wearer when walking necessarily maintaining a sliding instead of an up and down movement, in order to keep the shoe on.

Japanese footgear nowadays may be divided roughly into two classes—that for outdoor wear, and that for easy indoor wear. What Nellie Bly described was the *geta* or wooden clog; worn in rainy weather, it raises the feet well above the muddy ground. (The *geta* comes in many different styles and colors— some lacquered, some their tops covered with finely plaited rushes, and the thongs of velvet, silk brocade, cotton or velveteen.) The sandal-like *zori*, composed of straw and reeds, is made for wear inside and outside the house, but never on

210

the soft surface of the *tatami* or the thick straw mats which cover the floor of rooms. The *tatami* were the only "furniture," as Nellie Bly discovered to her amusement when she visited the house of the *geisha* girls:

At the door we saw all the wooden shoes of the household, and we were asked to take off our shoes before entering, a proceeding rather disliked by some of the party, who refused absolutely to do as requested. We effected a compromise, however, by putting cloth slippers over our shoes. The second floor had been converted into one room, with nothing in it except the matting covering the floor and a Japanese screen here and there. We sat upon the floor, for chairs there are none in Japan, but the exquisite matting is padded until it is soft as velvet. It was laughable to see us trying to sit down, and yet more so to see us endeavor to find a posture of ease for our limbs. We were about as graceful as an elephant dancing.

The difficulty that the sitting Nellie Bly experienced confronts the visitor to Japan to this day. The universality of her observations is confirmed by *Baedaker's Tokyo* (1987):

It is only in comparatively recent times that chairs were introduced into Japan. In *ryokans*, at home and in restaurants people still sit on the floor on many occasions; the typical sitting position generally stops the flow of blood in Westerners' limbs. After they have ventured out to visit a restaurant foreigners (Gaijin) are frequently to be seen hobbling along the streets of Tokyo. They have to keep their limbs moving for a long time before they can walk normally. The little cushions that are spread out for guests are really no help at all.

The *ryokan* or traditional Japanese-style inn is usually a one-or-two-story small wooden structure with a garden or scenic view. Nellie Bly does not mention a *ryokan* but she must have stayed in one, or as guest in a home very much like one. She reported:

The Japanese homes form a great contrast to the European bungalows. They are daintily small, like play houses indeed, built of a thin shingle-like board, fine in texture. The first wall is set back, allowing the upper floor and side walls to extend over the lower flooring, making it a portico built in, instead of on the house. Light window frames, with their minute openings covered with fine rice paper instead of glass, are the doors and windows in one. They do not swing open and shut as do our doors, nor do they move up and down like our windows, but slide like rolling doors. They form the partitions of the houses inside and can be removed at any time, throwing the floor into one room.

Nellie may well have sampled the refined but Spartan living of the *ryokan* and, like the Japanese, slept on a *tatami* mat in a room devoid of furniture—after having taken a long hot bath, donned a *yukata* or simple cotton kimono, and been served a cup of green tea in her room. She may have even rested her head on a wooden pillow, for she reported as follows on the Japanese women:

> Their bed is a piece of matting, their pillows, narrow blocks of wood, probably six inches in length, two wide and six high. They rest the back of the neck on the velvet covered top, so their wonderful hair remains dressed for weeks at a time. Their tea and pipe always stand beside them, so they can partake of their comforts the last thing before sleep and the first thing after.

There had to have been moments during her trip when Nellie Bly wondered whether anybody knew or cared who she was and why she was traveling around the world. But her public image continued to catch up with her: A Japanese reporter from Tokyo came to Yokohama to interview her, his newspaper having translated and published her story of her visit to Jules Verne. Japanese journalists obviously lacked the aggressiveness of their American counterparts:

> Carefully he read the questions which he wished to ask me. They were written at intervals on long rolls of foolscap, the space to be filled in as I answered. I thought it ridiculous until I returned home and became an interviewee. Then I would conclude it would be humane for us to adopt the Japanese system of interviewing.

Nellie was to visit Tokyo and spend a day there, but first she went to Kamakura (thirty-one miles south of the capital city, on the Bay of Sagami) to see Daibutsu, the one-hundred-ton, forty-foot-tall bronze statue of the Great Buddha. Thirteen years later, in 1903, Lafcadio Hearn, one of the first foreigners to respect Japanese art, would write that visitors absolutely must not miss seeing this majestic sculpture. Although Nellie Bly must have been impressed by the smiling serenity of the great god sitting cross-legged in his flowing robes, hands touching in his lap to symbolize constancy in faith, she contented herself with cataloguing his dimensions:

...it is sitting Japanese style, ninety-eight feet being its waist circumference; the face is eight feet long, the eye is four feet, the ear is six feet, six and one-half inches, the nose three feet, two and one-half inches, the diameter of the lap is thirty-six feet, and the circumference of the thumbs is over three feet. I had my photograph taken sitting on its thumb with two friends, one of whom offered $50,000 for the god.

To compound their impiety (although it should be noted that many tourists, including the Japanese, do the same nowadays), Nellie Bly and her companions walked inside the Great Buddha to examine its innards. Here, Nellie reported, human beings were once offered up to him:

Years ago at the feast of the god, sacrifices were made to Daibutsu. Quite frequently the hollow interior would be heated to a white heat, and hundreds of victims were cast into the seething furnace in honor of the god. It is different now, sacrifice being no longer the custom, and the hollow interior is harmlessly fitted up with tiny altars and a ladder stairway by which visitors can climb up into Daibutsu's eye, and from that height view the surrounding lovely country.

However barbarous those ancient Buddhists might have been (Buddhism first entered Japan in 552 A.D.), they bequeathed to the Japanese civilization the exquisite refinement of the *Cha-no-yu* or tea ceremony. Nellie Bly partook in one, spending some time in a delightful tea-house where two little Japanese girls served her in this time-honored ritual which demanded of them a meticulous poise, courtesy, and precision and whose function was to induce a state of composure and tranquility. Nellie must have drunk from crockery ware that appeared crude but was valued at thousands of yen. She must, as well, have participated in either the thick-tea ceremony called *Koi-cha* (the tea is made of powdered green tea-leaves and has the consistency of pea soup) or the less formal *Usu-cha* (mild and fragrant green tea is made with lukewarm water, and the bowl refreshed each time, after having been rinsed out with water). Nellie must, finally, have enjoyed immensely the nuances of the tea-house observance, for while her view of the Japanese was more realistic than Elizabeth Bisland's, for her as well as for Miss Bisland, Japan was a series of fleeting, delicate impressions:

> The prettiest sight in Japan, I think, is the native streets in the afternoons. Men, women, and children turn out to play shuttle-cock and fly kites. Can you imagine what an enchanting sight it is to see pretty women with cherry lips, black bright eyes, ornamented, glistening hair, exquisitely graceful gowns, tidy white-stockinged feet thrust into wooden sandals, dimpled cheeks, dimpled arms, dimpled baby hands, lovely, innocent, artless, happy, playing shuttle-cock in the streets of Yokohama?

Nellie Bly's sojourn in Tokyo introduced her to big-city ways in Japan. "The people in Tokyo are trying to ape the style of the Europeans," she reported. She saw a street-car line ("a novelty in the East"), carriages of all descriptions, and several men in native costumes riding bicycles. The effort to imitate European dress produced, to Nellie's Western mind, some strange effects:

> The European clothing sent to Japan is at least ready-made, if not second hand. One woman I saw was considered very stylish. The bodice of a European dress she wore had been cut to fit a slender, tapering waist. The Japanese never saw a corset and their waists are enormous. The woman was able to fasten one button at the neck and from that point the bodice was permitted to spread. She was considered very swell. At dinner one night I saw a "Jap" woman in a low cut evening dress,

214

with nothing but white socks on her feet.

Like Elizabeth Bisland before her, Nellie Bly rode past the Mikado's Japanese and European castles, which were enclosed by a fifty-foot stone wall and three wide moats. And like her, Nellie visited the great Shiba temple—but there the similarities cease. For while Miss Bisland's description of the shrine to the shogun king Ieymitsu was ornate and reverential, Nellie's was sparse, mocking, disrespectful:

> At the carved gate leading to the temple were hundreds of stone and bronze lanterns, which alone were worth a fortune. On either side of the gate were gigantic carved images of ferocious aspect. They were covered with wads of chewed paper. When I remarked that the school children must make very free with the images, a gentleman explained that the Japanese believed if they chewed paper and threw it at these gods, and it stuck, their prayers would be answered, if not, their prayers would pass unheeded. A great many prayers must have been answered. At another gate I saw the most disreputable-looking god. It had no nose. The Japanese believe if they have a pain or ache and they rub their hands over the face of that god, and then where the pain is located, they will straightway be cured. I can't say whether it cured them or not, but I know they rubbed away the nose of the god.

As elsewhere in Japan of 1890, Tokyo was, Nellie Bly reported, a place where girls were taught not only English in the schools but deportment—how to serve tea and sweets gracefully, how to receive, entertain, and part with visitors, and how to use chopsticks:

> It is a pretty sight to see a lovely woman use chopsticks. At a tea-house or at an ordinary dinner a long paper laid at one's place contains a pair of chopsticks, probably twelve inches in length, but no thicker than the thinner size of lead pencils. The sticks are usually whittled in one piece and split only half apart to prove that they have never been used. Everyone breaks the sticks apart before eating, and after the meal they are destroyed.

Japan was also a place where clothing was sewn with what Americans called the basting stitch ("but it is as durable as if sewed with the smallest of stitches")...where the women regarded their charms in round, highly polished steel plates and knew nothing of glass mirrors...where children at play always looked happy and never seemed to quarrel or cry...where the people were "not only pretty and artistic but obliging," ever cooperative when a tourist asked to snap their picture (Nellie, in her haste to depart from New York, had, much to her regret, forgotten to bring her Kodak)...and where, thoughtfully, the trade of massage bathing was taught to and reserved for the blind alone, who went through the streets "uttering to a plaintive melody these words: 'I'll give you a bath from head to toe for two cents.'"

With nothing much left to report in Tokyo, Nellie Bly, in the time-honored journalistic tradition, tried to make the best of her slow-news situation. Like Elizabeth Bisland, she visited the great park of Uyeno, but unlike Miss Bisland, she did not soulfully contemplate the view. Rather, she became intrigued with yet another monkey. This one—very large with a scarlet face and gray fur—was chained to a fence. One of the young men in Nellie's party went up and talked to him; the monkey "looked very sagacious and wise." At which point, in the little crowd that had gathered round but quite out of the simian's reach, a young Japanese, in a spirit of mischief, tossed a pebble at "the red-faced mystery, who turned with a grieved and inquiring air to my friend."

"Go for him," Nellie's friend urged, responding sympathetically to the look, and the monkey strove with all his might to do so. The Japanese withdrew; the monkey quieted down, gazing expressively at the spot where his tormentor had stood, then at Nellie's friend "for approval, which he obtained." Nellie watched the keeper give the monkey his dinner, which consisted of two large boiled potatoes; her friend broke one in two and the monkey "greedily ate the inside, placing the remainder with the other potato on the fence between his feet." If the action had stopped there, the incident would have possessed no human interest, but stories have a way of fulfilling their potential when a reporter is inquisitive. With an understanding eye, Nellie described what happened next:

Suddenly he looked up, and as quick as a flash he flung, with his entire force, which was something terrific, the remaining potato at the head of someone in the crowd. There was some loud screaming amid a scattering, but the potato missing all heads, went crashing with such force against a board fence that every particle of it remained sticking there in one shapeless splotch. The Jap who had tossed the pebble at the monkey and so earned his enmity, quietly shrunk away with a whitened face. He had returned unnoticed by all except for the monkey, who tried to revenge himself with the potato. I admired the monkey's cleverness so much that I would have tried to buy him if I had not already owned one.

Nellie Bly concluded her account of the Japanese experience by tossing off a rather grisly anecdote involving the native method of cremation—as told to her by an American resident of Japan who had witnessed one such form of burial. In terse, unrelenting detail, she reported, among other things, that as soon as the breath left the body, it was undressed, doubled up (head to feet), and fitted into a small, expensive box which was carried on two poles through the streets to the place of cremation...that when the box was heated over a fire in a pit, the body straightened out, the lower half being soon cremated (except for the feet and knee-joints), the upper half being pulled over the fire, and with the same large fork the half-consumed feet and knee-joints then being put under the arms. "In less than an hour," Nellie relayed to her readers, "all that remained of the body were a few ashes in the bottom of the pit." As a final touch of the macabre, she reported the hospitality of the cremator, who invited the American to his neat little home to dine with his pretty and charming daughters and who "jumped into a boiling bath in the open garden, from which he emerged later red as a lobster" then toweled his naked body while he talked to them and watched them eat.

Back in Yokohama, Nellie Bly visited the Hundred Steps, at the top of which lived "a Japanese belle, Oyuchisan, who is the theme for artist and poet, and the admiration of tourists." She ate rice and eel; she browsed in the curio shops and was charmed by the art therein; she was feted by United States dignitaries with a luncheon aboard the *U.S.S. Omaha*.

On the bright sunny morning of January 7th, Nellie Bly left Yokohama. She had made new friends in Japan, and a number of them in launches escorted her to the *Oceanic*. Nellie described the scene:

> ...and when we hoisted anchor the steam launches blew loud blasts upon their whistles in farewell to me, and the band upon the *Omaha* played "Home, Sweet Home," "Hail Columbia," and "The Girl I Left Behind Me," in my honor; and I waved my handkerchief so long after they were out of sight that my arms were sore for days. My feverish eagerness to be off again on my race around the world was strongly mingled with regret at leaving such charming friends and such a lovely land.

Nellie Bly had been out of New York fifty-four days now. She must travel the remaining eight-thousand miles in twenty-one days—to keep her promise to encircle the globe in seventy-five days. She must do even better than that—if the Other Woman was ahead of her.

CHAPTER TWENTY-TWO

FLIGHT TO OBSCURITY

Elizabeth Bisland had meant to stay overnight in London, and take the North-German Lloyd steamer out of Southampton the next day. But the unexplained withdrawal of that ship forced a change in her plans. Her one chance now was the night mail train to Holyhead (off the west coast of Wales) and to catch the *S.S. Bothnia*, which was scheduled to touch at Queenstown, Ireland, next morning. It was now the evening of January 18th; she had not slept since the day before, nor eaten since the breakfast yesterday morning in Calais.

For two months now, Miss Bisland had been traveling a globe on which the English tongue, laws, customs, and manners reigned from sea to sea, and when she set foot on the tiny island from which had sprung, in Shakespeare's words, "this race of kings," her soul filled with what she described as a "passion of pride that, I, too, am an Anglo-Saxon." In her veins, too, ran the blood of "this clean, fair, noble English race!" It was worth a journey round the world, she reported, to see "this royal throne of kings, this sceptred isle...this other Eden, demi-paradise...this happy breed of men." But now in London, the fabled seat of the mighty, far-flung empire, she felt her courage nearly at an end. Friends rushed to her aid;— the exhausted Miss Bisland was helpless to fend for herself:

> One of my fellow-travellers, who has been most kind to me all the way from Ceylon, comes to my rescue and assumes all responsibilities. I am sent off to the hotel to dine in company with two kind and charming fellow-voyagers, a Sir William Lewis and his daughter, while he arranges my difficulties. I am far too tired and disturbed, however, to eat, and can only crumble my bread and taste my wine. At half-past eight my friend appears and carries me off to the Euston Station. He has snatched his dinner, got rid of the dust of travel, and into evening clothes. He has brought rugs and cushions that I may have some rest during the night, a little cake in case I

grow hungry, and heaps of books and papers. My foot-warmer is filled with hot water, the guard is induced to give me his best care and attention, and then I go away alone again, somewhat comforted by the chivalrous goodness of the travelling man to the uncared-for woman.

Elizabeth Bisland's trials were only just beginning. The train thundered through a raging storm toward Holyhead more than two-hundred miles away. She tried to read the books but the words kept dancing up and down the page. The guard came in now and then to see if she needed anything. Deep in the black, howling night, the train reached Holyhead, a Welsh port on Holy Island from which ferries departed across the Irish Sea to Ireland. The town and island bore many evidences of Celtic, Roman, and prehistoric occupation (including Bronze Age "fertility" stones), but that was of no concern to the cultured but desperate Miss Bisland now:

Gathering up my multitudinous belongings, I run through the rain and sleet to the little vessel quivering and straining at the pier. The night is a wild one, the wind in our teeth, and the journey rough and very tedious. The cold and tempestuous day has dawned before we touch Kingstown and are hurried—wretched for lack of sleep and the means of making a fresh toilet—into the train for Dublin. The Irish capital is still, unawake, when I rattle across it from station to station this Sunday morning, and immediately I am off again at full speed through a land swept with flying mists and showers—a beautiful land, green, even in January.

Elizabeth Bisland was now out of New York sixty-five days. She must have been kept informed by *Cosmopolitan* of the progress of her rival, and known that Nellie Bly had crossed the Atlantic in seven days and seventeen hours. If the *Bothnia* could match that performance, Miss Bisland would reach New York on January 26th—having gone around the world in an incredible record-shattering seventy-three days! Now that the race was in its climactic stages, she discerned that despite the missed connections at Le Havre and Southampton, she still stood a good chance of winning. She tried to keep in mind that her rival too had been set back by delays; the race hung in the balance now—it could go either way. The same woman who had scorned hustling around the world as a "ridiculous wild-goose chase" now longed to finish first. She knew that in the end it would all come down to a competition between a ship steaming westward on the Atlantic and trains roaring eastward across the American continent, with the weather quite possibly the determining factor. If winning had meant nothing to her, might she not have already—anywhere along the route—called it quits and resigned herself to coming in second-best? Might she not have—after she was told the *Le Champagne* would not wait for her at Le Havre, dallied a day or two in Paris and sampled the delights there, instead of going straight through to Calais? Or when she learned that the ship at Southampton would not sail until late in the week, might she not have spent a few days in London touring the city she adored and enjoying the warm hospitality of Sir William Lewis and his daughter? Elizabeth Bisland saw that she could win, but she knew that the only way she could do so was by grabbing hold of the opportunity. She felt driven now to press forward and prevail, whatever the obstacles. There was simply no quit in her. Meanwhile, all she could do was lose herself in idle fancies. From the window of her train bound for Queenstown on the southern coast, she watched the Irish peasants walking to Church and wondered how soon those sturdy young men would become "New York aldermen and mayors of Chicago," those rosy girls in their queer, bunched, provincial gowns "leaders of society in Washington and dressed by Worth." She was ravenous. There was, of course, the little spice cake her friend had given her while taking her to the Euston Station. She tried to eat, but with no liquid save a bit of brandy in a flask, she soon choked upon the cake and abandoned it. Owing to the late arrival of the Channel Boat (Miss Bisland does not say which Channel—English, North, St. George's?), her train was behind time and stopped only for the briefest moments. Time was becoming an obsession with her.

Time....Time.

Her hopes were running high. She reported:

> At noon we reach Queenstown, having curved around a fair space of water and past the beautiful city

of Cork. The ship has not yet arrived, but will doubtless be here in a few moments, the bad weather having delayed her; and my luggage is all hurried down to the tender, where I should be sent, too, did I not wail with hunger.

Queenstown (now Cobh), the chief Irish port of call for transatlantic liners, was named in honor of Queen Victoria and was the place from which the *Sirius* (in 1838) set out to become the first steamship to cross the Atlantic, in eighteen and one-half days. But the famished Miss Bisland was not much interested now in historical associations. She went in search of food:

The Queen's Hotel is not far from the station but the evil luck which has pursued me for the last few days ordains that the kitchen of this hostelry should be undergoing repairs at this particular moment, and no food is to be had. By dint of perseverance, in frantic protest and reckless objurgation, I finally secure a cup of rather cold and bitter tea and a bit of dingy bread that looks as if it had been used to scrub the floor with before being presented to me as a substitute for breakfast. I am warned to hold myself in readiness for an instantaneous summons to the tender, for when the steamer is signalled there is no time to waste. So hastily I make such toilet as is possible with my dressing-bag aboard the tender, and sit alone in the waiting room attendant on the summons.

Hour after hour went by, but no summons came. Elizabeth Bisland was afraid to leave the dreary waiting room lest the call to the tender come during her absence. She sat there "hopeless, helpless, overwhelmed with hunger, lack of sleep, and fatigue." Six o'clock that evening arrived, and her patience deserted her; she was furiously demanding more food when they brought her the long-expected notice: The ship had been signaled, and the tender must be off. Miss Bisland reported:

It rains in torrents, mingled with sleet, and the wind blows a tempest. The tender puts out from the shore and is whirled about like an eggshell. The wind drives us back, and over and over again we essay the passage before we can make head against the wild weather. It is two hours and a half later when we get alongside the ship, and I am chilled to the bone, sick and dizzy for want of food and sleep, and climb stumblingly across the narrow, slippery, plunging path that leads from one ship to the other. No sooner have I set foot on the glassy deck than the push of an impatient passenger sends me with a smashing fall into the scuppers, where I gather bruises that last a week. A compassionate stewardess comes to the rescue and puts me to bed—speechless and on the verge of tears.

The *S.S. Bothnia* put out to sea the evening of January 18th on a voyage that was to subject Elizabeth Bisland to harrowing distress. Warnings of trouble on the North Atlantic were already appearing in the New York press; the *Sun*, in an age before wireless (ship-to-shore communication was optical, via semaphore to land stations or to other vessels at sea) reported on January 14th (while Miss Bisland was on the Mediterranean):

THREE BIG LINERS LATE

Three big passenger steamships, the *Umbria* from Liverpool, *La Bourgogne* from Le Havre, and the *Elder* from Bremen, were overdue a day yesterday. This delay would hardly matter in the case of the ordinary ocean-crossing steamship but it indicates with a tolerable certainty that these three boats have run into some very nasty weather. The *Umbria*, even in winter weather, manages to get her nose into Quarantine about seven days after she leaves Queenstown.

However little knowledge Elizabeth Bisland may have possessed regarding weather conditions far out on the Atlantic, she was made to understand very quickly what she was getting into. She reported on her first few days out to sea:

The waves toss our ship back and forth among them like a football. Even were I not too miserable to move, the plunging of the vessel would make it impossible to keep one's feet. The ship laboriously climbs a howling green mountain, pauses irresolute a moment on the crest, and then toboggans madly down the farther side, her screw out of water, and kicking both heels madly in the air to the utter dislocation of one's every tooth and joint. Down, down, she goes as if boring for bottom, and when it is perfectly certain that she can never by any chance right herself she comes nose upmost with a jerk, shakes off the water, and attacks a new mountain to repeat the same performance on the other side.

Two-thirds of the passengers were terribly seasick. Although Miss Bisland had apparently developed an immunity to the malady, the recent series of hardships she had suffered made her feel just as wretched as they. The jolting news at Villeneuve, the missed connections, the frenzied race across Britain to catch the ferry at Holyhead, the fearful passage across the Irish Sea, the humiliating wait at Queenstown where she suffered unendurably from hunger and fatigue—the cumulative impact of these experiences reduced Elizabeth Bisland to a mental and physical wreck. She tried, at length, to help herself:

> It is the third or fourth day out, and I am beginning to take heart of grace and to long to leave my stuffy little cabin. The ship is rolling frightfully still, and while revolving in my mind an attempt to rise, a sudden lurch sends the heavy jug of water flying out of its basin and into the berth, where it smashed into twenty pieces upon my face and chest, and drenches me with icy water. The doors of the gangway are left open lest they freeze together, and therefore a bitter wind sweeps through the cabin, so that when hauled from my dripping bed—and it is discovered that the key of my box, where are the only dry changes of garment, is mislaid—I am stabbed through and through my wet and clinging clothes by this terrible cold.

To appreciate the dimensions of Miss Bisland's solitary ordeal one needs to see it within the context of the catastrophe that was developing on the North Atlantic in January, 1890. She had been out to sea four days when the *New York Sun* reported (dateline Queenstown, January 21):

- The steamship *Catalonia* from Boston was badly battered by a hurricane-and-snowstorms that lasted twenty hours. The seas entered the funnels and quenched seven fires, as well as flooded the cabins. A steampipe burst and exploded, killing firemen Calvin, Fear, and Jones, who were asleep in the forecastle. Several seamen and two steerage passengers were injured in the hurricane and storm.

- The *Erin*, twenty-four hours out of New York and carrying a load of cattle in pens as well as a cargo of cotton, was presumed lost. The ship, commanded by Captain Tyson, had a crew of sixty to seventy men and about fifteen cattlemen.

- The steamship *Gallia* from New York lost five of her boats, her saloon bulkheads were stove in and the staterooms flooded several feet deep. Many of the occupants of the rooms were asleep at the time and panicked at the sudden entrance of the water. A number of the seamen narrowly escaped being washed overboard, and the sea burst through the engine-room skylight and nearly swamped the machinery. Captain Murphy said that the weather was the worst he had ever experienced.

- The steamer *Deerholme*, from Liverpool to New York and being twenty-two days at sea, had her boats stove, sails split, and decks swept. She was forced to put back to Moville, Ireland.

- As of January 20th, nothing was heard from the *Servia* of the Cunard Line, which in ordinary weather would get from New York to Queenstown in seven days.

The storms on the North Atlantic were to redouble in fury over the next week. Ships ran aground or were hammered into hulks by wind and sea; sailors were injured or swept overboard; passengers told of awful hardships (including holding on with benumbed hands to the mast of a wrecked schooner while others, their strength finally exhausted, were washed away in the night.) Compounding the dangers that confronted Elizabeth Bisland was a flu epidemic that raged in America and with whose perniciousness—in those days before the influenza vaccine—physicians were virtually helpless to cope. No less an authority than the president of one of the leading U.S. medical colleges proclaimed in the January 22nd *New York Times*:

> La Grippe, the Russian influenza, is a more severe affliction than most people think. It last visited America in 1803, and it came then as now from Asia. Whatever may be the cause, it is a strong congestion of the blood vessels and mucous membranes, principally in the head and throat and nothing but strong stimulants will check the congestion and keep the blood actively circulating. For this purpose I know of nothing better than pure whiskey, and I believe Duffy's Pure Malt is the best and purest whiskey in the world.

The January 26th edition of *The Times* carried an advertisement for Ayer's Sarsaparilla headlined, "No Fear of Grippe." Such recommended remedies, however efficacious, only served to highlight the universal desperation. According to the *Sun*, New York City reported that on January 7th a record single-day number of 235 persons died of the "grip" (pneumonia, pulmonary tuberculosis, bronchitis, or influenza), and the flu continued to be very serious abroad (160 boys aboard the training ships *Exeter* and *Plymouth* suffered from it, and 398 deaths caused by it were reported in Paris for January 6th).

It was not until the *Bothnia* had been about seven days out on the Atlantic that the storm abated and Miss Bisland was able once more to stand on her feet. The woes they had shared, she reported, brought the passengers closer together, made them "sympathetic and considerate," thankful they had survived the storm, and they were even able to get up in time a concert to benefit the orphans of seamen. Their good cheer extended to playing shuffleboard for prizes on the still shaking deck. Elizabeth Bisland's underlying mood, however, was one of disappointment;—any hopes that she might cross the Atlantic without losing yet more precious time had been shattered by the elements. She would later report:

> But this crossing of the zone of storms has greatly delayed us, and it is late in the evening of the eleventh day when we take our pilot aboard. The morning of the twelfth day is cold, but evidently has some thought of clearing, and the sea is rough.

226

Twelve days; under normal weather conditions, the *Bothnia* would have done it in seven. It was January 29th—one day past John Brisben Walker's confident prediction of when she would, at the very worst, arrive back in New York. But something else must have gnawed at her: Where, at this very moment, was Nellie Bly? If only, Elizabeth Bisland must have lamented, she had caught the *Le Champagne* out of Le Havre or the North German Lloyd liner out of Southampton! She probably was not yet aware that no ship out of the storm-lashed French or British ports was reaching New York without delay. (The French steamer *La Gascogne* out of Le Havre took a more southerly course than usual but *still* arrived two days late.) Elizabeth Bisland must have felt cruelly cheated of her triumph by the agent who gave her false information at Villeneuve (an incident whose cause, she would later declare back in America, was "never ascertained.") Yet the tone with which she described her return to New York harbor was poignantly subdued, as if however anguishing her defeat, she knew that she had given her all. She was relieved to be home, albeit home later than she had wanted:

A rim of opaque film grows on the horizon that the emigrants on the forward deck regard with eager interest and hope. The passengers stand about in furs, pinched and shivering, their noses red, but their eyes full of pleased anticipation. Any land would be dear and desirable after near a fortnight of this cold and frantic sea—but when it is one's own—! The film thickens and darkens, and suddenly resolves itself into Coney Island, where, as we swiftly near the shore, the plaintive reproachful eyes of the great wooden elephant are turned upon us as if to deprecate our late coming.

The water smoothed itself into a bay, Elizabeth Bisland reported, and the emigrants gazed in wonder at "the huge gray lady" with torch uplifted, her "benignant countenance turned towards all the outer world." The sight of the Statue of Liberty filled Miss Bisland with pride in her homeland. As the *Bothnia* sailed past Staten Island, a pretty English girl who had braved the winter storms to follow her husband to a foreign country remarked that all this looked much like England. Miss Bisland described the girl as "evidently having expected log-cabins and a country town," then added:

> But I have no time to be amused at her ignorance—I
> am saying joyously to myself
> "Is this the hill, is this the kirk,
> Is this mine ain countree?"

An air of unreality surrounds Elizabeth Bisland's account of her homecoming. It gives the impression that winning the race around the world meant nothing to her, but the tone of muted regret suggests otherwise. As she neared the great city, she must have known that Nellie Bly had arrived ahead of her. No cannon boomed on the Battery to salute her; no crowds showered her with bouquets and gave her a roaring welcome, shouting "Hurrah for Bessie Bisland! She's a winner!" No dignitaries honored her with speeches and lauded her feat as epochal. The anonymity she had once so dearly cherished was now a crushing weight upon her. But she put on a happy face, smiling through the tears:

> Suddenly a great flood of familiarity washes away the memory of the strange lands and people I have seen and blots out all sense of time that has elapsed since I last saw all this. I know how everything—the streets, the houses, the passers-by—are looking at this moment. It is as if I had turned away my head for an instant, and now looked back again. My duties, my cares, my interests, which had grown dim and shadowy in these last two months, suddenly take on sharp outlines and become alive and real once more. I feel as if I had but sailed down the bay for an hour, and was now returning.
>
> The ship slides into the dock. I can see the glad faces of my friends upon the pier. My journey is done. I have been around the world in seventy-six days.

Elizabeth Bisland had done something remarkable;—she had beaten the record set by the legendary Phileas Fogg in Jules Verne's fantastical *Around the World in Eighty Days*. But in her heart of hearts she knew that the very world she had just encircled couldn't care less. *The New York Times* buried on its back pages the notice of her return.

If only....

CHAPTER TWENTY-THREE

THEY BOTH WERE WINNERS!

The officers and crew of the *Oceanic* regarded Nellie Bly as somebody special and wanted to help her make history. They knew all about her mission and were much taken with her charm and winning smile. Chief Engineer Allen, her most fervent rooter, had the following message written over the engines and throughout the engine room:

"For Nellie Bly,
We'll win or die.
January 29, 1890.

Allen counted on the *Oceanic* to cross the Pacific in thirteen days, reaching San Francisco January 20th or two days ahead of the itinerary the *New York World* had arranged for her. He and Nellie radiated confidence that the voyage across the immense ocean would be a pleasant and rapid one...the Chief Engineer's expectation of fair winds and smooth sailing was based on an averaging of weather conditions previously reported over an extended period of time for this particular season and part of the world. In those days before wireless and means by which to measure upper-atmospheric pressure, anticipating the weather could be a chancy business. During the first two days out, the 3,707-ton ocean liner made extraordinarily good time; Nellie Bly was elated. (The *Oceanic* may seem small by modern standards, but it accommodated 166 persons in first-class; 1,000 in third, and a crew of 143 persons.) Then the ship ran into a storm that raged undiminished. An anguished Nellie reported on the loyalty she inspired in the officers and crew:

> They tried to cheer me, saying it would only last that day, but the next day found it worse, and it continued, never abating a moment: head winds, head sea, wild rolling, frightful pitching, until I fretfully waited for noon when I would slip off to the dining-room to see the run, hoping that it would have gained a few miles on the day before, and always being disappointed. And

they were all so good to me! Bless them for it! They suffered more over the prospect of my failure than I did.

Nellie felt profoundly depressed. "If I fail," she would tell the officers and crew, "I will never return to New York. I would rather go in dead and successful than alive and behind time." Doubtless, she envisioned what it would be like to come home a loser—the handful of people waiting to greet her...the city going about its concerns as if she didn't exist...the look in every eye that mortified her by trying to commiserate. To Nellie Bly's mind, second-best was no better than worst.

Chief Allen tried to cheer her. "Don't talk that way, child," he would plead, "I would do anything for you in my power. I have worked the engines as they have never been worked before; I have sworn at this storm until I have no words left; I haven't prayed before for years—but I prayed that this storm may pass over and that we may get you in on time."

As ever, laughter was Nellie's defense against impending disaster. She laughed now—hysterically. "I know—that I am not—a sinner," she gasped. "Day and night—my plea has been, 'Be merciful to me a sinner,' and as the mercy has not been forthcoming—the natural conclusion is—that I am not a sinner! It's hopeless, it's hopeless!"

The purser begged her not to be discouraged; he said he would jump overboard this instant if doing so could bring her success and happiness. The jovial, good-hearted captain said he would bet his every penny that Nellie Bly arrived home in New York "at least three days ahead of time."

"Why do you try to cheat me?" Nellie moaned. "You know we are way behind time." But she longed to be deluded still further into fresh hope. The ship's doctor refused to indulge her despondency. He responded, dryly:

"Look here, Nellie Bly, if you don't stop talking so I'll make you take some pills for your liver."

"You mean wretch," Nellie upbraided, "you know I can't help being blue. It's head sea, and head winds, and low runs—not liver!"

Nellie laughed and so did they, and Chief Allen, who had been pleading with her to "smile just once, give us but a glimpse of your smile," went away content.

Meanwhile the *Oceanic* bucked the screaming winds;

lashed by torrents of rain and buffeted by mountainous seas, the vessel rolled, pitched, tossed, plunged through day after direful day. The ordeal was enough to stretch taut the nerves of the hardiest seaman. A rumor spread throughout the ship that there was a Jonah on board. Nellie Bly learned much to her dismay that the sailors on the *Oceanic* wanted to toss her monkey overboard. Monkeys, they said, were Jonahs;—they brought bad weather to ships, and as long as her monkey remained on the ship the storm would continue. Somebody asked Nellie if she would consent to the monkey's being thrown overboard to appease the wrath of the supreme powers. Nellie's own superstitious nature fought with her feelings of justice for her pet. When she spoke to Chief Allen he advised her—with gusto—not to surrender her monkey:

> He said the monkey had just gotten outside of a hundred weight of cement, and had washed it down with a quart of lamp oil, and he, for one, did not want to interfere with the monkey's happiness and digestion! Just then someone told me that ministers were Jonahs; they always brought bad weather to ships. We had two ministers on board! So I said quietly, if the ministers were thrown overboard, I'd say nothing about the monkey. Thus the monkey's life was saved.

To the sacrilegious Nellie it must have seemed a fair exchange!

The distance from Japan to San Francisco by air is close to 5,200 miles and the flight time about nine hours. For Nellie Bly on a four-masted steamship plowing the storm-racked Pacific in 1890 each day was an agonizing eternity. She filled the hours by reporting on the foibles of the crew and her fellow passengers. Chief Allen had a boy who was very clever at tricks; he was able, for example, through sleight-of-hand, to make a bottle rise into the air without his appearing to lift it. But Walter was a spiteful cuss who, shortly, sure enough, would receive his comeuppance. Nellie reported:

> One evening, when the ship was rolling frightfully, everybody was gathered in the dining-hall; an Englishman urged Walter to do some tricks, but Walter did not want to be bothered then so he said: "Yes, sir; in a moment, sir," and went on putting the things upon the

table. He had put down the mustard pot, the salt cellar, and various things, and was wiping a plate. As he went to put the plate down the ship gave a great roll, the plate knocked against the mustard pot and the mustard flew all over the Englishman, much to the horror of the others. Sitting up stiffly, the mustard dotting him from head to knees, he said sternly:

"Walter! What is this?"

"That, sir, is the first trick," Walter replied softly, and he glided silently and swiftly off to the regions of the cook.

The Shakespeare-loving Miss Bisland might have said that Walter was about to be hoist on his own petard. A sailor told him that he could hide an egg on him so that no one could find it. Walter was dubious but willingly gave the sailor a test. Nellie Bly's gift for dramatizing a funny incident and giving it a moral came into play (the sailor was, of course, in cahoots with the aggrieved Englishman):

The egg was hidden and a man called in to find it. He searched Walter all over without once coming upon the egg. The sailor suggested another trial to which Walter, now an interested and firm believer in the sailor's ability; gladly consented. The sailor opened Walter's shirt and placed the egg next to the skin in the region of his heart, carefully buttoning the shirt afterwards. The man was called in, he went up to Walter, and hit him a resounding smack where Sullivan hit Kilrain. He found the egg and so did Walter!

John L. Sullivan, the popular Boston Strongboy, knocked out Jake Kilrain at Richburg, Mississippi, on July 8, 1889, in the 75th round of what was to be the last heavyweight title fight under London Prize Ring [bareknuckle] rules.

Nellie Bly's capacity for finding human interest in ordinary daily life was tested to the utmost by the remainder of the voyage across the vast Pacific. There was more scourging in store for the *Oceanic*, but the worst of the storms was over. With no hard news to report, Nellie described the harmonizing of the Chinese sailors and the legerdemain of the Japanese waiters:

Japanese "boys" serve in the dining-hall on the *Oceanic*, but the sailors are Chinese. They chant in a musical manner when hoisting sails: It sounds as if they say "Ah-Oh-Eh-Oh! Ah-Oh-Eh-Ah-Oh!" The "boys" shake the tablecloths into a plate. They put a plate in the tablecloth which two of them shake once or twice and then slide to the floor. The plate will be seen to have gathered all the crumbs.

Nellie's sharp eye for the crochets of humanity focused now on the dining habits of an Oriental passenger:

One Chinaman and one Japanese traveled first-class coming over. The Chinaman was confined to his cabin with sea-sickness all the time, so we saw very little of him. The Japanese wore European dress and endeavored to ape the manners of the European. Evidently he thought it the custom to use tooth-picks. It is—with some people. After every meal he had a tooth-pick so that the whole table might see, as if wishing to show he was civilized! Then after a great deal of gorging he always placed the tooth-pick pen-like behind his ear.

Nellie Bly chafed in despairing silence at the day-after-day monotony of the voyage across the Pacific. As the *Oceanic* steamed toward the American continent, she doubtless brooded about the progress of the Other Woman across the face of the globe. Day after day on the seemingly boundless watery expanse, Nellie yearned for an end to the torment of Hurry-Up-And-Wait. At last it came;—the *Oceanic* arrived in San Francisco harbor January 21st or only one day later than Chief Allen and his crew in the engine room had been shooting for in Nellie's behalf. She was, however, in for a rude shock. She reported:

But even with low runs our trip was bound to come to an end. One night it was announced that the next day we would be in San Francisco. I felt a feverish excitement, and many were the speculations as to whether there would be a snow blockade to hinder my trip across the Continent. A hopefulness that had not known me for many days came back, when in rushed the purser, his face a snow-white, crying:

"My God, the bill of health was left behind in Yokohama."

"Well—well—what does that mean?" I demanded, fearing some misfortune, I knew not what.

"It means," he said, dropping nerveless into a chair, "that no one will be permitted to land until the next ship arrives from Japan. That will be two weeks."

Two weeks! Nellie Bly's alarm at hearing this gave some indication of how badly she wanted to win:

The thought of being held two weeks in sight of San Francisco, in sight of New York almost, and the goal for which I had been striving and powerless to move, maddened me.

She quietly informed the purser that she would cut her throat if she was delayed two weeks in the harbor. That spurred him to make another search; to Nellie's enormous relief, he found the report safely lodged in the desk of the ship's doctor. But she was far from being home free;—word spread that there was a smallpox case on the *Oceanic* and that everyone might have to be quarantined. Nellie's anxiety soared when the revenue officers came aboard bringing the morning newspapers and she read of an impassable snow blockage which for a week had put a stop to all railroad traffic. "My despair knew no bounds," she reported.

According to Nellie Bly, the scare about smallpox proved to be only a rumor; nevertheless, the *Oceanic* did continue to wait for the quarantine officer to come aboard and examine the passengers and crew for that highly contagious disease. Nellie's dream of success hung in dementing suspension. The questions persist to this day: Who started the rumor of smallpox? Was it concocted by John Brisben Walker's *Cosmopolitan* in a last-ditch effort to sabotage Nellie's efforts to win the race? (Such a tactic was certainly not beyond the capability of a publisher who had already sought to bribe a steamship company to alter the departure date of one of its vessels and thereby gain Elizabeth Bisland an edge.) Did Nellie Bly demand that she be put ashore? (Given her aggressiveness, it would seem likely she did.) Equally provoking became the question of by whose agency Nellie was able to get off the *Oceanic* that same morning of January 21st while all the other passengers were held aboard. In this regard she reported simply:

> While the *Oceanic* was waiting for the quarantine officer, some men came out on a tug to take me ashore. There was no time for farewells. The monkey was taken on the tug with me, and my baggage, which had been increased by gifts from friends, was thrown after me. Just as the tug steamed off, the quarantine doctor called to me that he had forgotten to examine my tongue, and I could not land until he did. I stuck it out, he called out "all right"; the others laugh, I wave farewell, and in another moment I was parted from my good friends on the *Oceanic*.

Who were the men on the tug? Had they been hired by Joseph Pulitzer's *New York World* to rescue Nellie Bly from confinement on the *Oceanic*? (A publication that spared no expense to research the countries she was to visit, printed huge maps for its readers to hang on their walls and follow her journey step by step, insisted that she send her stories on a frequent basis by costly cable, and arranged a network of steamers, pilot ships, trains, and special couriers for the conduit of her reports, was not likely to let such trifling considerations as a quarantine prevent Nellie from winning.) Even the passengers left aboard the *Oceanic*—who knew she was Destiny's Darling—colluded, cheering her blithe defiance of the health authorities. The breach of regulations was amended when she got ashore; a doctor examined her and she was passed. He, too, knew who she was, giving her his arm and escorting her out to the waiting room. Thanks to the advance build-up in the press, they all knew who she was; thousands of them jammed the wharf and greeted their stunned heroine with a roar of acclaim. "Nellie! Nellie Bly!" they screamed. "Hurrah for Nellie Bly!" Bands played; people sang "My Nellie's Blue Eyes" (despite the fact her eyes were green) and the Stephen Foster song that had given her her pen-name; the flowers she was proffered were crushed as the masses strove to touch her and shake her hand. A welcoming committee that included the Deputy Collector of the Port of San Francisco, the Inspector of Customs, the Superintendent of the Occidental and Oriental steamship line, and the West

Coast correspondent for the *World* rode with her in a blocks-long parade past the cheering throngs that lined the streets of the city. Amid the excitement, Nellie asked him:

"What about Elizabeth Bisland? Has she really beaten me?"

"Where did you ever hear such a thing?" Nellie's inquiry startled him. Then: "Wait a minute—yes, there was a woman who started out—right after you left. She had to give up and come back."

He couldn't have been more wrong! But apparently, because Nellie Bly wanted to believe him, she did believe him. She must have been thrilled to hear that the Other Woman had dropped out. (Nowhere in her account of her trip around the globe does she report this incident, but her cock-sureness of victory as she crossed the American continent suggests that the incident did occur.) Nellie was conducted to the railroad station where, to her amazement, a special train awaited her. After she had landed in San Francisco, she had no idea what was to be done with her and thought she must be somebody's guest. The special train consisted of one handsome sleeping car, the San Lorenzo, and the engine, The Queen, was one of the fastest on the Southern Pacific Railway.

"What time to do you want to reach New York, Miss Bly?" Mr. Bissell, General Passenger Agent for the Atlantic and Pacific system, asked her.

"Not later than Saturday evening," she said, never thinking they could get her there that soon.

"Very well, we will put you there on time," he said quietly. His tone and manner made Nellie rest confident he could keep his word. She delighted in the fragrance that filled her beautiful car as the crack train raced "straight as a sunbeam" across three-hundred miles of the level, green San Joaquin Valley. It stopped at Merced where she saw a great crowd of people dressed in their Sunday best gathered in the station. While Nellie Bly was already famous, she did not yet *feel* famous; when she remarked they must be having a picnic, she was told they had come there to see her. She reported:

Amazed at this information, I got up, in answer to calls for me, and went out on the back platform. A loud cheer, which almost frightened me to death, greeted my appearance and the band began to play "My Nellie's

236

Blue Eyes." A large tray of fruit and candy and nuts, the tribute of a dear little news-boy, was passed to me, for which I was more grateful than had it been the gift of a king.

For herself, Nellie felt like royalty. The train, she reported, "tore like mad" through valleys dotted with flowers and over mountains capped with snow. On—on—on! She exulted: "It was glorious! A ride worthy of a queen!"

On the special train with Nellie Bly were two other persons whose names she did not mention but who, in any case, were not making history. The three of them had nothing to do but admire the scenery, read, count telegraph poles, or pamper and pet her monkey. It was yet another episode of Hurry-Up-And-Wait, but under more relaxing circumstances than those on the stormy Pacific Ocean. She saw herself as entering the last lap; she felt reassured by Bissell's promise of success; the smoothness of the ride over the rails lulled her into a state of content:

> I felt little inclination to do anything but to sit quietly and rest, bodily and mentally. There was nothing left for me to do now. I could hurry nothing, I could change nothing; I could only sit and wait until the train landed me at the end of my journey. I enjoyed the rapid motion of the train so much that I dreaded to think of the end. At Fresno, the next station, the town turned out to do me honor, and I was the happy recipient of exquisite fruits, wines and flowers, all the product of Fresno County, California.

Quite probably, this very moment when Nellie Bly was being feted, her rival was cramped in her little cabin on the S.S. Bothnia freezing from the onslaught of bitter wind and icy water. Apparently, everybody in America believed to be true what the West Coast correspondent for the New York World told Nellie Bly—that Elizabeth Bisland had given up the race. Everybody, that is, except John Brisben Walker and Cosmopolitan. What, then, caused the widespread ignorance that Miss Bisland was still competing? As an expensive magazine of limited appeal that came out but once a month, Cosmopolitan could not hope to match the barrage of publicity given Nellie Bly by Joseph Pulitzer's two-cent daily New

York World newspaper. Still, it must have released news of Miss Bisland's trip to other periodicals. (From November, 1889 through January, 1890, the *World* and the *Sun* gave her no ink, and the only heed paid her by *The Times* was that minor story in its January 31st issue about her arrival home.) And she was certainly well known in San Francisco where the editors of William Randolph Hearst's *Examiner* received her on her out-going journey with such cordiality. Yet from the time Nellie Bly set foot again on the American continent, she was welcomed as though there was no Other Woman still racing her. Shallow, capricious Fame liked to play favorites;— while Nellie was busy gripping the imagination of the U.S. populace, Elizabeth Bisland was embroiled in her grim, lonely struggle against the elements. The men who spoke to Nellie in the Fresno railroad station were interested in her sunburned nose, the delays she had experienced, the number of miles she had traveled (over 18,500 thus far). The women "wanted to examine my one dress in which I had traveled around, the cloak and cap I had worn, and were anxious to know what was in the bag, and all about the monkey."

Not that Nellie and her special train didn't run into difficulties, but they seemed to her and others connected with her, merely inconvenient interruptions to her victorious progress. The first day, she heard the whistle shriek and the train strike something. The brakes jammed on; Nellie went out to see what had happened:

> It was hailing just then, and we saw two men coming up the track. The conductor came back to tell us that we had struck a handcar, and pointed to a piece of twisted iron and a bit of splintered board—all that remained of it, laying alongside. When the men came up, one remarked, with a mingled expression of wonder and disgust upon his face:
> "Well, you are running like h——!"
> "Thank you; I am glad to hear it," I said, and then we all laughed. I inquired if they had been hurt; they assured me not, and good humor being restored all around, we said good-bye, the engineer pulled the lever, and we were off again.

Nellie Bly's celebrity caught on like Western wildfire.

When the train stopped at another station and she appeared on the rear platform, a man from the outskirts of the crowd yelled, "Nellie Bly, you must touch my hand!" He pushed forward, all excited. Anything to please the fellow, she reached over and touched his hand, and then he shouted: "Now you will be successful! I have in my hand the left hind foot of a rabbit!"

She could not vouch, Nellie reported, for the powers of the left hind foot of a rabbit; all she knew was that no sooner had her train safely crossed a bridge which was held in place by jackscrews, the span collapsed under the weight and fell.

Nellie Bly basked in the adulation of her fans, who yearned to share in her stardom and become her familiar. One place where another large crowd greeted her, a man cried, "Did you ride an elephant, Nellie?" and when she said she had not, he lowered his head and walked away. At another place, the police fought to keep the crowd back:

> ...everybody was wanting to shake hands with me, but at least one officer was shoved aside, and the other seeing the fate of his comrade, turned to me, saying: "I guess I'll give up and take a shake," and while reaching for my hand was swept on with the crowd. I leaned over the platform and shook hands with both hands at every station, and when the train pulled out crowds would run after, grabbing for my hands as long as they could. My arms ached for almost a month afterwards, but I did not mind the ache if by such little acts I would give pleasure to my own, whom I was so glad to be among once more.

Nellie Bly had become—almost overnight, it must have seemed to her—a symbol of the promise of young, questing America. As her train sped through the deserts of Arizona and New Mexico, Indians waved to Nellie from their ponies; ranchers came from hundreds of miles away to catch a glimpse of her in Colorado. By the time she reached Kansas, she was a living legend. "Come out here," a man told her, "and we'll elect you governor." Nellie believed they would have done it, judging from the welcomes they gave her. Telegrams addressed merely to "Nellie Bly, Nellie Bly's Special Train" and filled with words of cheer and praise poured in upon her day and night from all parts of the country. Over ten thousand people greeted her at Topeka; the mayor of Dodge City conferred upon her, in behalf of its citizens, resolutions of commendation; at Hutchinson, the Ringgold Cornet Band was so magnetized by her presence that they forgot to play and instead shouted along with the rest of the crowd. Nellie was up until 4 a.m. one morning talking with a young newspaper woman who had come 600 miles from Kearney, Nebraska, to meet and interview her, and dictating a report of her trip to her stenographer, who was, Nellie asserted, "seasick from the motion of the train." After but two hours of sleep and a quick cup of coffee, Nellie was met, at Joliet, Illinois, by members of the Chicago Press Club, who had come out to escort her to their city. She reported that after she answered all their questions "we joked about my sun-burnt nose and discussed the merits of my one dress, the cleverness of the monkey, and I was feeling happy and at home wishing I could stay all day in Chicago."

Nellie Bly arrived in Chicago January 21st (she had been out of New York sixty-eight days.) While Elizabeth Bisland continued to suffer from the brutal cold in her tiny stifling cabin on the storm-ravaged *S.S. Bothnia*, Nellie was feted by the Press Club with breakfast at Kinsley's then escorted to the Chicago Board of Trade where the pandemonium of business was already at its height. One of the brokers spotted her in the gallery and instead of roaring a bid cried "There's Nellie Bly!" Nellie describes what followed:

> In one instant the crowd that had been yelling like mad became so silent that a pin could have been heard to fall to the floor. Every face, bright and eager, was turned up toward us, instantly every hat came off, and then a burst of applause resounded through the immense hall. People can say what they please about Chicago, but I do not believe that anywhere else in the United States a woman can get a greeting which will equal that given by the Chicago Board of Trade. The applause was followed by cheer after cheer and cries of "Speech!" but I took off my little cap and shook my head at them, which only served to increase their cheers.

Nellie changed trains in Chicago; instead of a fine sleeping car at her disposal, she now had only a state-room, and space was so limited that floral and fruit tributes had to be left behind. She received, to her profound pleasure, a cable that had missed her in San Francisco:

Mr. Verne wishes the following cable to be handed to Nellie Bly the moment she touches American soil:

M. and Mme. Jules Verne address their sincere felicitations to Nellie Bly at the moment when that intrepid young lady sets foot on the soil of America.

Verne's book *Around the World in Eighty Days* had gone into its tenth printing since Nellie Bly started on her journey around the world, and now it was to be revived as a play at the Châtelet Theatre in Paris, with Nellie written into the epilogue, if she could beat the record of Phileas Fogg.

The new train, Nellie reported, was "rather poorly appointed," and the passengers had to get off for their meals. At Logansport, Indiana, Nellie being the last in the car, was the last to detrain for dinner. A young man recognized her and sprang toward her waving his hat and shouting, "Hurrah for Nellie Bly!" She reported:

The crowd clapped hands and cheered, and after making way for me to pass to the dining-room, pressed forward and cheered again, crowding to the windows at last to watch me eat. When I sat down, several dishes were put before me bearing the inscription, "Success, Nellie!"

At Columbus, Ohio, the depot was packed with men and women waiting for America's heroine, and a delegation of railroad men presented her with beautiful flowers and candy; at Harrisburg, Pennsylvania, she was welcomed by thousands including the local Wheelsmen's Club which gave her a floral offering in remembrance of her being a wheelman (she had, from time to time taken the throttle during those reckless sixty-miles-per-hour train rides across the great Southwest); at Philadelphia, she was again called upon to make a speech and was met by Jules Chambers and other *World* editors who were to escort her to New York. But the celebration really erupted when her train rumbled into Jersey City:

I was told when we were almost home to jump to the platform the moment the train stopped at Jersey City, for that made my time around the world. The station was packed with thousands of people, and the moment I landed on the platform, one yell went up from them, and the cannons at the Battery and Fort Greene boomed out the news of my arrival. I took off my cap and wanted to yell with the crowd, not because I had gone around the world in seventy-two days, but because I was home again.

Actually, it was seventy-two days, six hours, eleven minutes, and zero seconds. Three stopwatches clicked the historic moment as the train lurched to a final stop and Nellie alighted. "She's a winner! She's a winner!" cried the timekeepers. The crowd went wild; the police were unable to stop them; the men carried floral testimonials which were crushed in the massive surge toward Nellie Bly who stood at the train entry, her sunburned face aglow, her eyes sparkling. It was 3:15 p.m. Saturday, January 25th.

Elizabeth Bisland had been out to sea seven days;. Now that the storms on the Atlantic had let up she was able to receive visitors. Friends solicitous about her health called on her in her cabin. About that time, Mayor Cleveland of Jersey City, who was having trouble making himself heard above the roar of the crowd, welcomed the radiant Nellie Bly home in the "Name of Progress." In a sonorous, oratorical tone, he told her that she had revolutionized distance and that the world would never be as big again. "The American Girl will no longer be misunderstood," he proclaimed. "She will be recognized as pushing, determined, independent, able to take care of herself wherever she may go. You have added another spark to the great beacon light of American liberty that is leading the people of other nations in the grand march of civilization and progress."

The crowd strained on tiptoe for a glimpse of their great "Nell." "Passing rapidly by them," the Mayor went on, with patriotic bombast, "you have cried out in a language they could all understand, 'Forward!' and you have made it the watchword of 1890. The American people from every part of this great and glorious country shouted back to you, 'Forward! And God speed you on your wonderful march!'"

242

The horde of people broke through the cordon of police; they tore at Nellie's gloves and handkerchief for souvenirs; they pleaded for her autograph. The Mayor shouted above the din:

"'Forward!' comes the cry of the restless and toiling masses from every quarter of the globe. 'Forward' is the very essence and the spirit of the age and times in which we live. In that spirit...."

Nellie Bly struggled to disentangle herself from her delirious admirers.

"...you have carried safely and splendidly the interest of a great newspaper more than twenty-five thousand miles over sea and land; but there is something higher and greater as a result of your achievement than the interests of a single enterprise. People the world over have been taught that they are not so far apart as they had imagined; and that is a great lesson. You have set the whole world to thinking about it, and so have brought mankind closer together....Welcome home!"

The triumphant Nellie struck just the right balance between pride and humility: She smiled and bowed and said, "From Jersey to Jersey is around the world, and I am in Jersey now!"

In New York, the streets were a mass of people. They surged in from lower Broadway and blocked Nellie's carriage. A way was forced and she proceeded uptown. People hung from windows, stood on overturned horsecars to catch a glimpse of her. A throng followed her carriage all the way to Park Row and the *World* building whose windows were filled with faces; small boys shinnied up the pillars for a better look. Joseph Pulitzer was there to acclaim her feat and tell her that he knew she would win. Nellie was given a champagne reception at the Astor House. Congratulations came from overseas: Jules Verne said that what made her accomplishment incredible was she succeeded during the Winter in a trip wholly north of the equator; Phillip Gille, an editor of *Figaro* in Paris, said it was extraordinary a young girl had done fearlessly what so few men would have ventured to do; the big London newspapers which—perhaps out of loyalty to their own admirable Phileas Fogg?—had predicted Nellie Bly would fail, now applauded her success. (Dissenters to the prevailing mood of accolade opined that she had trivialized

243

travel by racing from country to country without pausing to contemplate their essence and that Woman was not made to live and act without the assistance of Man.)

How much praise, if any, was accorded Elizabeth Bisland when she returned to New York remains unknown. It would be nice to think that in honor of her own sublime achievement, the friends with the "glad faces" who welcomed her at the pier took her out to dinner, or that John Brisben Walker and his staff at *Cosmopolitan* toasted her with champagne at an office party. She deserved at least that much.

What makes a winner? Is it luck? Might not Elizabeth Bisland, with a break here and there, just as easily have been the one to receive the plaudits of the multitude and Nellie Bly the one to be greeted by a few good friends? Or is it true that winners make their own luck? Was it her aggressiveness that got Nellie Bly off the quarantine ship in San Francisco harbor and gained her the edge over Miss Bisland, who quietly accepted misinformation that the vessel at Le Havre would not wait for her? (The *New York World* was to maintain that even if she had caught the *Le Champagne*, she would not have beaten Nellie Bly.) Is character "fate," and "luck" the result of design? Or is winning a matter of self-confidence and maintaining a positive attitude? (Did Nellie win the race because the idea of losing never entered her mind whereas Elizabeth Bisland didn't want to go in the first place?) Or was Nellie Bly simply fated to be a winner in the cosmic crapshoot that cruelly singles out a favored few for fame and relegates the rest to oblivion? There seems to be but one answer to all this speculation: More truly, both Elizabeths won! Both outdid Phileas Fogg, and both struck a blow for the right of women everywhere to be daring, independent, free-spirited. Both covered themselves with glory.

EPILOGUE

Nellie Bly, now internationally famous, was earning $25,000 a year as a reporter. She was in great demand on the lecture circuit; songs were written about her, games were named after her and so was a race horse; "Nellie Bly" was printed on testimonials to everything from Pear's Soap to Dr. Morse's India Root Pills. Her *Nellie Bly's Book: Around the World in 72 Days*, was published by Pictorial Weeklies in 1890. As a crusader for social reform, she went on to bring to light the squalid living conditions in New York tenements, expose a noted woman mind-reader as a quack, interview a murderer facing capital punishment and get his side of the story, and cover the bloody Pullman strike, interviewing Socialist Eugene V. Debs in jail, and railroad workers and their families. As a wealthy celebrity, Nellie became an intimate of the rich and the powerful, including Hetty Green the "Old Lady of Wall Street" and Edwin Gould, brother of financier Jay Gould. At the age of twenty-eight, she married Robert L. Seaman, prosperous Brooklyn manufacturer of metal products ranging from hot-water heaters to oxygen tanks, who was more than forty years her senior. (She was accused of being a gold-digger, but Seaman loved, respected, and admired her.)

Elizabeth Bisland returned to *Cosmopolitan* and wrote features on such cultural subjects as the Cologne Cathedral and Dancing as "the eldest of the arts." Her *In Seven Stages: A Flying Trip Around the World* was published by Harper & Brothers in 1891. That same year, she married Charles W. Wetmore, financier and a lawyer for a prominent New York law firm, as well as a Harvard grad and well-known yachtsman. (Wetmore, then thirty-seven, was described as a witty, delightful companion and a man of courageous intellect who worked zealously for the betterment and benefit of the civic and business interests with which he was associated.)

Nellie Bly—Elizabeth Cochrane Seaman—was presented the Iron Clad Manufacturing Company by her husband as a gift. He died in 1904, and Mrs. Seaman, now in complete charge of the firm, turned it into a multi-million-dollar enterprise, pioneering improvements in the steel barrel in particular to carry oil (wooden barrels leaked) and revamping outmoded facilities. But ironically, the same woman who had been such a shrewd reporter showed a lamentable lack of awareness when it came to business. She worked long, hard hours in the plant, and expected her personnel to do the same. Trusted male employees, using a system they alone could fathom, over the years forged her signature on checks and looted the company to the brink of bankruptcy. Mrs. Seaman took them to court in a long, painful litigation during which, she claimed, she was continually harassed by the male judge and the battery of male defense attorneys. Enjoined to show the firm's books, she refused and fled to Europe to escape indictment.

Elizabeth Bisland Wetmore and her husband moved to Washington, D.C., where they enjoyed hobnobbing in diplomatic circles. The woman who had been so self-absorbed in her youth began to develop a sense of social responsibility. She became a leader in the Women's National Democratic Club, campaigning for such programs as college courses in home economics. Between 1902 and 1916, she published several books including an edition of the letters of Lafcadio Hearn, who wrote about Japan and whose talents as a journalist she was among the first to recognize. Charles Wetmore, who had become a corporation executive and helped develop the Mesabi Iron Mines in Minnesota and consolidated the Bethlehem Steel Company, was stricken with an ailment (not named by Mrs. Wetmore in her affecting letters) that ruined his mental and physical health. For the next ten years, his wife cared for him; ultimately he was admitted to a sanatorium where, in 1919, he died without her having been permitted to visit him. Mrs. Wetmore sold her home in Washington, D.C., and went to live on a twenty-five-acre plantation in Charlottesville, near the University of Virginia.

Elizabeth Cochrane Seaman—Nellie Bly—worked in Austria as a war correspondent and enjoyed the affection of Oscar Bondy, a wealthy Viennese manufacturer. In 1919, she returned to New York and surrendered herself to the courts, which finally cleared her of the indictment against her. Now penniless and in poor health, she pawned the brooch and earrings Bondy had given her but refused—despite his insistence that she put her own welfare first—to sell the 150 shares of common stock he had given her. (She preferred to suffer privation than to deny him access to assets that might help him in his own country where soaring inflation and tremendous income taxes loomed.) Mrs. Seaman—Nellie—was hired by one of her closest friends, the great editor Arthur Brisbane, to work for William Randolph Hearst's *New York Evening Journal*. The papers were full of women reporters now, and the woman who helped pave the way for them was now largely forgotten. But she covered brilliantly the Republican National Convention of 1920. (When Leonard Wood, who commanded with valor in the invasion of the Philippines, was nominated for the presidential candidacy, there ensued a thirty-minute ovation and the fall of millions of colored feathers from the ceiling. Nellie, not taken in, reported, "I fear that they have plucked poor Wood bare"; Harding, sure enough, was nominated.)

Nellie Bly, who loved children but had none of her own, devoted her last years to the care and shelter—in her rooms in the Hotel McAlpin—of abandoned youngsters until they could be legally adopted. She died on January 27, 1922, of pneumonia, in St. Mark's Hospital in New York City, at the age of fifty-four. The obituary on page 13 of *The New York Times* read, in part:

> She went down into the sea in a diving bell and up in the air in a balloon and lived in an insane asylum as a patient; but the feat that made her famous was her trip around the world in 1889. She was sent by the *World* to beat the mark of Phineas *(sic)* Fogg, Jules Verne's hero of *AROUND THE WORLD IN EIGHTY DAYS*, and she succeeded in making the tour in seventy-two days, six hours, and eleven minutes. Everyone who read newspapers followed her progress and she landed in New York a national character.

During World War I, Elizabeth Bisland Wetmore cared for the sick and wounded in an army hospital in London, England. After the war, she became president of an evening clinic, in Washington, D.C., that served the health needs of working girls of moderate means. She conducted an extensive private correspondence with poet Charles Woodward Hutson in which she commented shrewdly on such matters as the madness of post-war international politics and the deficiencies in Shelley's poetry. She died suddenly on January 6, 1929, of pneumonia, at her home in Charlottesville, Virginia, at the age of sixty-seven. The obituary in the *New Orleans Times-Picayune* described her as "the Bessie Bisland who raced against Time and Nellie Bly around the world in the 80's pledging the stories of her journey in the *Cosmopolitan* magazine against those of Nellie Bly in the *New York World* and losing by a few hours."

Despite the unpredictable Elizabeth Bisland Wetmore's demise, she was not through with surprises. In her will, she bequeathed the bulk of her estate to her three sisters and their survivors, to be paid them from a trust. At their deaths, a sum of $10,000 per year would be paid quarterly to Elizabeth Tallant Owen, a niece. If Owen died, the trust was to end and the trustees were to transfer $250,000 to her surviving issue. An added clause, however, stipulated that if at any time she became a member of the Roman Catholic Church, she and her heirs would be cut off without a cent. In that case, if Owen left no survivors, the will provided, the net income from the trust should go to "the care of indigent native sufferers from tubercular consumption in and about New Orleans." How the money should be distributed would be determined by representatives of the First Methodist and First Presbyterian Churches and the Christ Church Episcopal Cathedral. The will further mandated that no part of the fund should be used for construction of any building. Elizabeth Tallant Owen did not join the Roman Catholic Church. Distant heirs challenged the terms of the will, and the Internal Revenue service held that the money was now taxable inasmuch as tuberculosis had been "cured" and was no longer a problem. For years, the will was in litigation while the trust went untouched, accumulating more money from investments. Then, in the 1960s, the U.S. Court of Appeals ruled in favor of the trust and the Charles and Elizabeth Wetmore Foundation was allowed to begin meeting the needs for which it was designed. There was then already in New Orleans, a tuberculosis clinic. Today, operated by the city's and Louisiana State's health departments, it is one of the best-equipped community services in the country for combatting a disease that far from being "cured" and no longer a problem has shown an alarming increase, especially among Asian-Americans and the homeless. The Wetmore Foundation works closely with the clinic, helping needy patients through grants. That may not have been Elizabeth Bisland Wetmore's prime intent when she drew up her will, but doubtless she would have been pleased with the end-result.

Would the imposing Mrs. Wetmore and the strong-willed Mrs. Seaman have hit it off if they ever met? So far as is known, neither woman—when married or when single— ever spoke to the other or ever mentioned the other by name in her written work. But from the time each first learned that the other was going around the world, she must have had the other very much on her mind.

THE END

BIBLIOGRAPHY

PRIMARY SOURCES

Bisland, Elizabeth, *In Seven Stages: A Flying Trip Around the World*. New York: Harper & Brothers, 1891.

Bly, Nellie, *Nellie Bly's Book: Around the World in 72 Days*. New York: Pictorial Weeklies Company, 1890

Bly, Nellie, *Ten Days in a Mad-house; or, Nellie Bly's Experience on Blackwell's Island*. New York, Munro, 1887.

SECONDARY SOURCES

Baker, Nina Brown, *Nellie Bly*. New York: Holt, 1956.

Brown, Lea Ann (Southern Illinois University), *Elizabeth Cochrane (Nellie Bly). Dictionary of Literary Biography.*

Cott, Jonathan, *Wandering Ghost: The Odyssey of Lafcadio Hearn.*New York: Alfred A. Knopf, 1990.

Eaton, John P., historian, Titanic International. *Titanic: Destination Disaster*, 1987, *Falling Star*, 1989, co-author of *Titanic: Triumph and Tragedy*, 1986, now in second printing. New York: W.W. Norton, Ltd.

Elizabeth Bisland Wetmore Collection, Manuscripts Section, Special Collections Division, Howard-Tilton Memorial Library, Tulane University, New Orleans, La.

Emery, Edwin and Emery, Michael, The Press and America: *An Interpretative History of the Mass Media* (fifth edition). Englewood Cliffs, N.J.: Prentice-Hall, 1984.

Hynes, Terry (California State University, Fullerton), *Joseph Pulitzer. Dictionary of Literary Biography.*

Myers, John, *The Story of Nellie Bly*. New York: American Flange & Manufacturing Company, 1951.

National Cyclopedia Biography, on Charles W. Wetmore.

Noble, Iris, *Nellie Bly, First Woman Reporter*. New York: Messner, 1956.

Rittenhouse, Mignon, *The Amazing Nellie Bly*. New York: Dutton, 1956.

Sante, Luc, *Low Life: Lures and Snares of Old New York*. New York: Farrar, Straus and Giroux, 1991.

Verne, Jules, *Around the World in Eighty Days*. New York: Bantam Books, 1988.

We Japanese. Published by Fujiya Hotel, Miyanoshita, Hakone, Japan, and printed by Yamagata Press, Yokohama. 1964 edition.

PERIODICALS

Fallows, James, "The Mind of Japan," *U.S. News & World Report*, December 2, 1991.

Moore, Edith Wyatt, "Girlhood Home of Author Who Wrote Life of Hearn Will Be Shown at Natchez," *New Orleans Times-Picayune*, March 28, 1937.

Natchez Democrat, Natchez, Miss., "Mount Repose," March 5, 1983.

New Orleans Times-Picayune, "Woman Writer's Death Is Sudden," January 8, 1929.

New Orleans Times-Picayune, "Anniversary Recalls Race Round Globe," November 12, 1939.

New York Sun, November, 1889, through January, 1890.

New York Times, November, 1889, through January, 1890

New York World, November 1889, through January, 1890.

Nolan, Paul T., "The Louisiana Belle Who Beat Phogg," *New Orleans Times-Picayune*, September 22, 1957.

Roehl, Marjorie, "Bessie Bisland Was Fast, But She Couldn't Beat Nellie Bly," *New Orleans Times-Picayune*, April 20, 1986; "Bessie's Will Kept Them Guessing," *Times-Picayune*, April 17, 1986.

Rogers, Jaque, "Bisland Sisters Return Thanks for Sharing Retirement Together," *News-Commercial*, Collins, Miss., November 21, 1990.

Washington Evening Star, "Good Health Home Changes Quarters," July 14, 1920.

INDEX

Adam, 129
Aden, 81-85, 167-171, 173
A Flying Trip Around the World by Elizabeth Bisland, 245
Agostino, Dom Leopoldo, 144
Ah Cum, 181, 183, 184, 185, 186, 190, 191, 192
Captain Albers, 24, 25, 26
Chief Allen, 229, 230, 231, 233
Arabian Sea, 166
Arnold, Sir Edwin, 205
Around the World in 72 Days by Nellie Bly, 245
Around the World in Eighty Days by Jules Verne, 15, 29, 112
    228, 241
Astor House, 243
S.S. *Augusta Victoria*, 24, 25

Bay of Bengal, 130
Betel-nut habit, 138, 147, 149
Bisland, Elizabeth
    background, 22
    offered opportunity to race Nellie Bly, 22
    declines to go, 22
    her appearance, 22
    itinerary, 23
    arrives in Chicago, 31
    colors her prose, 32, 33, 34, 51, 88, 92, 101, 148-149
    her personality, 31, 32-33, 34, 35, 37, 38, 48, 49, 50, 51,
        52-53, 54, 59-63, 65, 66, 69, 88, 89, 90, 91, 92, 101, 103,
        105, 106, 108, 109, 124, 125, 126, 128, 144, 145-146, 147,
        148, 149, 150, 151, 166, 168, 169-170, 195-196, 198, 200,
        201, 219, 221, 227, 228, 244, 246, 247, 248, 249
    arrives in Council Bluffs, Iowa, 33
    her writing ability, 32, 36, 63, 67-68, 87, 93-94, 103, 124,
        129, 148
    crosses Rockies, 35
    her romantic nature, 31, 32-33, 34, 66, 69, 103, 109, 129,
        151, 167, 170, 174
    arrives in Ogden, Utah, 36
    stays in San Francisco, 37
    meets William Randolph Hearst's editors, 37
    crosses the Pacific, 48-51, 53

Fujiyama, 53-54

Gabler, Hedda, 52
geishas, 207-209
gharry, 125, 137
Ghormley's, 18
Gille, Phillip, 243
Gordon, Charles George, 198
Gould, Edwin, 245
Gould, Jay, 17, 245
Gounod, Charles, 118
Grant, Hugh J., 98
Greece, 173
Green, Hetty, 245
Captain Grogan, 180, 181

Mr. Harmon, 94, 159-164, 175
Harrison, Benjamin, 25, 97-98
Harrison, William Henry, 97
Hayes, Rutherford B., 16
Hearn, Lafcadio
    works with Elizabeth Bisland on New Orleans
        newspaper, 59
    his appearance, 59, 63
    his personality as described by Miss Bisland, 59, 63
    his feelings toward her, 59-63
    his love of Japan, 60, 61, 213
Hearst, William Randolph, 19, 21, 37, 238
Highlanders, 90, 91, 94-95
Hindus, 105, 106, 125
Hohenzollern dynasty, 90
Hong Kong, 87-94, 103, 155, 157, 158, 175-179
Howells, William Dean, 21
Hutson, Charles Woodward, 247

Ibsen, Henrick, 52
Ieymitsu, tomb of, 66-68, 79
India, 30, 111, 173

Jeremiah, 168
jewelry, Colombo, 113, 145
jinricksha, 105, 119
juggler on Bay of Suez, 79-80

Owen, Elizabeth Tallant, 248

Pantheism, 168
Paris, Exhibition of 1855, 197
Parsees, 88; theatre, 117-118
Pasa, Emin, 171
Pascal, Blaise, 163
Passepartout, 29
Penang, 124-127, 130-132
Peninsular and Oriental Steamship Line, 46, 165
Perry, Commodore Matthew, 60, 205
Phelps, Ed, 74, 98
Phoenicians, 167
Pidgin English, 176-177
Pinkerton, U.S. Naval Lieutenant, 210
Pittsburgh Dispatch, epigraph, 12, 13
Port Said, 74, 76, 77-78, 172
Portuguese, 88
The *Powan*, 180, 181, 194
Puccini, Giacomo, 210
Pulitzer, Joseph
   his failing health, 16
   his background, 16-17
   his principles and policy, 17, 27, 188-189
   his rivalry with Walker, 21, 160-161, 234-235
Pullman Strike, 245

Quay, Matt, 98
Queenstown, Ireland, 219, 221, 222

Republican National Convention of 1920, 247
Richards, William L., 40-41
Robert Elsmere, 43
Robinson, Sir William, 144
Roebling, John Augustus, 56
Rousseau, Jean Jacques, 34
Ryokan, 211-212

Sago, 146
St. Theresa, 52
Sampan, 125, 130
Samurai, tradition, 61, 205
San Francisco Examiner, 47, 238

Victoria Peak, 92, 178
Queen Victoria, 96, 165, 222
S.S. *Victoria*, 58, 70, 73, 74, 75, 80, 81, 83, 85, 96
Villeneuve, 197, 198, 199, 200, 201

Walker, John Brisben, 20-23; principles and policies, 20-22; 35, 37, 86, 199, 237, 244
Wanamaker, John, 97, 98
Ward, Humphry Mrs., 43
Washington Chronicle, 21
Washington, George, 97
Wedderburn, Sir William, 177
Weller, Samuel, 102
Westliche Post, 16
Wetmore, Charles W., 63, 151, 245, 246
Wetmore, Elizabeth Bisland, 245, 246, 247-249
Wilde, Oscar, 150
William Wordsworth's grandson, 144, 150
Wilson, A.D., 23, 200
Wilson, Woodrow, 21
Wood, Leonard, 247
Women's National Democratic Club, 246
Wrenfordsly, Sir Henry, 144

Yokohama, 64, 65, 68, 69, 205, 217, 218